Politics, Society,
and Nationality
Inside Gorbachev's Russia

An East-West Forum Publication

Politics, Society, and Nationality Inside Gorbachev's Russia

EDITED BY

Seweryn Bialer

Westview Press
BOULDER & LONDON

Copyright © 1989 by The Samuel Bronfman Foundation, Inc.

Published in 1989 in the United States of America by Westview Press, Inc., 5500 Central Avenue, Boulder, Colorado 80301, and in the United Kingdom by Westview Press, Inc., 13 Brunswick Centre, London WC1N 1AF, England

Library of Congress Cataloging-in-Publication Data
Politics, society, and nationality inside Gorbachev's Russia / edited
  by Seweryn Bialer.
    p. cm.
  "An East-West Forum publication"—P.
  Bibliography: p.
  Includes index.
  Contents: Introduction/Edgar M. Bronfman—Ideology and
political culture/Archie Brown—Politics before Gorbachev: de-
Stalinization and the roots of reform/Peter Hauslohner—The
Yeltsin Affair : the dilemma of the Left in Gorbachev's revolution/
Seweryn Bialer—State and society : toward the emergence of civil
society in the Soviet Union/Gail W. Lapidus—The sobering of Gorbachev :
nationality, restructuring, and the West/Alexander J. Motyl—
Politics and nationality : the Soviet Jews/Laurie P. Salitan—
The changing Soviet political system : the Nineteenth Party Conference
and after/Seweryn Bialer.
  ISBN 0-8133-0752-X
  ISBN 0-8133-0753-8 (pbk.)
  1. Soviet Union—Politics and government—1982–   . 2. Soviet Union—
Ethnic relations. 3. Soviet Union—Social conditions—1970–   .
I. Bialer, Seweryn.
DK288.P66 1989
947.085′4—dc19   88-21024
                                                                   CIP

Printed and bound in the United States of America

The paper used in this publication meets the requirements of the American National
Standard for Permanence of Paper for Printed Library Materials Z39.48-1984.

10   9   8   7   6   5   4   3   2

Contents

About the Contributors vii
Preface ix
Introduction, *Edgar M. Bronfman* xi

1 Ideology and Political Culture, *Archie Brown* 1

2 Politics Before Gorbachev: De-Stalinization and
the Roots of Reform, *Peter Hauslohner* 41

3 The Yeltsin Affair: The Dilemma of the Left in
Gorbachev's Revolution, *Seweryn Bialer* 91

4 State and Society: Toward the Emergence of Civil
Society in the Soviet Union, *Gail W. Lapidus* 121

5 The Sobering of Gorbachev: Nationality,
Restructuring, and the West, *Alexander J. Motyl* 149

6 Politics and Nationality: The Soviet Jews,
Laurie P. Salitan 175

7 The Changing Soviet Political System: The
Nineteenth Party Conference and After, *Seweryn Bialer* 193

Selected Bibliography: Recent Works on
the Soviet Union 243
Index 247

About the Contributors

Seweryn Bialer is the Robert and Renee Belfer Professor of Social Sciences and International Relations and director of the Research Institute on International Change at Columbia University. He is the author of *Stalin's Successors* and *The Soviet Paradox*, as well as the editor of several collected works on Soviet foreign and domestic policies—the most recent of which is *Gorbachev's Russia and American Foreign Policy* (Westview, 1988).

Archie Brown is a Fellow of St. Antony's College and a lecturer on Soviet institutions at Oxford University. He is an export on Soviet politics, ideology, and political culture, and is the author of numerous works, the most recent of which is *Political Culture and Communist Studies*.

Peter Hauslohner is assistant professor of political science at Yale University and the author of a forthcoming work on the origins, maintenance, and decline of the first post-Stalin "social contract."

Gail W. Lapidus is professor of political science at the University of California at Berkeley and directs the Berkeley-Stanford Program on Soviet International Behavior. She is the author of numerous studies on Soviet politics and foreign policy and the author of a forthcoming work on Soviet nationality policy.

Alexander J. Motyl is assistant professor of political science at Columbia University and director of the program in nationality and Siberian studies of the W. Averell Harriman Institute for Advanced Study of the Soviet Union. He is the author of *Will the Non-Russians Rebel?* and of the forthcoming study, *Sovietology, Rationality, Nationality: Coming to Grips with Nationalism in the USSR*.

Laurie P. Salitan is assistant professor of political science at The Johns Hopkins University and chair of the W. Averell Harriman Institute's Seminar on Soviet Republics and Regional Issues. She is the author of the forthcoming book, *The Politics of Contemporary Soviet Emigration*.

Preface

The East-West Forum is a New York–based research and policy analysis organization sponsored by the Samuel Bronfman Foundation. Its goal is to bring together experts and policy leaders from differing perspectives and generations to discuss changing patterns of East-West relations. It attempts to formulate long-term analyses and recommendations.

In preparing the chapters of this book, the authors, as with our earlier work *Gorbachev's Russia and American Foreign Policy*, drew upon a series of workshops initiated by the Forum. Aside from the authors, workshop participants included Jeremy Azrael, Donna Bahry, Joseph Berliner, Robert Campbell, Timothy Colton, Robert Cullen, Fritz Ermarth, Sheila Fitzpatrick, John Gaddis, Gregory Grossman, Thane Gustafson, Mark von Hagen, Arthur Hartman, Grey Hodnett, Stanley Hoffmann, Robert Hormats, William Hyland, Alex Inkeles, Robert Legvold, William Luers, I. Mac Destler, Michael Mandelbaum, Mary McAuley, Joseph S. Nye, Jr., Robert Osgood, William Schneider, Jutta Scherrer, Helmut Sonnenfeldt, S. Frederick Starr, Fritz Stern, William Taubman, and Ted Warner.

As in the past, the East-West Forum would like also to express thanks to Stephen E. Herbits, Executive Vice President, Joseph E. Seagram and Sons, Inc.; William K Friedman, Trustee of the Samuel Bronfman Foundation; and David E. Morey, Associate Executive Director, the East-West Forum, as well as to Thomas Sherlock, the Forum's rapporteur, and to Anne Mandelbaum for her editorial work.

James M. Montgomery
Executive Director
East-West Forum

Introduction

As all the world knows, Mikhail Gorbachev, since assuming power in March 1985, has pursued a program of reform that—even if its major objectives should fail—will change fundamentally the social, political, and economic character of the Soviet Union.

The Gorbachev Era has already begun to provide opportunities for improved superpower relations. To be sure, there remains a serious gap between Soviet rhetoric and Soviet reality. Many more political events must unfold and survive the test of time before we see reliable signs that the historical patterns of military threat and global political competition have begun to change. Yet, clearly, the landscape has been altered. The challenge to U.S. policy leaders is to exploit the opportunities, while recognizing and avoiding the dangers.

The East-West Forum seeks to advance a clear and accurate understanding of today's Soviet Union and contribute thereby to the long-term management of East-West relations. In its first book, *Gorbachev's Russia and American Foreign Policy*, the Forum examined the implications of Gorbachev's proposed reforms in light of the aims of U.S. policies. In this volume the authors look at the dynamics of those reforms from within the Soviet system itself.

To what extent can these policies gain acceptance and succeed? What, in fact, does success mean? What are the fundamental political, societal, and nationality factors that might influence Gorbachev's program? And finally, to what extent might his reforms be reversible?

Developments in Gorbachev's Soviet Union pose a particular problem for Americans. They must steer a careful course between unwonted optimism and cynicism. Much of what Gorbachev is doing and saying resonates comfortably with U.S. observers: "openness," "democracy," "restructuring." In Soviet terms, by contrast, these concepts are startling and revolutionary. They presage a dramatic change in Soviet conditions and Soviet thought. In this sense, some optimism—or at least an acknowledgment that things are different—is in order.

But as encouraged by the reform rhetoric as Americans may be, they must also recognize that what is happening in Moscow, measured in U.S. terms, remains very limited. Gorbachev is not proposing to change the Communist Party's exclusive political control over all aspects of Soviet life. He is instead urging that it be more responsive to the people's needs and desires. He is not saying that the Communist Party should be accountable to Soviet citizens in any fashion that Americans understand. Rather, to those with entrenched interests and privileges who see his actions as a threat he is saying that the Soviet Union can have the economic benefits of a more open, competitive society, without its leadership's losing exclusive political control. For the U.S. part, cynicism may not be in order. But caution is.

Contributors to this volume have focused on four central aspects of continuity and change within the Soviet Union: politics, political culture, society, and nationality. Politics continues to command all aspects of life in the Soviet Union. Politics determines Gorbachev's design of *perestroika*, as well as his chance of implementing it. His leadership recognizes that the Soviet Union's current crisis was brought about by the stagnation and destructiveness that the political system imposed upon Soviet society. In Gorbachev's view, radical political change is fundamental to the reforms he sees as necessary to develop a progressive Soviet society. And he is clearly determined to alter the deadening effects the political system he inherited has had on Soviet society.

Gorbachev is opposed, as the pages following will describe, by vested bureaucratic interests buttressed by tradition, inertia, and a fear of political commitment. He must thus pursue several important goals in order to overcome this, including:

- Transforming the Communist Party, almost 20 million strong, into a genuine political movement, as opposed to an appendage of the party bureaucracy
- Reducing that bureaucracy's political power while removing it entirely from the daily management of the urban and rural economy
- Creating checks and balances in the political order by strengthening the national parliament and the governing bodies in the republics, provinces, and cities
- Promoting grass roots pressure against the party bureaucracy, partly through greater freedom of expression

The principal enemies of Gorbachev's reform effort are the "conservatives." His most loyal supporters are the "liberals," represented by many in the creative and technical intelligentsia—such as writers and scientists. To become powerful enough to implement *perestroika*, however, Gorbachev will need the support of the still-uncommitted centrists who are often made uneasy by his liberal supporters. The liberals constantly test the limits of the new dispensations of freedom and thus provide the conservatives with ammunition to frighten the centrists.

To make *perestroika* work, the General Secretary must find ways of controlling the bureaucracy. He has begun to appoint officials who support his program, particularly in the Central Committee. But it is clear that mere personnel changes will not be enough. Gorbachev needs also to impose structural changes that will curb the bureaucrats' power and force them to act in accord with his program. Such structural changes began only with the June 1988 Nineteenth Party Conference and the Plenum Central Committee that followed. Soon, we will be able to measure their effects in the results of elections to the Party's ruling bodies in November 1988, and to the new Soviet Union National Deputies in November 1989.

Faced with the Soviet Union's pervasive tradition of Russian authoritarianism and Soviet mass conformity, Gorbachev knows that if people are to act differently they must think differently. As in the past, at least the initial impulse for change has come from above. Now we are seeing also an outburst of new ideas from below.

Such new thinking is represented most clearly in the area of political culture—those rules of behavior based in Marxist-Leninist ideology and Russian history and tradition. Changes in this culture will be a valid indicator of just how far Gorbachev has succeeded in stimulating new thinking. Gorbachev and his followers have examined and criticized many of the basic principles of Soviet political culture. Furthermore, many of the more creative members of the intelligentsia have followed this lead and turned the Soviet media into an arena for an intense clash between traditional and new ideas. Here, they question the infallibility of the party and criticize mistakes made recently, as opposed to those made forty years ago. Spontaneity—the dirtiest word in the Bolshevik vocabulary—is tolerated, if not encouraged. Individual creativity and entrepreneurship are praised. And it appears that the open expression of different opinions is no longer a certain one-way ticket to the Gulag.

Despite the fact that many Soviet officials are still reading the old script, recent changes in culture represent a real statement of Gorbachev's intention. Put permanently into practice, they would effect a sea change in Soviet political life.

Gorbachev is clearly seeking a significant transformation in the relationship between the Soviet state and the Soviet society. The society that Gorbachev inherited differs dramatically in some ways from Stalin's: It is younger and better educated and has the world's largest professional and middle classes. But despite such changes, Stalin's successors did not significantly shift the relationship between the Soviet citizen and the state. The interests of social groups and of individuals remained entirely subordinate to those of the state, as defined by the political oligarchy.

Although Brezhnev continued Khrushchev's moderation of Stalin's brutalities, he left a plundered economy, a parasitic party, and a body politic generally disdainful of the work ethic. Gorbachev wants to change this without fundamentally changing the single-party system that allowed it to happen. It remains to be seen whether he can have one without the other.

Gorbachev appears to sense he can no longer simply decree that things be done, as did Stalin, and that a revolution imposed from above— even a peaceful one—will not work. Gorbachev is not out to crush any class or group but to create conditions that will stimulate and engage everyone's energies in the modernization challenge. The General Secretary hopes he can bring about a new reconciliation between the state and the society—and from that will come stability and progress. But there are limits to what he is offering. Will it be enough? Will he get the burst of participation and creativity he is seeking by offering Soviet society increased responsiveness, but not accountability, from the Party?

The outcome is uncertain. *Perestroika* has already produced many "unintended consequences." Gorbachev, to his probable consternation, and his critics, to their certain satisfaction, are discovering it is difficult to calibrate the parceling out of freedom and critical privileges. Unanticipated social forces can come forth. Indeed, nowhere is this more evident than in the relations with the many nations that compose the USSR. Since the Revolution, the Russians have ruled a multinational imperial system from Moscow. Relations between those nations and the Russians, and among those nations themselves, are extremely sensitive. And the Russians' ability to maintain control over this is fundamental to the present system's stability.

The recent nationalistic turmoil in Armenia, Azerbaijan, Kazakhstan, and the occupied Baltic states demonstrates that conditions having a direct impact on Gorbachev's chances for success can get out of control. In fact, strained relations between the dominant Russians and the non-Russian peoples constitute probably the single most difficult obstacle to *perestroika*'s success. They threaten to foster dangerous, newly awakened, centrifugal tendencies along with the economic and political decentralization that Gorbachev believes necessary for the Soviet Union's revitalization. The question is simple. Can the Russian leadership transform peacefully its present imperial system into a genuine multinational state?

I am particularly interested in the Jewish aspect of the nationality question. Can the Soviets cope with this issue, which is so important both in Soviet terms and in U.S.-Soviet relations? Gorbachev's response to the struggle for the right to emigrate, for the release of all prisoners of Zion, and for religious and cultural freedom for Jews who wish to remain Soviet citizens will be an important litmus test of the extent of his liberalization.

The prospects are exciting. But serious questions remain. Can Gorbachev succeed with his plans, and are his plans enough?

Edgar M. Bronfman
President
East-West Forum

1

Ideology and Political Culture

Archie Brown[1]

Some of the deepest skepticism in the West concerning the possibility of significant change for the better in the Soviet Union is based on the belief that the ideology of the Soviet state and the political culture of the Soviet elite and of the mass of the people are in essence unchanging. If the Soviet leaders' way of looking at the world stays the same and the fundamental values and beliefs of the elite and the people remain as they were, what hope can there be for either meaningful reform at home or a more constructive relationship with the West?

Thus, the issue of continuity and change in ideology and political culture—although seemingly at some remove from the everyday world of political decisionmaking—is of critical importance for the success or failure of the project on which Mikhail Gorbachev has embarked in the second half of the 1980s. Because the concepts of ideology and political culture can mean different things to different people, it should be made clear what is meant by them here.

Ideology has been defined in so many different ways[2] that some meanings are almost the precise opposite of others. The term *political culture*, although not the subject of quite as many definitions as its parent anthropological concept of *culture*,[3] has also generated argument concerning its scope as well as its utility. What matters is that analytical distinctions be made that will pave the way for useful discussion of the important political phenomena embraced by the concepts.[4]

As far as ideology is concerned, I adopt the definition propounded by Malcolm B. Hamilton in a recent article[5] and hold to my own earlier definition of political culture.[6] Thus, an *ideology* "is a system of collectively held normative and reputedly factual ideas and beliefs and attitudes advocating a particular pattern of social relationships and arrangements, and/or aimed at justifying a particular pattern of conduct, which its proponents seek to promote, realise, pursue, or maintain."[7]

Hamilton supports the idea that ideology takes the form of a system or a relatively coherent pattern of ideas and beliefs not only because that notion appears in almost all previous definitions but also because this is one of the features that can usefully distinguish ideology from ideas and beliefs more generally.[8] A *political culture*, as I see it, "consists of the subjective perception of history and politics, the fundamental beliefs and values, the foci of identification and loyalty, and the political knowledge and expectations which are the product of the specific historical experience of nations and groups."[9]

A majority of the political scientists who have made use of the notion of political culture have adopted a similar "subjective," or psychological, view of the concept. Apparently because it is easier to obtain evidence on the public conduct of citizens of Communist states than on their values and beliefs,[10] a number of specialists on Communist politics have, however, adopted a much broader definition of political culture that includes behavior[11] or even organization.[12] But there is much to be said for defining political culture so stringently that it does not become a virtual synonym for "politics" but rather so that it facilitates discussion of the relationship between the complex of subjective factors—political perceptions, political knowledge, values and beliefs—on the one hand, and political activity and the potential for political change, on the other.[13]

It should be clear from the definitions of ideology and political culture I have adopted that the substance of one can impinge upon and intertwine with the other, notwithstanding some important differences between the two concepts. In the concluding section of this chapter, I shall return briefly to this point, but before then I examine Soviet ideology and political culture in turn, paying attention to the ways in which they may, in fact, have changed or be changing. I shall also consider the relationship of both ideology and political culture to Soviet policy and to the prospects for serious reform of the system.

Soviet Ideology

The definition I have adopted for ideology is applicable to all ideologies (as distinct from ideas and beliefs more generally, including some of the deep-rooted ones that come within the rubric of political culture). Ideologies, moreover, are to be found in all states, not just Communist ones. But Soviet ideology fits particularly well with this emphasis on a *system* of ideas and beliefs and on advocacy of a particular pattern of social relationships and of political conduct. The Soviet Union has an acknowledged official ideology, Marxism-Leninism, and devotes vast resources to its promotion. While there are many perceptions and fundamental political beliefs of both the elite and the Soviet people that have little or nothing to do with Marxism-Leninism, they may appropriately be considered under the heading of political culture.

Although there is broad agreement that Marxism-Leninism is an "ideology," the very term *Marxism-Leninism* is far from free of ambiguity. Karl Marx *could* not have used the expression and V. I. Lenin *did* not. The term *Marxism-Leninism* dates from the early Stalin period of Soviet history, and Iosif Stalin himself made his own contribution to the body of doctrine, some elements of which (such as the idea that classes continue in the socialist stage of development of society but that they are "nonantagonistic classes") remain part of the ideology to this day. Marxism-Leninism is both more and less than the sum of all the works of the remarkably prolific Marx and Lenin. It is *more* not only in the sense that subsequent politically authoritative interpreters have added to (or "creatively developed") the arguments of Marx and Lenin, but also inasmuch as the doctrine has been codified into a set of binding rules and principles applicable in contexts often very different from those in which Marx and Lenin wrote. It is *less* in that, for most of the Soviet period, Marxism-Leninism has consisted of a conscious selection from the works of Marx and Lenin by the Soviet political elite, with particular political leaders or theoreticians acquiring great power *over* Marxism-Leninism. Most of what has been produced (especially for mass consumption) is a slimmed-down and simplified Marx and Lenin, in which some parts of their writings are deliberately accorded greater weight than others. This is what has formed the official ideology known as Marxism-Leninism.

The question of the part played by the thought of Marx and Lenin themselves in contributing to the highly authoritarian (or, as some would have it, "totalitarian"[14]) character of the Soviet state is too large to be dealt with here, except in passing. There are strong participatory-democratic (although hardly pluralist-democratic) strands in the thought of Marx and Lenin, especially in their vision of socialism as distinct from the period of struggle against the capitalist state. But as Leszek Kolakowski has observed, "Marxism was a combination of values which proved incompatible for empirical though not for logical reasons, so that some could be realized only at the expense of others."[15]

It could be argued that the absence in Marx and Lenin of a place for the idea of legitimate conflict and political competition was particularly important for later Soviet developments.[16] Although Lenin's *State and Revolution* has been interpreted as an example of the democratic and libertarian side of Lenin's thought, as distinct from the authoritarian *What Is to Be Done?*,[17] A. J. Polan has based an entire book-length condemnation of Leninist authoritarianism on an analysis of *The State and Revolution* and its implications. In Polan's words:

"in the main" being built during the next two decades (by about 1980). The revised Party Program adopted at the Twenty-seventh Party Congress in 1986 made no such rash prediction, for Khrushchev's venture into futurology had been a considerable source of embarrassment to his successors. As Gorbachev said recently, in an unmistakable reference to that period, "Superficial notions of communism and various prophecies and abstract views gained some currency. This in turn detracted from the historical significance of socialism and weakened the influence of socialist ideology."[23]

In the years of Brezhnev's ascendancy—his power was substantially greater following the Soviet military intervention ending the 1968 Prague Spring and especially after the Twenty-fourth Party Congress in 1971 when he consolidated his position within the leadership by adding four new voting members to the Politburo—the official ideology acquired a more cautious, complacent, and yet somewhat defensive tone. The notion of "developed socialism," which when first launched in the 1960s was deemed to be still in the early stages of construction and embodying ideas of reform, including the use of the profit motive and material interest and "the transformation of the entire superstructure,"[24] degenerated into an apologia for the status quo once it had been through the hands of more orthodox theorists and had been adopted personally by Brezhnev as the name for the stage of development reached during his General Secretaryship. Discussion of the nature and periodization of "developed socialism" became a major scholarly industry under Brezhnev, whereas critiques of the deficiencies of the system and society were discouraged both by conservative holders of power and by the conservatism of the ideological construct that placed such emphasis on how "developed" Soviet society had become—regardless of the lines, shortages, inefficiencies, and injustices that persisted in the real world of the Soviet Union.

The first authoritative, albeit oblique, critique of "developed socialism" came from Yuri Andropov, who emphasized that the Soviet Union was only "at the beginning" of the stage of "developed socialism," which would be a "historically long one" with its "own stages and phases of growth."[25] Gorbachev, in a major speech several months before his accession to the General Secretaryship, in which he first raised many of the reformist themes on which he has elaborated since becoming leader,[26] similarly referred to the task and "problems of *perfecting* developed socialism."[27] Since then, he has abandoned "developed socialism" as a central concept. In his speech to the Twenty-seventh Party Congress, he noted how it had become a cloak for conservatism,[28] and it was doubtless "developed socialism" that, inter alia, he had in mind when he spoke to the January 1987 Plenum of the Central Committee about the way in which "all manner of scholastic theorizing, having no bearing on anyone's interests and vital problems, was often even encouraged in the country, while attempts to carry out a constructive analysis and put forward new ideas were not supported."[29]

Gorbachev's Key Concepts

Gorbachev's own catchwords are *perestroika* (reconstruction or restructuring), *uskorenie* (acceleration), *glasnost'* (openness), and *demokratizatsiya* (democratization). The first of these concepts occupies pride of place and has increasingly come to stand for political and economic reform; indeed, Gorbachev has more than once spoken of the need for "radical reform" and on other occasions has referred to the "revolutionary" character of the changes under way. He has made it plain that *perestroika* means a program of action, in contrast to "developed socialism," which became a rationalization for inactivity. The very real resistance that "reconstruction" and greater openness are encountering within the Soviet system and society is sufficient evidence that this time more than concept-mongering and cosmetic changes are involved.

The idea of "acceleration" means, in effect, "getting the country moving again" following the economic stagnation of the later Brezhnev years. The stress on acceleration has led to the setting of economic targets that may be unrealistic and that may, to some extent, be induced by the imperative of "overtaking" capitalism. Gorbachev, however, is aware that if acceleration leads to Soviet industry being judged solely by the crude, old indices of gross output, nothing will have improved. It is less clear that the Soviet leadership as a whole is willing to accept with equanimity that in the transitional period of adaptation to what is now called a "new economic mechanism" the closing of uneconomic factories (if the economic reform is really implemented) and a much greater emphasis on quality could mean several years of low quantitative growth.

The change to *glasnost'* is one of the most striking features of the contemporary Soviet Union. *Glasnost'* has been virtually incorporated in the official ideology and, as such, must not be confused with total freedom of publication.[30] *Glasnost'* indicates a definite widening of the limits of the possible in the release of information and in debate, but the limits are thus far characteristic of a more enlightened authoritarian regime rather than those of a pluralist political system. The greater frankness of the mass media has also, as Gail Lapidus has noted, a preemptive aspect: "It is intended to reduce the reliance of the Soviet population on foreign and unofficial sources of information."[31] If maintained, however, even the present level of *glasnost'* has implications of great significance for Soviet political culture (which I shall address later in this chapter).

Gorbachev's adoption of the term *democratization* now in common use in the Soviet Union, raises still broader issues. As I noted earlier, there are participatory democratic elements in the thought of Marx and Lenin, and Gorbachev draws upon the later works of Lenin—specifically, from the New Economic Policy period—to justify not only his economic policy but also a more conciliatory relationship to different groups and legitimate interests within the society.

The question arises, however, whether democratization, in a sense that would be meaningful in the West, is compatible with official Soviet ideology. In *The Yawning Heights*, the Soviet émigré writer, Alexander Zinoviev, has a character who is a spokesman for the author's views say, "The leadership is powerless to change the official ideology of any society at will, even if they wanted to, even if they didn't believe in the ideology. . . . A society like ours would be unthinkable without some form of ideology. It is an ideological society at its very base."[32]

It can be argued that the store of concepts within Marxism-Leninism— even when the latter is defined broadly enough to include not only the complete works of Marx and Lenin but also some of the more innovative writers within that tradition, such as Antonio Gramsci, who has been quoted with increasing frequency by Soviet theorists in recent years— is insufficient to analyze all that is wrong with the Soviet system. This is a view that commends itself to most Western observers, but it would be utterly unrealistic to expect a General Secretary of the Soviet Communist Party to believe it to be often necessary to step outside the official ideology to provide an adequate critique of Soviet society's deficiencies.

This does not mean that a leader of an innovative and reformist cast of mind—a description befitting Gorbachev—need be as ideologically hamstrung as Zinoviev appeared to suggest. Not all options are open, but a combination of the prolific and somewhat diverse nature of the "classics" of Marxism-Leninism and the injunction that this body of doctrine be "creatively developed" leaves substantial scope for ideological innovation.

Socialist Pluralism

A remarkable example of this innovation is Gorbachev's adoption of the term *socialist pluralism*. He used it on at least three occasions in 1987, although his first usage of the term at an authoritative Party forum did not occur until the February 1988 Central Committee Plenum. These were the first times in Soviet history when a General Secretary had employed the word *pluralism* (albeit "socialist pluralism") other than critically.

Soviet politicians, theorists, and propagandists have indeed been anathematizing the concept ever since it entered their consciousness in 1968, when it was adopted by leading Party intellectuals in Czechoslovakia. (The concept has also been accepted in principle by many Yugoslav, Polish, and Western European Communists.)[33] The context in which Gorbachev first used the term *pluralism* positively—in his July 1987 speech to leading representatives of the mass media and creative unions— was that of criticism of the control of access to the columns of Soviet newspapers by narrow cliques. "Let us vary the output," he said, "so that the whole of society participates, and the whole of socialist pluralism [*plyuralizm sotsialisticheskiy*] so to speak, is present."[34]

The second occasion on which Gorbachev used pluralism as a concept with positive connotations was at a meeting with a large group of French public figures who visited the Soviet Union at the end of September 1987. Responding to the expression of approval from a French Communist of the greater "pluralism of opinion" that was "now more and more openly tolerated" in Soviet society, Gorbachev said, "It is true, but to the word pluralism we add only one adjective—socialist pluralism. That means that our democracy and our pluralism are based on our socialist values."[35] Although it should not be overlooked that Gorbachev was placing limits on pluralism, in the Soviet context that was not what was new. Rather, the novelty lay in the fact that he was prepared to accept a "socialist pluralism" (as distinct from monism or monolithism) as a positive goal and, insofar as it has begun to emerge, as a desirable achievement.

That these were not chance endorsements of pluralism—albeit "socialist pluralism"—by Gorbachev was demonstrated when he used the term (in a similar context to the first occasion) in his book *Perestroika*, published in late 1987.[36] These new uses of pluralism reflect, rather, his endorsement of the views of some of the reformers around him that the time has come for a revision of Soviet attitudes to pluralism and that the concept has much of value to offer reformers in their own fight against dogmatism and political intolerance. Such doctrinal innovation also reflects the fact that under Gorbachev some elements of de facto pluralism have been tolerated within Soviet society.

Thus, for example, Soviet newspapers and journals have become increasingly differentiated in their attitudes toward reform and toward the past, with editors having a much greater say in determining the line of their periodicals and with fewer instructions being handed down from above. These de facto elements of pluralism are illustrated, too, by the existence of many unofficial groups,[37] some of which have been attacked in the mass media although not suppressed. The most notable example is the Russian nationalist association, Pamyat' (Memory), which, although it is subject to criticism by the press, has continued to function. Notwithstanding the fact that Pamyat' is, in its way, a very conservative (and also anti-Semitic) organization, conservatives of a different sort (those who pride themselves on their Marxist-Leninist orthodoxy) have been pressing for its suppression. Thus, Pamyat' has become a test case, and Soviet party reformers have thus far resisted proposals to crush it because they hold that this would be used as a precedent to eliminate every other independent group and would lead to a more comprehensive trampling of the tender shoots of political pluralism that have emerged.

Gorbachev's most unambiguous espousal of the concept of pluralism came when he used it at the February 1988 Central Committee Plenum. In his major speech on that occasion, he observed, "For the first time in many decades we are really experiencing a socialist pluralism of opinion."[38] He also made it clear that the phenomenon of pluralism—and, by implication, the concept—was evaluated in different ways within the Party, but he left his listeners in no doubt that his own attitude toward both the concept and at least a limited pluralism in reality was a positive one. Thus, in the space of eight months, what had seemed to some to be no more than a throwaway remark had come close to being elevated into new Party doctrine, notwithstanding the traditional monist theory of the Soviet state, and the oft-repeated claim of the "monolithic unity" of the Party and the people.

The fact that Gorbachev's support for pluralism is qualified by his use of the adjective "socialist" and that the party leadership retains the power to define the boundaries of socialism both in theory and in practice indicate that this is not Western-style pluralism. Such elements of pluralism as do exist are far from sufficient to make it meaningful to describe the present Soviet system as one of a pluralist type. Nevertheless, Gorbachev's remarks, although somewhat elliptical, bring him closer to the views of Prague Spring or Polish Communist reformers who have so often been excoriated by Soviet leaders and propagandists for offering theoretical and practical defense of a socialist pluralism.[39]

Thus, these remarks made by Gorbachev have considerable ideological significance, even though it would clearly be a mistake to interpret them to mean that a full-fledged political pluralism is even on the near-term agenda of the Soviet leadership. But the use of concepts that have, at best, a tenuous place within the Marxist-Leninist tradition and the change of emphasis within the ideology should not be dismissed as unimportant—least of all by those who hold that Marxism-Leninism is still of vital significance in Soviet political life.

In a number of respects, Marxism-Leninism is indeed of vital importance. There are, perhaps, three elements of the ideology that have been elevated to a higher pinnacle than the rest. Historically, their preservation has imposed limits upon the possibilities of fundamental change in other aspects of the doctrine, in the power structure, and in some areas of policy. It is worth examining each of the three elements separately to see whether there is any sign of change even there.

These central tenets of Soviet ideology are (1) the fundamental importance of class consciousness and of the class struggle; (2) the "leading role" of the Communist Party; and (3) democratic centralism. In the sense that these have remained principles on which great stress is laid—and principles interpreted in such a way that they have great practical import—they have been constants throughout virtually all of Soviet history. Yet here, too, there has been some variation of interpretation from the Stalin to the post-Stalin era, and there has also been change within that latter period, not least since the death of Brezhnev.

Class Consciousness and the Class Struggle

Unlike the other two elements of Marxism-Leninism, the idea of class struggle is a concept that derives from Marx himself, although he can hardly be held responsible for some of the subsequent interpretations of it. Stalin's theory of the intensification of the class struggle as completion of the building of socialism approached was used as an excuse to brand countless real and imaginary opponents (usually imaginary) as "class enemies," which in many cases was tantamount to pronouncing a death sentence. The importance of the "all-people's state," to which I have already referred, was that it signified an end to even the theoretical need for class struggle within the Soviet Union itself. Soviet citizens have continued to be urged, however, to adopt a "class approach" in their analysis of social phenomena and thus to be suspicious of, for example, "bourgeois" or "abstract" rights as distinct from rights that will strengthen the socialist system.

A "class approach" has also frequently been applied in the analysis of events in other Communist states. Thus, Brezhnev's public interpretation of the culmination of the reform movement within Czechoslovakia between January and August 1968 was that this was a particularly sharp instance of class struggle. He did not satisfactorily explain why, if this class struggle was, in fact, taking place within a socialist state, the working class was losing—and losing so badly, apparently, that it required reinforcement from approximately 500,000 foreign troops. The class approach has also been extensively used in analyses of the Soviet Union's relations with capitalist states. Thus, although goodwill toward the "toiling masses" under capitalism has traditionally been encouraged by the Soviet leadership, implacable hostility toward the bourgeois states as such has also been a concomitant of the approved class consciousness and of the interpretation of the meaning of class struggle within the international arena.

Yet even here, notable changes are occurring in Soviet ideology. The notion of the leading role of the working class took the place of the more drastic concept of the dictatorship of the proletariat, although in Brezhnev's time even the former, less authoritarian concept was often used as a rhetorical stick with which to beat an intelligentsia suspected of independent thought. The Party leadership in the post-Brezhnev era is, however, no longer deliberately fostering distrust between workers and intellectuals, although both the theoretical possibility and the concrete reality of actual conflicts of interest between different social and institutional groups have increasingly been recognized.

Particularly important is the fact that some Soviet theorists have in recent years moved away from an emphasis on a "class approach" to international relations, and there are signs that this "new thinking" has been incorporated in the official ideology. For some years, there has been a school of thought in Soviet writing holding that in the nuclear age "all-human considerations" take precedence over class concerns. One way of formulating this is to say, as has Georgiy Shakhnazarov (formerly a prominent official in the Central Committee apparatus and since early 1988 a personal assistant to the General Secretary), that because nuclear war could not, by any conceivable stretch of the imagination, be beneficial to the working class of one or another country, it follows that a pursuit of class goals to the endangerment of world peace is irrational. Shakhnazarov formulated as a maxim for the nuclear era the proposition that "political ends do not exist which would justify the use of means liable to lead to nuclear war."[40]

Other Soviet theorists have in recent years gone even further and have elevated peace higher than socialism as an absolute value, although defenders of the traditional orthodoxy have been quick to attack these theorists for adopting "supraclass" positions. Gorbachev himself has spoken of "the priority of the all-human value of peace over all others to which different peoples are attached,"[41] and some of the new thinking he has espoused provides a theoretical basis for a low-risk foreign policy in which military means are further subordinated to political ends defined in less narrow terms than before. Although it is too early to say that "all–human considerations" have definitively triumphed over the so-called class approach in Soviet analyses, Stephen Shenfield, who has made the most careful study of the "peace and socialism" debate published thus far, has appositely pointed out that "Gorbachev's 'new thinking' has enabled moral absolutism to establish a precarious foothold in the fortress of official ideology."[42]

The Leading Role of the Communist Party

The leading role of the party, a concept that owes much more to Lenin than to Marx and that has, in one way or another, always played an important part in Soviet political life, connotes the hegemonic power and superior authority of the Communist Party vis-à-vis all other institutions and groups within the society. Under Stalin, however, it was a moot point whether the Party had a superior authority to the security forces, although the vastly superior power and authority of the party *leader*, Stalin himself, were beyond dispute. Under Khrushchev, the "leading role" of the Party meant, in part, a revitalization of the Party and the much firmer subordination of state institutions—in the first instance, the security organs—to Party control. In Brezhnev's time, the power of many state organs, including the ministries, grew again, and a further revitalization of the Party may be regarded as one element of the Gorbachev reforms.

Gorbachev's reconstruction clearly excludes anything that would diminish the leading role of the Party as he understands it. Although there have been moves toward strengthening the legal system (so that, for example, Party members cannot enjoy immunity from prosecution for criminal actions, such as bribe taking), it is not likely that the present Soviet leadership would wish to see its own political powers significantly curbed. Yet Gorbachev *is* attempting to redefine the leading role of the Party as far as its involvement in the economy is concerned. Although the Party has long been enjoined not to engage in petty tutelage in its supervision of economic activity, this injunction would become more meaningful to the extent to which the economy became more self-regulating—that is to say, as far as it included a significant market element. Given that such an economic reform is now at least on the political agenda and could become a reality during the next few years, a concomitant redefinition of the leading role of the Party is a distinct possibility. The Party in China and in Hungary has in a significant sense retained its "leading role," but the way it exercises that role in relation to economic management has in recent years been very different from the role of the Soviet Party in the economy of the USSR.

The leading role of the Party also now involves much less petty tutelage of the mass media, literature, and the arts than has generally been the case during the past seventy years. Here, as in the social sciences, the *legitimacy* of diverse viewpoints on many important issues of the day has been more fully accepted than at any time since the

1920s. In reality, as well, the conflict of opinion within the same newspaper or journal and between one such publication and another is greater than it has been since then. This broadening of the limits is not yet insti-tutionalized and still depends upon the goodwill or tolerance of de-partment heads within the Central Committee apparatus, on their ov-erlords within the Secretariat, and, ultimately, on the General Secretary, Gorbachev, himself. In that sense, of course, the leading role of the Party is maintained, but the way it is interpreted has already changed, in actual practice, more from the Brezhnev era to the Gorbachev period than has the role of the Party in the economy.

In addition, the widening of the boundaries of the permissible has led not only to conservative attacks on "muckraking" writers but also to radical demands from within the literary establishment for a true freedom of publication. Thus, for example, in May 1987 a member of the editorial board of the prestigious journal *Novy mir* argued that the press should be "independent of the party bureaucracy and the state apparatus" and that freedom should not be viewed as a means but as an end in itself.[43] If such a view were ever to be fully accepted at the highest political level, a radical change indeed would have occurred in the understanding of the leading role of the Party. But even the expression of such an opinion by a prominent literary figure addressing Komsomol activists at Moscow University is a sign that things are not as they were.

Democratic Centralism

The third concept I have singled out as a central tenet of the official ideology, democratic centralism, postdates Marx but was accepted as a key principle by Lenin. Given that Lenin believed in persuasion of Party members as well as in a highly centralized Party structure, both parts of the notion had some meaning in his time. Subsequently, the doctrine of democratic centralism was used for long periods of time to strengthen the predominance of the Party leadership and of the full-time professional apparatus; to sustain strict discipline within the Party; and to prevent any frank criticism of major policy or attempts from below to exercise real influence over leading Party officials. In Party language, a distinction was made between democratic centralism and bureaucratic centralism (with the former, unlike the latter, connoting, in principle at least, a willingness on the part of higher Party organs to listen to views emanating from below). In practice, that distinction has become blurred, for the doctrine has been used to reinforce the overwhelmingly hierarchical nature of the Party with the centralistic component all too clearly prevailing over the democratic.

One change in the post-Stalin period was the extension of this principle from Party life to the society as a whole. Whereas democratic centralism has served as the organizational basis of the Party throughout the entire Soviet era, it was only in 1977, with the promulgation of the fourth Soviet constitution, that democratic centralism was applied as well to all state structures. In practice, however, Soviet state bodies probably remained no more and no less hierarchical than before.

A more important change in the concept of democratic centralism has occurred in recent years. Soviet theorists have once again emphasized the democratic as well as the centralistic component of the concept, arguing that the former had been downgraded and was in need of enhancement.[44] When Gorbachev speaks of democratization it is, indeed, not pluralist democracy in the conventional Western sense that he has in mind, but it may not be going too far to attribute to him an actual desire to return to those "Leninist norms" to which all Soviet party leaders have paid at least lip service and to impart meaning to the democratic part of democratic centralism. With his support for competitive party elections and his references to the need for control from below as well as from above, Gorbachev may be undertaking a more far-reaching reinterpretation of this concept than occurred even in Khrushchev's time.[45]

New Thinking

The new thinking in the Soviet Union has enabled reformers to put forward ideas as compatible with socialism that only a few years ago would have been condemned as antisocialist or anti-Soviet. Indeed, many of the current reform proposals advocated by Gorbachev himself—from the encouragement of new forms of cooperative enterprise to the recognition that the market must play a much greater role in the Soviet economy as a whole—have been greeted with the accusation that the principles of Soviet ideology are being undermined.[46] The acceptance as a central feature of reform of the principle of self-management is a case in point. For years, it was condemned as a revisionist Yugoslav notion. But now one especially sensitive part of it—the principle of electing factory managers—is receiving the enthusiastic support even of the Director of the Institute of Marxism-Leninism of the Central Committee of the Communist Party. This former bastion of conservatism is, in fact, now headed by a reformer, Georgiy Smirnov, who in a Soviet television discussion program in July 1987 replied to the criticism that electing managers could lead to "errors." "Of course there can be errors," he said. "But there were even more of them when they were appointed!"[47]

One of the most significant areas of ideological innovation concerns the ownership of property in Gorbachev's Soviet Union. Since the 1930s, the highest form of socialist ownership had, in effect, been defined as state ownership (with its concomitant layers of bureaucracy). But now those who are influential in the Soviet Union, such as Smirnov, pose the rhetorical question, "Who said that socialism is linked only with the form of organization and only with the form of property which took shape in our country in the 1930s?"[48] A sector head in the Institute of Economics of the World Socialist System was more specific.

> I would lay particular emphasis on the need for a multiplicity of forms of ownership. . . . There is a keen discussion currently underway over the rehabilitation and revival of co-operative ownership and individual ownership, and I think that masses of other types of ownership will also arise on the experience of the other socialist countries. Joint stock capital investment is probably also possible. Indeed, why should not working people use their savings to participate in stimulating the kinds of products they are crying out for—why not?[49]

What all of this suggests is that although Soviet Marxism-Leninism makes some doctrinal claims or policy options more difficult than others to justify within terms of the ideology, that ideology can be quite flexible if the Party leadership wishes it to be. The top leader himself is not entirely unconstrained by the ideology, for if he is an innovator, he is also forced to justify himself against accusations from more conservative colleagues that he may be departing from the principles of Soviet-style socialism. Thus, Gorbachev must cite Lenin in his support and must answer the question that he concedes is being posed, "Doesn't our restructuring drive mean a departure from the foundations of socialism or at least their weakening?" His reply is,

> No, it doesn't. On the contrary, what we already are doing, planning and proposing should strengthen socialism, remove everything holding back its progress, bring out its potential for the people, give play to all advantages of our social system, and lend it the most modern forms.
>
> But what does boosting socialism actually mean? The essence of our revolutionary teaching and all our vast experience demonstrate that socialism should not be seen as an ossified, unchanging system or the practical work to refine it as a means of adjusting complex reality to fit ideas, notions and formulas adopted once and for all.
>
> Views on socialism and its economy are developed and enriched all the time, with account taken of historical experience and objective conditions. We should follow Lenin's example in creatively developing the theory and practice of building socialism, adopt scientific methods and master the art of specific analysis of a specific situation.[50]

Marxism-Leninism provides a language and framework for Soviet political discourse, but these are much more elastic and subject to change than is often assumed. The differences among those who speak this language may be no less than those that separate members of the major political parties in the West. Drawing on different parts of Marx and Lenin and different elements in Soviet experience can produce quite radically dissimilar bodies of doctrine, for each of which the claim can be made that it is "socialist." Conservative Communists make more frequent use than do reformers of the label "Marxist-Leninist" to describe their thoughts and endeavors (perhaps because of the Stalinist origins of the conjunction of Marxism and Leninism), but that term can also be pressed into the service of innovation because in the Soviet context, realistic reformers cannot allow the mantle of Marx and Lenin—even in the form of Marxism-Leninism—to become the exclusive garb of their hidebound opponents.

Political Culture

The Soviet Union does not have a unified political culture, but it does have a dominant one. By that I mean that there are certain values, fundamental political beliefs, perceptions of history, and understandings of politics shared by a majority of the population.[51] It is a dominant Soviet political culture that draws heavily from the dominant Russian one.

There are various subcultures that coexist, with more or less facility, with the dominant political culture. In certain respects, the subcultures are based upon nationality, but although there are *some* political cultural differences separating one ethnic group from another—especially in the areas of perception of history, the foci of identification and loyalty (different symbols and national heroes)—it does not follow that values and fundamental beliefs differ radically along ethnic lines. Among nationalities with experience of living together under the same authoritarian rule during a long period of time—stretching back beyond the Soviet period into the Russian empire—even those ethnic groups that may harbor ideas of greater national independence do not necessarily differ fundamentally from the Russians in terms of their attachment (or more precisely, lack of attachment) to political pluralism and Western ideas of political freedom and individualism.

Thus, the best evidence available, that of the Harvard Project on the Soviet Social System, suggests that there are not significant differences between Russians and Ukrainians in terms of their understanding of politics. The results of the large-scale Harvard survey of "displaced persons" of various Soviet nationalities after World War II indicate that there are many striking similarities in the attitudes of these, the largest and second largest of Soviet nationalities, toward the role of government and toward political liberties as well as a "relative absence of strong class-linked variation." This suggests that "attitudes toward the ideal government and social and economic organization of society are a general cultural trait shared by both Russians and Ukrainians."[52]

That does not rule out the consideration that a heightened national consciousness on the part of Ukrainians may have been developing,[53] nor does it exclude the possibility that differences between the values and fundamental political beliefs of Russians and Ukrainians may have become more pronounced since the Harvard Project was conducted.[54] A verdict on that must remain open. One would expect to find more significant deviation from Soviet norms on the part of those inhabitants of the western Ukraine whose territory belonged to Poland or Czecho-slovakia between the world wars and who thus did not go through the Stalin school of political education. Similarly, of all the Soviet nationalities that have their own republic, there seems little doubt that the differences in political culture between the three Baltic republics (independent states between the wars) and the Russians are greatest. Different value systems in these cases are associated too with Western religious traditions, most notably in respect of the Protestant Estonians and Roman Catholic Lithuanians. Numerically, however, the Baltic nationalities hardly loom large in the Soviet population of some 280 million people. At the last census (1979), the combined numbers of Lithuanians, Latvians, and Estonians made up 4.2 million compared with 137.4 million Russians and 42.3 million Ukrainians. Among the faster-growing Asian peoples of the Soviet Union, there are also foci of identification and loyalty and, of course, traditions different from those of the Russians, but there is no evidence of a greater attachment to individual political liberties or of rejection of an authoritarian political system.[55]

Political Culture and Obstacles to Reform

There is no getting away from the predominantly authoritarian nature of Soviet and Russian political experience. Because values and funda-mental political beliefs evolve in a complex relationship with social and institutional developments, the relative absence of pluralist and democratic political structures during a historically long period should make it less than surprising that attachment to individual political liberties, and support for their institutionalization, remains weak. It is important not to overstate this point. There have been many sustained attempts to demonstrate the unremittingly authoritarian character of *The Russian Tradition*, to cite the title of Tibor Szamuely's posthumously published book on the subject.[56] The authoritarian tradition is a stark reality, but it is better stated in terms of a dominant political culture that does not exclude subcultures or alternative traditions even among the Russian population.

Yet the political-cultural obstacles to reform of a democratizing, especially pluralizing, type may be even more formidable than those posed by Marxism-Leninism. We are concerned here with values and attitudes based on long historical traditions and on direct experience. Although the diversity of values and beliefs both in prerevolutionary and in Soviet society is greater than has sometimes been suggested, centuries of autocratic or, at best, oligarchical rule have left their mark on the Russian and Soviet population, even if the scope for more or less independent political activity has not been uniformly limited and was, for instance, much greater under Nicholas II than under Stalin. If there has been one period of pluralist democracy in all of Russian history, it was the chaotic months between March and November 1917. Very few people now alive have adult memories of that time, and, given the value Russians have traditionally placed upon order, it would hardly strengthen attachment to pluralist and democratic values if they had.

Because political cultures are historically conditioned, the long-term authoritarian character of the Russian and Soviet state constitutes a serious impediment to political change of a pluralizing, libertarian, or genuinely democratizing nature. Often, too little emphasis is placed on the extent to which a number of central features of traditional Russian political culture have been reinforced in the Soviet period. Such elements as acceptance of strict political hierarchy; the taking for granted of political police powers, administrative exile, and restrictions on travel; great deference to the top leader; loyalty to a person rather than to political, and particularly legal, institutions; and reluctance to engage in autonomous political activity could only be strengthened by the Soviet experience and, above all, by what happened in Stalin's time.

Another central value of the dominant Soviet political culture is the emphasis placed upon order (*poryadok*). Indeed, the extent to which fear of disorder, of chaos, has been one of the strongest bonds of unity, drawing together all social groups—workers, peasants, intellectuals, and power-holders—in the Soviet Union has been remarked upon both by Western analysts[57] and by perceptive observers within the USSR. Nadezhda Mandelstam, commenting on the intelligentsia's fear of what would happen if ever "the mob" got out of hand ("We should be the first to be hanged from a lamppost"), observed, "Whenever I hear this constantly repeated phrase, I remember Herzen's words about the intelligentsia which so much fears its own people that it prefers to go in chains itself, provided the people, too, remain fettered."[58] Andrey Amalrik recalled the response of one Russian worker to the political turmoil, as he saw it, of Czechoslovakia in 1968: "What sort of government is it," the worker asked, "that tolerates so much disorder? Power must be such that *I* live in fear of it—not that *it* lives in fear of me!"[59]

This may be regarded as unpromising soil for the growth of democracy. If intellectuals distrust the mass of the people—the *demos*, or Russian *narod*—and if workers perceive spontaneous or autonomous political activity as "disorder," what hope can there be for the process of democratization that Gorbachev and Soviet writers and spokesmen claim is under way? It would appear that to the serious institutional, interest-based, and, to a lesser extent, ideological obstacles to far-reaching political reform should be added at least as fundamental a political-cultural one—the lack of experience of the mass of the Soviet people with democratic institutions and processes and their degree of distrust of "spontaneity" and of relaxation of controls.

The changing of attitudes and practices does not come easily. Two of the more remarkable recent examples, judging by the standards of the past, of the Soviet authorities practicing a new tolerance were when the police refrained (or were restrained) from breaking up a large demonstration by Crimean Tatars in Moscow in July 1987 and demonstrations in the Baltic republics the following month. Reporting on the first of these events for *The Times* of London, Mary Dejevsky wrote, "Comments heard on Red Square yesterday suggest there would have been a popular mandate for the police to have broken up the demonstration with whatever force they considered necessary."[60] Writing a month later, following the further demonstrations in the Baltic cities, Dejevsky elaborated, "It is not just the authorities which have to educate themselves as to the need to tolerate other opinions and listen to argument if Soviet society is to become more democratic, it is the Russian public as well. . . . During the Tatar protests, the police had to ensure not only that they kept the demonstration under control but that they restrained the crowd of onlookers as well."[61] Public protests of this kind, or, indeed, any act of overt political dissent or opposition, represent a significant deviation from Soviet norms of behavior and can be relied upon to provoke widespread hostility. More than one Soviet dissident, on being questioned and warned by the security police in Brezhnev's time, was told, "You should be grateful to the KGB. We stand between you and the wrath of the people!"

A striking feature of the contemporary Soviet Union is, however, the realization on the part of reformers that although political-cultural change is far from easy to effect, it must be achieved if their efforts are ultimately to be successful; it would be in part a concomitant but also a condition of lasting improvement in the nature and functioning of the Soviet political system. One of the most prominent reformers among Soviet Party intellectuals, Fedor Burlatsky, when invited to explain why Khrushchev's reforms had failed and the process begun at the Twentieth and Twenty-second Party Congresses had given way to a conservative tendency, adduced "the traditional thinking, the political culture of the population" as among the major reasons.[62] Asked why he thought that this time there would be no turning back, he noted both the urgency of the problems and public understanding of their scale, adding, "Now we have a new society, a more educated society, and we have new cadres, cultured cadres. It is not the same as after Stalin's time. And last, but not least, the political will of our leadership. It is traditional in Russia, you know, that the reform must be supported first of all from our leadership. That is the case now."[63]

Burlatsky has elaborated his views in a significant article in *Pravda*, the newspaper he was forced to leave twenty years earlier for his support of *glasnost'* at a time when such advocacy was unfashionable.[64] Entitled "To Study Democracy," the theme of the article (published in the summer of 1987[65]) was the issue of the development of Russian and Soviet political culture. Burlatsky suggested that this political culture has "a rather contradictory tradition," and "tradition," he adds (quoting Aleksandr Pushkin), "is the soul of power." He considered the major areas of prerevolutionary Russian history and observed that Pushkin's words, "the people are silent" (*narod bezmolvstvuet*)[66] reflect "a political tradition of authoritarianism." This legacy could not but have its effect in the Soviet period, and "the inadequacy of the general and political culture" was a significant factor in the transformation of the vision of government by the working people into government for the working people. Taking note of the "cruel repressions" and "human tragedies" of the Stalin period, Burlatsky observed that "the cult of personality itself was not only implanted from above. Alas, it reflected the phenomenon of the specific level of political culture of the masses."[67]

Since the April 1985 Plenum of the Central Committee (the first substantive plenum of the Gorbachev era), said Burlatsky, "a new Soviet political culture has begun to be formed to a significant degree before our eyes." But he emphasized "how much lies ahead" in terms of fostering "the political culture and authentic civilization" ("to which," he added by way of ideological justification, "Lenin attached such enormous significance").

Although an advocate of far-reaching reform who specifically observed that the most useless result of *perestroika* would be a "microreform" (the kind of half-hearted measures, half-heartedly applied, characteristic of the two previous decades), Burlatsky also went out of his way to warn against extremes, seeing "democratization" as the key to political-cultural change because "it is precisely democracy which rules out the swinging from one extreme to another that has cost our country so dearly." He was critical of immediate, maximalist demands, such as that for unlimited freedom of demonstration. The people who want this, he suggested, are the single-issue fanatics, among whom he numbered (perhaps for the sake of political symmetry) both the "narrow nationalists and extremists" from Pamyat' and "refuseniks." He was particularly severe about national*ism*, as distinct from preservation of national consciousness. He fully endorsed the desire to preserve Russian culture, including ancient monuments and the old names of towns and streets, but rejected the views of "people who have attached themselves to that movement" and who operate from "positions of nationalism and chauvinism."[68]

Another key to political culture change, in the eyes of a good many reformers, is to be found in the exposure of Soviet history to the searchlight of serious analysis and scholarly debate. One of the foremost advocates of *glasnost'* in history, the Rector of the Moscow State Historical-Archival Institute, Yuriy Afanas'ev, has written of the divergence between a "domestic" knowledge of history and "history for general use" as something that "each of us experiences for himself." These discrepancies are, in his view, "the source of spiritual torment, moral trauma and bitterness."[69] In criticizing the persistence of "white spots" in Soviet historiography, Afanas'ev said, "The full truth is needed" (*nuzhna polnaya pravda*).[70] This echoes, virtually verbatim, the words of the senior party secretary responsible for ideology, Yegor Ligachev, but it reverses Ligachev's meaning. Whereas Ligachev, who has acted as a brake on *perestroika*, warned in an article in 1986 entitled, "We Need the Full Truth" (*nam nuzhna polnaya pravda*),[71] against an excessive concentration on negative aspects of the Soviet experience, Afanas'ev was, much more pertinently, using the phrase to draw attention to the way historical writing in the Soviet Union became "propaganda of successes." He was stressing the need to remove old taboos and engage in honest analysis of all periods and all important personalities in Soviet history.[72]

Gorbachev, Perestroika, *and Political-Cultural Change*

Although it is far more difficult than once was assumed to engineer or plan cultural change,[73] it is interesting to note that some Soviet reformers, indeed Gorbachev himself, have addressed themselves to the issue of changing deeply entrenched habits of thinking, values, and beliefs. When Gorbachev equated the concept of *perestroika* with revolution, it was, as Robert C. Tucker has observed, "a cultural revolution" the Soviet leader had in mind, "in the sense of a fundamental transformation of a great many customary Soviet ways of acting and thinking."[74]

Gorbachev is not the first General Secretary to use the terminology "political culture." Leonid Brezhnev did so, and Yuri Andropov and Konstantin Chernenko followed suit, but for Brezhnev and Chernenko at least, the concept seems to have held no special significance. At times, the words put into previous General Secretaries' mouths by their speech-writers reflected the views of reformers and were not strikingly different from some of the sentiments expressed more recently by Gorbachev. Thus, in what appears to have been the first use by a General Secretary of the term *political culture*, the idea of the broadening of participation of working people in political life and in management was linked by Brezhnev in June 1974 to the need for "raising the political culture of the workers and of extending the degree of openness [*glasnost'*] of the work of the Party, soviet and economic organs."[75] Given, however, that the General Secretary had more power than anyone else in the society to translate at least the latter part of those words into action, it must be concluded that Brezhnev was doing little more than reading a text placed in front of him, whereas Gorbachev actually appears to believe in the ideas put into Brezhnev's mouth more than a decade ago.

Gorbachev has made increasing use of the term "political culture." Addressing leading figures in the mass media and the creative unions in July 1987, he identified as a major defect of existing Soviet political culture the lack of tolerance and respect for contrary opinions. Gorbachev told them, "We are now going through the school of democracy afresh. We are learning. Our political culture is still inadequate. Our culture in debate is insufficient, and also inadequate is our respect for the point of view even of our friend and comrade. We are an emotional people. All this we shall doubtless pass through. We shall grow up."[76]

Gorbachev has also been careful to address himself to some of the objections of opponents of reform, among them those rooted in the values of the dominant Russian political culture—not least of which is the devotion to order and control. In a speech in February 1987, he recognized that "further democratization" might lead some to suggest that control was being weakened and standards of discipline and order lowered. His reply to such critics was that those with doubts about the wisdom of further democratization suffered from a serious shortcoming of great political significance: "They do not believe in our people."[77] Arguing that stepping further down the path of reform should give no cause for alarm, Gorbachev held that the choice facing the Soviet Union was "either democracy or social inertia and conservatism." While suggesting in only general terms what he meant by "democracy" (it is worth noting that the concept has far from the same connotation for all who use it in the Soviet Union), he went out of his way to say what it was *not*.

Democracy is not opposed to order. On the contrary, it is order of a higher level, being based not on unquestioning obedience, the mindless execution of instructions, but on the active participation of members of society in all affairs. Democracy is not the opposite of discipline. On the contrary, it is conscious discipline and organization of people's work, the foundation of which is the sense of being a real master of the country, together with collectivism and the solidarity of the interests and efforts of all citizens. Democracy is not the opposite of responsibility, not the absence of control or the permitting of everything. On the contrary, it is self-control on the part of society, based on faith in the civic maturity and understanding of social duty of Soviet people; it is the unity of rights and duties.[78]

In seeking political-cultural change, Gorbachev is clearly not attempting to overturn all existing Soviet norms and values; rather, he is trying to show that different attitudes and practices may be compatible with them. Doubtless, he himself shares many of the traditional values, but that does not mean that he is lacking in openness to new ideas or that his beliefs are unchanging in the light of experience.

Although it is useful, for the most part, to consider values and fundamental political beliefs together when discussing political culture, values are more resistant to change than are attitudes and even some important political beliefs.[79] Values—such as a commitment to egalitarianism, collectivism, or order—are not subject to falsification. But many political beliefs can be shown in the light of experience to rest on shaky empirical foundations. A good example is the Soviet belief in planning—at least planning by which an all-seeing political leadership can promote more efficient industrial organization and faster economic growth than market forces can. In the 1950s, that belief had a much stronger basis in comparative growth rates than it has today. The fact, however, that the Soviet rate of economic growth has been in decline from the 1950s to the 1980s, and dramatically so in the early 1980s, has led to a loss of faith in the omnipotence of "the plan." But this is unlikely to lead to a complete reliance on the market. Not only is the idea of planning too firmly entrenched in Soviet rhetoric for such a shift to be easy, but even those who are skeptical about old-style planning do not want to leave all investment decisions to the market because of the extent to which this would be liable to widen the economic gap between one part of their vast country and another and thereby risk increasing national tensions. Real-world trends have, however, been sufficient to lead a growing number of Soviet social scientists as well as Gorbachev and his political supporters to seek to redefine the meaning and role of planning and its relationship with the market.

Generational Subcultures and Support for Reform

Part of the explanation for the greater support for reform now must also be sought in terms of a generational subculture. The passage of time has brought, and the arrival of Gorbachev in the Kremlin has hastened, the coming to positions of power and influence of the generation that reached maturity in the early post-Stalin period and for whom the Twentieth Party Congress (which, at a stroke, destroyed so many sustaining myths) was the most fundamental political experience of their lives. This was particularly true of those who were already Party members (and who thus had more information on Khrushchev's speech and for whom the shock of it was, in any event, greater) and who were still young enough to alter their ways of thinking. Those who were in their late teens, twenties, and early thirties in 1956 are a full generation later in their late forties, fifties, and early sixties, and it is from this age cohort that the overwhelming majority of significant reformers within the Party apparatus and the intelligentsia is drawn.

It is of particular interest that so many people of this generation are now pressing their views and exerting influence, whereas those wielding equivalent power and influence during the second half of Brezhnev's General Secretaryship tended to be a full decade older. Even today, there are many in important positions who *are* older and who are, by and large, more conservative. As for Party members who are one political generation younger than those now in and around their fifties—that is to say, the people who matured in Brezhnev's time—they do not live up to the generalization holding that "the younger, the more radical," for they appear to include more cynics and careerists than the generation whose hopes were fired by Khrushchev, even though the dashing of those hopes doubtless reduced many of the latter group, as well, to cynicism.[80]

Mikhail Gorbachev himself is in that generation for whom Khrushchev's de-Stalinization was a decisive experience, and so are the most influential supporters of reform. One such person, who has commented explicitly on the impact the Twentieth Congress had on him, is the *Izvestiya* political commentator Aleksandr Bovin. Writing in the formerly staid and predictable pages of the journal *New Times*, Bovin has observed:

> I cannot but recall the 20th Congress of the C.P.S.U. I matured as a communist, a citizen, an individual under the impact of that congress. It was then that my own "restructuring," a lifelong restructuring began. For the young party functionaries of that time (I was 25 then and worked as head of propaganda department of a party district committee) the 20th Congress was a purifying storm-wind which made it possible to look to the future with hope. We began to learn to think, to act, to speak our

minds. And it was with bewilderment, pain, with a revolting sense of my own hopelessness that I and my generation saw the idea of one of the truly historic congresses of our Party sink into the quicksands of bureaucracy.[81]

In the same article, Bovin—borrowing a phrase from the Soviet writer and editor of *Novy mir*, Sergey Zalygin—described "homegrown bureaucratic Soviet socialist conservatism" as "our main enemy," adding that these Soviet socialist conservatives were afraid of openness. Bovin warned that this group of people "and their numerous hangers-on" had not lost hope: "They are biding their time. They have already reared their successors—younger functionaries, more sophisticated in manner, but thinking in terms of past decades, past practices. This kind of new functionary readily talks about turning over a new leaf but whether he is actually doing so is doubtful."[82]

The Soviet socialist conservatives described by Bovin represent a very different political subculture from that of the group of people radicalized by the Twentieth Party Congress. The existence and influence of these conservatives mean that there can be no guarantee that the forces favoring change in the Soviet system and society will succeed in achieving their goals. Yet, the very fact that socialist conservatives have been publicly identified as opponents of *perestroika* (in an abandonment of the myth of the Party's monolithic unity[83]) and as people who have "succeeded twice in barring the way to long-overdue and urgently needed changes"[84] makes it that much less certain that they will succeed again, especially given that the reformers are in positions of greater institutional power or proximity to power than ever before.

To place a value on reform, which has so often been attacked in the history of the communist movement, and on openness, when the Harvard historian Edward Keenan has appositely regarded *neglasnost'* (lack of openness) as part of the very essence of traditional Russian political culture,[85] could, if sustained by the top political leadership, have an impact even on the dominant political culture. For although political cultures certainly do not change overnight, or even within a year or two, they are not immutable. From the perspective not only of the continuing reality and prospects for success of the reform process now under way in the Soviet Union but also from the standpoint of the deeper imprint it might make on Russian political culture, it is of crucial importance that *glasnost'* be maintained and developed. If openness becomes "not a campaign, but a norm,"[86] that in itself will constitute change in the Soviet political culture and pave the way for other changes—institutional as well as cultural.

Democratic institutions and democratic values mutually reinforce one another, and an attempt to democratize, however gradually, Soviet institutions is unlikely to succeed if it is not accompanied by some change in values and by a shift from certain traditional political beliefs. It is probable that a majority of even the more radical Soviet reformers favor "democratization" rather than instant democracy. Because they do not yet wholly trust the mass of the people, they take the view that a period of preparation for the exercise of influence and power is required— hence the support for *glasnost'*, for factory-level democracy ("self-management"), and for competitive (albeit circumscribed) elections for deputies to soviets and party secretaryships.

Yet we should not underestimate the extent to which Soviet society has already changed compared with the period of Stalin's ascendancy or the immediate post-Stalin years. Although Gorbachev himself has noted that there is too much rote learning and not enough encouragement of independent thought in Soviet education (the context of his remarks was specifically that of teaching in the social sciences),[87] there is no denying the fact that the general level of Soviet education has greatly increased since Stalin's death and that today education is far less dogmatic than it was during the twenty years or so of "high Stalinism." Educational and social change have gone together. Workers are increasingly second- and third-generation workers, rather than displaced peasants. The peasantry as a social class has continued its absolute and relative numerical decline, whereas the intelligentsia has grown not only in size but also in knowledge of the outside world. Although the contemporary Soviet intelligentsia is doubtless much less closely integrated into world culture than was the much smaller intelligentsia of late imperial Russia, the contrast is certainly sharper between the former's level of knowledge of the outside world (its politics, its culture, and especially its level of development in their own particular discipline) and the level of the new, upwardly mobile intelligentsia in the 1930s and 1940s. It would be surprising if all this had not already been accompanied by some political-cultural change, and it is reasonable to argue that the climate for reform is less arid than the climate that confronted the immediate post-Stalin reformers.

Conclusions

Thus far, I have examined Marxist-Leninist ideology and political culture separately. Although political culture is the broader of the two concepts, there is an important sense in which Soviet Marxism-Leninism and Russian and Soviet political culture are intertwined and make an impact on each other. On the one hand, such values as attachment to "the collective" or to "order" have been reinforced and given a specific Marxist-Leninist form by the Soviet ideology. On the other, Marxism-Leninism has shown the influence of Russian political culture in, for instance, its acceptance of the concentration of unchecked power at the top of the political system (with the supreme leader placed on a pinnacle that puts him out of reach of *overt* criticism), the authority accorded to the Party-state bureaucracy, and the downplaying of the antistatist and more democratic elements in Marx's and Lenin's thought. A traditional Russian patriotism was, moreover, embodied in the idea of the Soviet Union as "the homeland of socialism" and in the development of an implicit outlook that could be summarized as, "What's good for the Soviet Union is good for socialism." Such a phrase suggests the nature of the interaction. The Party leaders' ideas of what is good for the Soviet Union have themselves been heavily influenced by Marxist-Leninist ideology, and yet, within fairly broad limits, these same leaders have felt free to redefine socialism to keep it consistent with what they think is good for their state.

There is an extensive Western literature that discusses the relative importance of Marxism-Leninism and "national interest" as determinants of Soviet foreign policy. But much of this writing overlooks the fact that Soviet ideology has been so refined throughout the years as to largely eliminate the clash of principle between one and the other. Moreover, when such a clash has seemed difficult to avoid, Soviet leaders have found themselves able to think in separate compartments and to offer different public and private explanations for their conduct without necessarily feeling weighed down by the discrepancy. Thus, as I noted earlier, Leonid Brezhnev publicly interpreted developments in Czechoslovakia in 1968 in terms of a class struggle and argued that the foundations of the socialist system were being undermined by enemies of the working class. But when he was speaking to a group of Czechoslovak Party leaders—a majority of whom had been brought to Moscow at gunpoint—in the Kremlin in August 1968 after the Soviet military intervention in Czechoslovakia, the terms of the discourse changed. Brezhnev was not expecting to be reported, but the meeting was recounted in some detail by Zdenek Mlynář,[88] a prominent member of the Czechoslovak leadership who was present, in his political memoirs *Night Frost in Prague*.[89] Brezhnev initially argued that the intervention was unavoidable because "the interests of socialism were paramount," but when the First Secretary of the Czechoslovak Communist Party, Alexander Dubček, attempted to defend the Prague Spring on the basis of his understanding of socialism, Brezhnev swept these views aside. With great force, he expressed the sentiments shared by the vast majority of Soviet citizens at the time—that the Soviet Union had paid with blood and sacrifice for the boundaries that were established in Europe after World War II and that these common borders would be defended whenever the Soviet leadership felt they were threatened.[90]

Neither Marxist-Leninist ideology nor "national interest" demanded, however, the action taken by the Soviet Union at that time. The ideology is open to a sufficiently wide variety of interpretations, provided the minds of the interpreters are not closed, to have accommodated the reform movement within Czechoslovak communism. It could, indeed, be argued that acceptance of developments in Czechoslovakia (which were "antisocialist" only on the most dogmatic interpretations of "socialism") was in the *enlightened national interest* of the Soviet Union. By taking the action it did, the Soviet Union not only undermined its own authority within the international Communist movement, but also strengthened conservative forces within the Party and state at home to such an extent that, ironically, it retarded the development of the USSR itself. The Prague Spring, and the Soviet reaction to it, was the final death knell for Aleksey Kosygin's economic reform, and many of the Soviet Union's current problems are traced by party reformers, from Gorbachev downward, to the failure to take decisive steps toward reform at the end of the 1960s and the beginning of the 1970s.

There are few policy options that are actually ruled out by Marxism-Leninism, although it is an ideology that makes it more difficult to defend some than others. As far as systemic change is concerned, the monist theoretical base of the ideology makes it, by definition, difficult to justify political reforms of a pluralizing tendency or anything resembling a separation of powers. Yet should the political support for such reform within the Party and society grow sufficiently, it is likely that the elasticity of "Marxism-Leninism" would turn out to be great enough to accommodate even political change of that type. I have already noted Gorbachev's significant, albeit qualified, support for the concept of pluralism. But in a more concrete (if less authoritative) manifestation of such support, it is noteworthy that the annual conference of the Soviet Association of Political Sciences (a body in which reformers predominate)[91] called in February 1987 for "the creation of a socialist 'theory of checks and balances,'" in which it would be "necessary also to use the experience of the development of the bourgeois state system and the corresponding theoretical material."[92] In the post-Stalin period, many Soviet social scientists have incorporated ideas from Western literature into their thinking, and to the extent that these ideas have been grafted onto "Marxism-Leninism," that body of doctrine has already become more malleable. But explicit recognition of the usefulness of Western political theory of checks and balances is a new phenomenon, even if in the recent past, implicit advocacy of such a viewpoint may be found in Soviet publications.[93]

Both the ideology and the political culture incorporate a number of different ideas, and important change in the meaning and significance of Marxism-Leninism and in the political culture can take place without the rejection of any one of them. Such change can be produced by a different weighting of the various elements of the ideology and of the variety of values and beliefs that form, in part, the political culture. Thus, the ideas of egalitarianism and of having material incentives (which may produce increased income differentiation) both have a place in the official ideology. The emphasis on one rather than the other has varied over time. Similarly, the ideology embraces the idea of democratic participation in the political process and the norm of strict political discipline and absolute acceptance of the decisions of the highest Party and state bodies. The extent to which one idea has prevailed over the other (usually the second over the first) has varied from one period of Soviet history to another.

Change in ideology, either through a different weighting (especially in the minds of the political elite) of its various components or through the abandonment of notions that have all too obviously not stood the test of time, is not as hopeless a task as is often assumed or as slow a process as change in political culture. Because a political culture is the product of a historically longer period of time as well as of more direct everyday life experience than ideology is (even though ideological education is a *part* of that experience and therefore an influence on the culture), political culture cannot change with the comparative suddenness of ideological change—as occurred, for example, at the beginning of the 1920s, the end of the 1920s, the mid-1950s, the mid-1960s, and the mid-1980s. Yet, as I argued earlier, it would be most implausible to suggest that the political culture of either the Soviet elite or of the mass of the people is the same today as in the 1940s or early 1950s. Indeed, if even the present level of *glasnost'* is maintained between now and the end of the century (and especially if *glasnost'* is further developed and accompanied by such measures of democratization as the spread of competitive elections, albeit within prescribed limits), it is unlikely that such an unusually prolonged period of reform in Russian and Soviet history could fail to have a significant impact on the political culture.

Again, this need not mean the abandonment of central values, but rather the placing of them in a different perspective or reweighting of one as compared with another. Thus, the fear of chaos and the desire for order are likely to remain, but there is something rather absurd about the fact that many Soviet citizens look back on the Stalin period as one in which "order" prevailed when this era embraced both forcible collectivization and mass and arbitrary arrests. To the extent that *glasnost'* permits the full story of the Stalin period to be told in the Soviet Union, these times are likely to be decreasingly valued for exemplifying order, even if they continue to be perceived in some respects as a heroic time. This perception is likely to continue to apply, above all, to the years of World War II.

The idea of freedom can serve as an illustration of the complex relationship among ideology, political culture, and political change. Soviet ideological and philosophical texts define freedom as "the recognition of necessity." The understanding of freedom within the dominant political culture has surely been influenced by this teaching as well as by the Russian and Soviet authoritarian tradition; therefore, freedom embodies at one level that deterministic connotation.[94] Yet the idea of freedom as the absence of constraints—as personal independence or the ability to act in some area without limitations or prohibitions, without hindrance— retains its place among the meanings published in ordinary Soviet dictionaries, thus reflecting the fact that this "nonideological" meaning lives on in Russian culture.[95] James Scanlan, in his book, *Marxism in the USSR*, gives an account of a group of Russian schoolchildren who, upon being released from a regimented tour of the Tret'yakov Art Gallery in Moscow, "burst out of the door with gleeful shouts of 'Freedom!'" Had they, Scanlan observes, "been thoroughly imbued with the Marxist-Leninist notion of freedom as the recognition of necessity, they would have exclaimed 'Freedom!' when they trooped into the museum, not when they were let out!"[96]

It is by no means impossible that in conditions of continuing or developing *glasnost'*, the idea of freedom as personal independence and absence of constraints already present in everyday discourse will not only gain ground but will also be accompanied by an increasing interest in the institutionalization of political liberties. There is no likelihood that this notion of freedom will supplant order as a value—and no logical reason why it should because criminal violence, after all, is the most blatant infringement of personal freedom. Yet the weighting between the two values might be changed so that more freedom could be seen to be compatible with "order of a higher level," in Gorbachev's phrase.[97] I am not suggesting that these particular changes are bound to happen or that they are the most likely political outcome in the short term. Rather, they *may* happen, and we should be alert to the possibility. The idea that Marxism-Leninism never changes is ahistorical nonsense, and the notion that "the Russians" never change is often thinly disguised racism.

There is certainly an important sense in which the dominant Russian political culture (with its passivity, acceptance of hierarchy, distrust of independent initiative, and strong strand of economic egalitarianism) appears resistant to even the kind of reform Gorbachev has already made clear he wishes to push through, not to mention more radically libertarian or pluralizing measures. But the political culture also provides several counterbalancing advantages. A controlled "liberalization from above"—or a gradual democratization—is more difficult in Eastern Europe, for the populations will push for change to go further and faster than the Communist Party leadership there can readily countenance. Poland and Czechoslovakia are clear cases in point, and if in Hungary there *has* been a considerable "liberalization from above," its success (insofar as it has been successful) rests on the limits imposed on expectations by the dire confrontation with Soviet tanks in 1956 and the several years of repression that followed the Hungarian uprising. Above all, the value placed upon patriotism in the Soviet Union (and the Soviet official political socialization efforts have been largely successful in linking love for the motherland with loyalty to the Soviet state) is one that Gorbachev can draw upon in the enormously difficult task of winning support for his changes (which can, after all, offer little in the way of improvement in material living standards in the short run).

Institutional change, ideological innovation, and political culture are, in the long run, closely interlinked. The one that is most intractable is political culture, but the advantage of the *concept* of political culture over the older idea of "national character" is that the former recognizes that values, fundamental political beliefs, political knowledge, and foci of identification are the result of concrete historical experience. On the content of that experience in the remainder of the 1980s and in the 1990s hangs a great deal—further change in the Soviet ideology and even in the political culture, and the possibility of a Soviet Union in the twenty-first century that will be easier both to live in and to live with.

Notes

1. In rewriting the paper I presented to the East-West Forum in New York on March 5–6, 1987, as a chapter for this volume, I have greatly benefited from the comments of all the participants in that conference, especially those of Jutta Scherrer, Seweryn Bialer, Joseph Berliner, and Gail Lapidus. I am grateful also for the observations of Stephen Welch in Oxford.

2. This is so even in the context of Western analyses of the Soviet Union. It was well illustrated in an interesting series of articles that appeared in the journal *Soviet Studies* between 1966 and 1970 (especially 1966 issues). The series was launched by Alfred G. Meyer with a contribution entitled, "The Functions of Ideology in the Soviet Political System" (17, no. 1 [January 1966], pp. 273–

285). See also a forthcoming volume edited by Stephen White and Alex Pravda, *Ideology and Soviet Politics* (London: Macmillan, 1988).

3. Well over a hundred definitions of culture had been produced by 1952, and there is no doubt that many more have been added since. See David Kaplan and Robert A. Manners, *Culture Theory* (Englewood Cliffs, N.J.: Prentice-Hall, 1972), p. 3, citing A. L. Kroeber and Clyde Kluckhohn, "Culture: A Critical Review of Concepts and Definitions," in *Papers of the Peabody Museum of American Archeology and Ethnology*, vol. 47 (Cambridge, Mass: Harvard University, 1952).

4. Thus, for example, Seweryn Bialer has made a distinction between "doctrine" and "ideology," seeing the former as "a set of highly general and internally consistent theoretical propositions" and holding that "ideology can best be understood as a part of culture, a slowly changing combination of doctrinal inputs and historical experience and predispositions that run parallel to doctrine" (Bialer, *The Soviet Paradox: External Expansion, Internal Decline* [New York; Knopf, 1986], p. 264) Although this distinction facilitates a very useful discussion by Bialer of the relationship of Marxist-Leninist to other Soviet beliefs (ibid., pp. 262–268), I find it helpful to adopt a definition of ideology that differentiates political culture from ideology while at the same time recognizing that the relationship between them needs to be discussed.

5. Malcolm B. Hamilton, "The Elements of the Concept of Ideology," *Political Studies* 35, no. 1 (March 1987), pp. 18 38.

6. Archie Brown, "Introduction," in Archie Brown and Jack Gray (eds.), *Political Culture and Political Change in Communist States* (London: Macmillan, 1977), p. 1.

7. Hamilton, "The Elements of the Concept of Ideology," p. 38.

8. Hamilton went on to note, however, "The interrelatedness of the elements in a belief system must surely be a matter of degree and it is difficult to draw a line which would demarcate highly consistent sets of beliefs from those which are not so, except arbitrarily. What matters is that there should be some interrelationship. For example, belief A may be consistent with belief B and B with C but not A with C. Contradictions and ambiguities of this sort are fairly common in those belief systems which most theorists have wished to call ideology" (pp. 22–23). Hamilton's route to his conclusions was to survey eighty-five major sources on ideology and then to identify twenty-seven definitional components or "elements" of the concept of ideology proposed by different authors and schools.

9. See note 6.

10. This is, however, a factor that varies a great deal from one Communist state to another. Excellent survey data on values and attitudes have been produced by sociologists in Poland and Hungary and (in the 1960s) in Czechoslovakia. Soviet sociological research is less developed, as was noted in the pages of *Pravda* by the distinguished sociologist-cum-economist, Tat'yana Zaslavskaya. (See Zaslavskaya, "Perestroyka i sotsiologiya," *Pravda*, February 6, 1987, pp. 2–3.)

11. See, for example, Robert C. Tucker, *Political Culture and Leadership in the Soviet Union: From Lenin to Gorbachev* (Brighton: Wheatsheaf, 1987), esp. pp.

3–6; Stephen White, *Political Culture and Soviet Politics* (London: Macmillan, 1979), esp. p. 1; and Stephen White, "Soviet Political Culture Reassessed," in Archie Brown (ed.), *Political Culture and Communist Studies* (London: Macmillan, 1984), pp. 62–69, esp. p. 62.

12. Kenneth Jowitt, "An Organizational Approach to the Study of Political Culture in Marxist-Leninist Systems," *American Political Science Review* 68, no. 3 (September 1974), pp. 1171–1191.

13. There are good reasons for making a conceptual distinction between the complex of subjective orientations (including values and attitudes), on the one hand, and behavior, on the other. The gap between attitudes elicited in surveys and behavior has proved to be disturbingly wide so often in relatively liberal societies that this phenomenon has become known among social psychologists as "the A-B problem"—the attitude-behavior problem—although many political scientists have continued in all innocence to assume that behavior neatly reflects attitudes and values. Given that quite frequently this is not the case within liberal democracies, it would be surprising if such a situation should turn out to exist when we are concerned with political behavior within authoritarian political systems.

Moreover, it is perfectly obvious that much political behavior in the Soviet Union specifically cannot be taken at face value. What is one to make of the fact that more than 99 percent of Estonians, Latvians, and Lithuanians apparently vote for the Communist Party candidate in elections to the Supreme Soviet (which are, thus far, uncontested elections)? Does this mean that such an overwhelmingly large proportion of the Balts are really convinced Communists? Are we not forced to make judgments about certain behavior that reflects people's values and other behavior that may not? If so, do we not need a concept that will act as an umbrella for the whole variety of subjective political perceptions and orientations?

14. I personally am willing to attach the label "totalitarian" to the period of "high Stalinism," although even there it can be somewhat misleading inasmuch as bureaucratic conflict existed and many orders went unfulfilled; moreover, in some variants, the "totalitarian model" accords to Stalin a superhuman power that even he could not possess. For the post-Stalin period, I am in no doubt that application of the concept to the Soviet Union is more misleading than helpful. It is a topic on which a great deal has been written, but my own reasons for holding that view are briefly set out in "Political Power and the Soviet State: Western and Soviet Perspectives," in Neil Harding (ed.), *The State in Socialist Society* (Albany: State University of New York Press, 1984), pp. 51–103, at pp. 55–57.

15. Leszek Kolakowski, *Main Currents of Marxism: The Breakdown*, vol. 3 (Oxford: Clarendon Press, 1978), p. 526.

16. This point is made by Jack Gray in Brown and Gray, *Political Culture and Political Change in Communist States*, p. 272.

17. Jack Gray, for example (ibid., pp. 259–260), stressed the fact that "Soviet politics developed in the spirit of *What Is To Be Done?* and not in the spirit of *State and Revolution*."

18. A. J. Polan, *Lenin and the End of Politics* (London: Methuen, 1984), p. 130.

19. M. S. Gorbachev, "O perestroyke i kadrovoy politike partii," *Pravda*, January 28, 1987, pp. 1–5, at p. 1.

20. Ibid.

21. Some of the writings for specialist readerships of Abel Aganbegyan, Evgeniy Ambartsumov, Fedor Burlatsky, Anatoliy Butenko, Ivan Frolov, Boris Kurashvili, Georgiy Shakhnazarov, and Tat'yana Zaslavskaya are among those that come to mind.

22. For a brief discussion of the genesis of the concept of the "all-people's state," see my "Political Power and the Soviet State," in Harding, *The State in Socialist Society*, pp. 98–99; and for more detailed discussion of the concept's place in Soviet ideological development, see Ronald J. Hill's chapter in the same book, "The 'All People's State' and 'Developed Socialism,'" pp. 104–128.

23. *Pravda*, January 28, 1987, p. 1.

24. Ernst Kux, "Contradictions in Soviet Socialism," *Problems of Communism* 33, no. 6 (November-December 1984), pp. 1–27, at p. 11.

25. Yu. A. Andropov, "Uchenie Karla Marksa i nekotorye voprosy sotsialist-icheskogo stroitel'stva v SSSR," *Kommunist*, no. 3 (1983), pp. 9–23, at p. 20.

26. M. S. Gorbachev, *Zhivoe tvorchestvo naroda* (Moscow: Politizdat, 1984). This booklet version of Gorbachev's speech is about twice as long as that published by *Pravda* and contains many interesting passages excluded from the newspaper report.

27. Ibid., p. 11 (italics mine).

28. M. S. Gorbachev, *Political Report of the CPSU Central Committee to the 27th Party Congress* (Moscow: Novosti, 1986), p. 117.

29. *Pravda*, January 28, 1987, p. 1.

30. While welcoming *glasnost'* as "undoubtedly important" and "a marked improvement on the earlier practice of secrecy and concealment," Alec Nove cast an interesting sidelight on its ambiguity and limitations by citing the remark of a radical critic of the regime during the reign of "that other major reformer, Tsar Alexander II." At that time, Nikolay Chernyshevsky wrote, "*Glasnost* is a bureaucratic expression, a substitute for freedom of speech." See Nove, in the symposium, "What's Happening in Moscow?" *The National Interest*, no. 8 (Summer 1987), pp. 3–30, at p. 15.

31. Gail W. Lapidus, "Gorbachev and the Reform of the Soviet System," *Daedalus* 116, no. 2 (Spring 1987), pp. 1–30, at p. 16.

32. Alexander Zinoviev, *The Yawning Heights*, trans. by Gordon Clough (Harmondsworth: Penguin, 1981), p. 289.

33. But the level of suspicion of the concept was such that as recently as 1983 a group of Soviet scholars came under high-level pressure from within the Central Committee apparatus to publish an attack on the prominent Polish sociologist and political scientist, Jerzy Wiatr, for his espousal of the concept of pluralism. This group did so under the pseudonym of A. V. Kuznetsov. See "his" article, "O teoreticheskikh kontseptsiyakh odnogo pol'skogo politologa," *Voprosy filosofii*, no. 12 (December 1983), pp. 26–39.

34. *Pravda,* July 15, 1987, pp. 1–2, at p. 2.

35. *Pravda,* September 30, 1987, p. 1.

36. Mikhail Gorbachev, *Perestroika: New Thinking for Our Country and the World* (London: Collins, 1987), p. 77.

37. By February 1988, there were, according to a Soviet author, "as many as 30,000 independent social groups and associations in the Soviet Union." This author added that "at present, non-official groups are considered by our society as a fact of pluralist reality," but he posed the question, "Can we treat that reality in a normal and civilized way, in keeping with the spirit of democratization?" See Eduard Khamidulin, "Pluralism Soviet Style," *Moscow News,* no. 9, February 28, 1988, p. 5.

38. *Pravda,* February 19, 1988, p. 1.

39. See note 33 for Soviet criticism as recently as 1983 of the viewpoint Gorbachev has espoused.

40. G. Kh. Shakhnazarov, "Logika politicheskogo myshleniya v yadernuyu eru," *Voprosy filosofii,* no. 5 (May 1984), pp. 62–74, esp. pp. 72–73.

41. Gorbachev was speaking in October 1986; the remark is cited by Stephen Shenfield, *The Nuclear Predicament: Explorations in Soviet Ideology* (London: Routledge & Kegan Paul and the Royal Institute of International Relations, 1987), p. 45.

42. Ibid., p. 47.

43. A. I. Strelyanyy, at that time the head of the Current Affairs (*publitsistika*) Department on Economic and Scientific Questions at *Novy mir,* addressed a meeting of Komsomol activists at Moscow University on May 15, 1987, and answered their questions. A report of the meeting was sent abroad and is published in *Russkaya mysl'* (Paris), August 7, 1987, p. 5.

44. See, for example, M. I. Piskotin, "Demokraticheskiy tsentralizm: problemy sochetaniya tsentralizatsii i detsentralizatsii," *Sovetskoe gosudarstvo i pravo,* no. 5 (May 1981), pp. 39–49; A. P. Butenko, "Protivorechiya razvitiya sotsializma kak obschestvennogo stroya," *Voprosy filosofii,* no. 10 (October 1982), pp. 16–29; and the more recent work of B. P. Kurashvili, *Ocherk teorii gosudarstvennogo upraveleniya* (Moscow: Nauka, 1987), esp. pp. 241–263.

45. Gorbachev speech to the January 1987 Plenum of the Central Committee, *Pravda,* January 28, 1987, pp. 1–5, at p. 3. For further discussion of this, see Archie Brown, "Gorbachev and Reform of the Soviet System," *The Political Quarterly* 58, no. 2 (April–June 1987), pp. 139–151, esp. pp. 147–149.

46. Gorbachev has quite frequently alluded to this. See, for example, his speech to the heads of social science departments published in *Pravda,* October 2, 1986, pp. 1–3; and his address to the Soviet Trade Union Congress in *Pravda,* February 26, 1987, pp. 1–3.

47. In a Soviet television discussion program, July 8, 1987, reported in BBC Summary of World Broadcasts: Soviet Union/8617/B/2-B/4, July 11, 1987.

48. Ibid.

49. Gennadiy Lisichkin, in a Soviet television broadcast on July 3, 1987, reported in BBC SWB: SU/8617/B6, July 11, 1987.

50. Mikhail Gorbachev, *On the Tasks of the Party in the Radical Restructuring of Economic Management*, Speech to the June 1987 Plenum of the Central Committee (Moscow: Novosti, 1987), p. 40.

51. I am distinguishing a "dominant political culture" (in the sense of one that actually dominates people's minds) from the "official political culture"—the norms for "correct" political behavior and beliefs laid down by successive Party leaders and ideologists. That body of writing has much to say about the "new man" (or "new socialist person") but not necessarily very much to do with what is going on inside the heads of most living people. These and other distinctions relating to the concept of political culture are elaborated in much greater detail in Brown, *Political Culture and Communist Studies*, particularly in my concluding chapter, pp. 149–204, esp. pp. 174–184.

52. Alex Inkeles and Raymond A. Bauer, *The Soviet Citizen: Daily Life in a Totalitarian Society* (Cambridge, Mass.: Harvard University Press, 1961), p. 348.

53. Some evidence of this is presented in the carefully documented study by Bohdan Krawchenko, *Social Change and National Consciousness in Twentieth-Century Ukraine* (London: Macmillan, 1985).

54. Surveys of the "third wave" of emigration—those who left in the 1970s and at the beginning of the 1980s—although useful in many respects, are not nearly as helpful regarding the contemporary perceptions of, for example, Ukrainians because of the overwhelming predominance of Jewish and German emigrants among those who have recently settled in the West. For such information as is available, see Rasma Karklins, "Nationality Policy and Ethnic Relations in the USSR," Working Paper no. 10 (Urbana: Soviet Interview Project, University of Illinois at Urbana-Champaign, 1986).

55. The slowness of "cultural change" in Soviet Central Asia is a major theme of Nancy Lubin, *Labour and Nationality in Soviet Central Asia: An Uneasy Compromise* (London: Macmillan, 1984), esp. Ch. 7 and 8. But one should also note that the spread of education produces advances in capacity for generalization and abstract thought. See the study (based on research in Kirghizia and Kazakhstan in 1931–1932, but published even in the Soviet Union only as recently as 1974) of A. R. Luria, *Cognitive Development: Its Cultural and Social Foundations* (Cambridge, Mass.: Harvard University Press, 1976), for discussion of change in the type of reasoning in Central Asia under the impact of schooling.

56. Tibor Szamuely, *The Russian Tradition* (London: Secker and Warburg, 1974).

57. See, for example, Seweryn Bialer, *Stalin's Successors: Leadership, Stability, and Change in the Soviet Union* (Cambridge: Cambridge University Press, 1980), pp. 145–146; and Archie Brown, *Soviet Politics and Political Science* (London: Macmillan 1974), p. 96.

58. Nadezhda Mandelstam, *Hope Against Hope* (London: Collins, 1971), p. 96.

59. Andrey Amalrik, interviewed in George R. Urban (ed.), *Eurocommunism* (London: Temple Smith, 1978), p. 239.

60. Mary Dejevsky, "Glasnost and the Tartars," *The Times* (London), July 27, 1987, p. 10.

61. Mary Dejevsky, "When Dogma Comes Up Against Demo," *The Times*, August 25, 1987, p. 8.

62. "The Gorbachev Revolution," Fedor Burlatsky interview in *Marxism Today* (London) (February 1987), pp. 14–19, at p. 15.

63. Ibid., p. 17.

64. See Angus Roxburgh, *Pravda: Inside the Soviet News Machine* (London: Victor Gollancz, 1987), pp. 46–47.

65. Fedor Burlatsky, "Uchit'sya demokratii," *Pravda*, July 18, 1987, p. 3.

66. These are the last words of Aleksandr Pushkin's play, *Boris Godunov*, first published in 1825.

67. Burlatsky, "Uchit'sya demokratii."

68. Ibid.

69. Yuriy Afanas'ev, "Vospitanie istinoy," *Komsomol'skaya pravda*, September 1, 1987.

70. Ibid.

71. Y. K. Ligachev, "Nam nuzhna polnaya pravda," *Teatr*, no. 8 (August 1986), pp. 2–7.

72. Afanas'ev, "Vospitanie istinoy."

73. See Samuel P. Huntington and Jorge I. Dominguez in Fred I. Greenstein and Nelson W. Polsby (ed.), *Handbook of Political Science, Volume 3: Macropolitical Theory* (Reading, Mass.: Addison-Wesley, 1975), pp. 31–32; and Brown, *Political Culture and Communist Studies*, pp. 174–184.

74. Tucker, *Political Culture and Leadership in Soviet Russia*, p. 157. For a more skeptical view of the possibilities for "a true cultural revolution: the creation of a novel form of social life informed by a new set of values," see Stephen F. Burant, "The Influence of Russian Tradition on the Political Style of the Soviet Elite," *Political Science Quarterly* 102, no. 2 (Summer 1987), pp. 273–293.

75. L. I. Brezhnev, *Voprosy razvitiya politicheskoy sistemy sovetskogo obshchestva* (Moscow: Politizdat, 1977), p. 315. Authorship of Brezhnev's first mention of political culture is attributed by well-informed Soviet sources to the *Izvestiya* political correspondent Aleksandr Bovin. As is clear from Bovin's subsequent writings, there is no need to doubt that the passage quoted represents *his* views, if not Brezhnev's.

76. *Pravda*, July 15, 1987, p. 1.

77. *Pravda*, February 26, 1987, pp. 1–2, at p. 1.

78. Ibid., pp. 1–2.

79. Milton Rokeach, *The Nature of Human Values* (New York: Free Press, 1973), esp. p. 217.

80. Although interesting in other respects, Donna Bahry's chapter, "Politics, generations and change in the USSR," in James R. Millar (ed.), *Politics, Work and Daily Life in the USSR* (Cambridge: Cambridge University Press, 1988), provides neither confirmation nor disconfirmation of my generalization about the greater reformism of the political generation now in or immediately around its fifties. Her data are drawn from the Soviet Interview Project (centered at the University of Illinois at Urbana-Champaign), which questioned approximately

two thousand eight hundred emigrants from the Soviet Union to the United States who arrived in the United States between January 1, 1979, and April 30, 1982. The emigrants were predominantly Jewish, and few admitted to Party membership in the Soviet Union. The young emerged in this study as the most politically deviant, but the measures of this were their engagement in various kinds of dissident activity in their "last normal period" in the Soviet Union. The political generation I am talking about is one that has remained within the parameters of the Soviet system as well as the boundaries of the USSR and is exercising influence today precisely because the key reformers who are its leading lights abided by the rules of the game even during the lean years for reform under Brezhnev, although some stretched those rules to just short of the breaking point. (On the methods and database of the University of Illinois project, see James R. Millar, "Emigrants as Sources of Information about the Mother Country: The Soviet Interview Project," Working Paper no. 5 [Urbana: University of Illinois at Urbana-Champaign, 1983]).

81. Aleksandr Bovin, *New Times*, no. 5 (February 9, 1987), pp. 9–10.

82. Ibid., p. 9.

83. Anatoliy Strelyanyy—a Soviet commentator already cited in note 43— went much further in his May 1987 talk to Komsomol activists at Moscow University. In answer to a question from the floor—"Does the Party need confrontation?"—he replied, "Today in the party itself there already exist two parties under the label 'CPSU.' The revolutionary character of *perestroika* rests in the fact that the people must have freedom" (*Russkaya mysl'*, August 7, 1987, p. 5).

84. Bovin, *New Times*, had in mind both the failure to persist with the de-Stalinization began under Khrushchev and the watering down and virtual abandonment of Kosygin's economic reform of 1965. A similar point about the Soviet opponents of reform having succeeded twice already was made by Fedor Burlatsky in an article in *Literaturnaya gazeta*, October 1, 1986, p. 10, which he developed into a play entitled, *Two Views in One Office*, shown on Soviet television on December 17, 1986.

85. Edward L. Keenan, "Muscovite Political Folkways," *The Russian Review* 45 (1986), pp. 115–181, esp. pp. 119–121, 145, 148, 154 and 170.

86. The words are Gorbachev's in his speech to the 1987 Trade Union Congress: "Socialism is a structure of the working people. Everything that happens in a socialist state is the concern of the people. That is why we are for openness. It must not be a campaign, but a norm" (*Pravda*, February 26, 1987, pp. 1–2, at p. 1).

87. *Pravda*, October 2, 1986, p. 1. For a more recent, extremely interesting critique and assessment of the social sciences in the Soviet Union, see the speech delivered to the Presidium of the Academy of Sciences by Gorbachev's close Politburo colleague, Alexander Yakovlev. It is published under the title, "Dostizhenie kachestvennogo novogo sostoyaniya sovetskogo obshchestva i obshchestvennye nauki," *Kommunist*, no. 8 (May 1987), pp. 3–22, and in a fuller version in *Vestnik akademii nauk SSSR*, no. 6 (June 1987), pp. 51–80.

88. By one of history's coincidences, Mlynář was a good friend of the young Mikhail Gorbachev when they lived in the same student residence and studied

together in Moscow University Law Faculty from 1950 to 1955. See Mlynář's article, "Il mio compagno di studi Mikhail Gorbaciov," *L'unita*, April 9, 1985, p. 9; and Archie Brown, "Gorbachev: New Man in the Kremlin," *Problems of Communism* 34, no. 3 (May-June 1985), pp. 1–23.

89. Zdenek Mlynář, *Night Frost in Prague: The End of Humane Socialism* (London: Hurst, 1980).

90. Ibid., pp. 237–241.

91. See Archie Brown, "Political Science in the USSR," *International Political Science Review* 7, no. 4 (October 1986), pp. 443–481.

92. S. E. Deytsev and I. G. Shablinsky, "Rol' politicheskikh institutov v uskorenii sotsial'no-ekonomicheskogo razvitiya," *Sovetskoe gosudarstvo i pravo*, no. 7 (July 1987), pp. 118–120, at p. 119.

93. See, notably, V. G. Kalensky, *Bill' o pravakh v konstitutsionnoy istorii SShA* (Moscow: Nauka, 1983).

94. For a discussion of "freedom" in Soviet thought, see James P. Scanlan, *Marxism in the USSR: A Critical Survey of Current Soviet Thought* (Ithaca, N.Y.: Cornell University Press, 1985), pp. 333–335.

95. Ibid., esp. p. 334.

96. Ibid., p. 335.

97. See notes 77–78.

2

Politics Before Gorbachev: De-Stalinization and the Roots of Reform

Peter Hauslohner

From the beginning of Mikhail Gorbachev's rule, Western specialists have been deeply divided about the prospects of state-led change in the Soviet Union. Part of this debate has centered on the scope and ambition of Gorbachev's own objectives, although many of these doubts dissipated in the wake of the General Secretary's extraordinary demands for political and economic reform at the January and June 1987 Plenums of the Communist Party Central Committee.[1] On the other hand, most of the disagreement has always had more to do with judgments about the ability of any Party leader, however skilled or well intentioned he or she might be, to carry through so dramatic a transformation of the Soviet system. Just prior to the June Plenum, Peter Reddaway suggested that Gorbachev would eventually have to curb his radicalism or else up the ante and "risk being removed from office à la Khrushchev." Yet, should Gorbachev "persist in his radicalism, and also fail to produce a steady improvement in the standard of living," Reddaway wrote, "then it is hard to see how he could survive for many more years." Although it was at least conceivable that Gorbachev's reforms might lead to "unprecedented changes," the Soviet system still seemed no more "susceptible of transformation today than it was thirty years ago."[2]

But what *is* the Soviet system that so desperately needs to be transformed? To understand the enterprise that Gorbachev has now embarked on, let alone to gauge its chances, we need a clear sense of the system he inherited. Surely the most popular view among specialists is that reflected in the remarks just quoted, which sees the "essence" of the Soviet political-economic system as largely unchanged from what Iosif Stalin left his successors when he died in March 1953. To be sure, proponents of this position do not maintain that everything is as it was in Stalin's time. On the contrary, virtually everyone agrees that the three decades following the dictator's death witnessed major changes that extended throughout society and often resulted in substantial improvements in the quality of ordinary people's lives. Most striking were the changes in state policy: an end to terror and the curtailment of unbridled police powers; the erection of a genuine, although austere, welfare state; and the shift to a foreign policy of "peaceful coexistence," which reduced the severe isolation of the Soviet public from the outside world. Specialists also acknowledge important changes in the manner in which policies were made: a greater degree of rationality and empiricism in the process and much increased opportunities for participation and influence by loyal specialists and lower-ranking officials. However, when one turns to basic institutions and the structure of power, it was and is the *lack of change* that impresses the most: the Communist Party's unqualified monopoly of power; the publicly owned, bureaucratically run "command economy"; and an omnipresent state that made whatever civil society existed practically invisible to the outside observer. It is, above all else, this astonishing yet persistent concentration of formally unaccountable power in the hands of a very few that makes the Soviet system seem so remarkable even today and that has led some writers to characterize "the transition of the Soviet Union from Stalinism to post-Stalinism as a change in the form of rule, not its basic substance."[3]

Yet the juxtaposition of far-reaching policy changes with an unchanging system seems odd, if not implausible. By way of analogy, suppose that one had an old car that was badly out of tune and getting only 15 to 20 miles to the gallon. If the car went into the shop to be tuned and came back a little peppier, now managing perhaps 25 miles to the gallon, one would not be surprised. But if the same car came back, getting 30 to 35 miles per gallon and accelerating from 0 to 50 miles per hour in six seconds rather than twelve, one would know without even looking under the hood that the mechanic had installed a different engine, for no amount of tuning could have changed the old engine's performance so dramatically. Broadly speaking, the same must be true of post-Stalin Soviet politics. Institutional stability and the cycling of policy changes across different administrations—the repudiation of much of Nikita Khrushchev's reformism by Leonid Brezhnev—may have helped to obscure this fact. On the other hand, an end to terror, the uneven but steady growth of a welfare state, and the pursuit of a foreign policy based on peaceful coexistence all represent dramatic departures from Stalinist practice, the duration of which through three decades of widely fluctuating political conditions makes sense only if one assumes that the equivalent of a new "engine of state" was installed somewhere along the way.

This analysis is not meant to suggest that the performance of the Soviet system under Stalin's successors was different in all important respects. On the contrary, from Stalin to Gorbachev, politics was still largely hidden from public view, censorship severe, official lies common, and dissenters harshly repressed. The economy remained extraordinarily wasteful in its use of resources and backward in much of its technology. Culture was drab and mediocre by world standards. Consumer goods and services were in chronic short supply, and their quality struck visitors as more likely the product of an early developing nation than of one of the world's two military-industrial superpowers. Repeated Soviet invasions of neighboring countries demonstrated that the successors could be as cynical and cruel as Stalin himself when it came to guarding or extending a geopolitical advantage. Yet the discontinuities with Stalinism were no less striking, and a good explanation of the similarities in performance must accommodate the differences as well. The key to constructing such an explanation is to recognize that power, although obviously crucial, is not the only thing that matters in politics. The rules according to which power is exercised also matter, as do the methods by which power customarily is applied and the purposes for which power is used. Even in the context of an unchanging distribution of power, little imagination is required for one to see how and why significant changes in the rules, methods, and purposes of power might lead to equally far-reaching changes in the chronic behavior of those who wield power and of the system itself.

In this chapter, I shall argue that despite the stability of major institutions and the structure of power, the Soviet political system changed after Stalin's death in fundamental respects. The differences emerge clearly when one considers three factors that are important for assessing any political system. One is the relative strength of political institutions, or the degree to which relatively constant, visible, and widely shared roles, norms, and expectations, as opposed to largely invisible and ever-shifting personal loyalties, shape the political process. A second is the relative strength and capacity of "the state," or the degree to which public authorities are able to ensure, through public institutions, the security of the state from foreign and domestic threats and to pursue the increasingly numerous and complicated policy objectives that all leaderships accumulate over time. Finally, a third factor is the nature of the relationship between state and society and the extent to which public authorities are able to exercise power without relying on coercion or intimidation to maintain public compliance. The far-reaching changes in policy and policymaking that have marked the post-Stalin era can be traced to important changes in each of these factors: the halting if incomplete institutionalization of politics; the continually expanding but awkward power of the Soviet state; and Soviet leaders' adoption of a more inclusive and conciliatory approach toward managing their relations with society. Taken together, these developments suggest that the political order evolving under Khrushchev and Brezhnev was not Stalinism *redux* but something quite different.

However, my argument is less about taxonomy—indeed, I have no substitute label to offer—than about the causes of political change after Stalin and the prospects for renewed change under Gorbachev. The crucial fact is that Stalin's successors could not have reproduced Stalinism even if they had wanted to: not only because the dictator himself was dead, a fact no less important for its being obvious, but because the circumstances that helped give rise to Stalinism had long since disappeared. The new rules, methods, and purposes of power did not emerge spontaneously but were instead stimulated by pressures and opportunities present in the radically different post–World War II world. These were problems and possibilities with which any of Stalin's successors would have had to contend. Even more important, these "adaptations" worked! Again, the crucial fact is that Soviet rulers coped, by and large successfully, with the great dangers and uncertainties associated with Stalin's passing; with the severe economic and social problems that were also Stalin's legacy; and with the Soviet Union's vulnerabilities in the complicated international situation of the early 1950s. Thereafter, the regime enjoyed more than two decades of uninterrupted domestic tranquility and unprecedented prosperity. But such good fortunes did not—in fact, could not—last. During the final decade of Brezhnev's rule, Soviet power began unmistakably to lose its effectiveness. If there appeared to be many reasons for this, most could be traced ultimately to the growing discordances between the now-entrenched rules, methods, and purposes of post-Stalin politics, on the one hand, and newly emerging challenges, pressures, and opportunities embedded in a permanently changing society and global environment, on the other. These discordances, I shall argue, gave rise to the "precrisis" situation Gorbachev has said was developing in the Soviet Union in Brezhnev's final years. At the same time, these discordances offer clues to the likely nature and direction of a new wave of change in the future.

Politics Without Terror

In a recent essay, T. H. Rigby argued that the basic "rules" of Soviet politics by which Khrushchev rose to power in the 1950s were essentially the same as when Stalin rose to power in the 1920s and little different, he suggested in an aside at the end of his essay, from those prevailing today.[4] Rule Number One is to acquire a patron and clients. One cannot get ahead in Soviet politics without the support of someone higher up or hope to get ahead without the assistance of loyal associates close by. Rule Number Two is to "deliver the goods," which, in the first instance, means to advance the interests of those persons higher up who will decide whether one does in fact get ahead. Delivering the goods requires one to manipulate whatever material and organizational resources are available, and that, Rigby observed, almost always leads one to violate an official norm or policy goal in the process. To do so without compunction is Rule Number Three.[5] Things change, of course, as one moves up the hierarchy. The need for friends (as distinct from clients) and of coalitions (including those based on shared policy interests) becomes relatively more important, and the building of coalitions and the tending of one's patronage ties may come to interfere with one another, thereby presenting the ambitious politician with increasingly complicated and uncertain choices. Delivery of the goods also grows more difficult. The interests of friends and policy coalitions must now be served as well as those of more traditional constituencies, although the interests of one's patrons (now there may be more than one) still take precedence. Finally, at the very top of the hierarchy, in the Party Politburo, the relevant audience consists of no hierarchical superiors at all, only clients, friends, and peers. That makes it easier to advance one's own agenda, especially for the General Secretary. But delivering the goods is also a less certain enterprise for someone at the top, not least because there is no longer a protector to ensure against one's errors.

Although it is difficult to imagine the evidence that would falsify these "rules," they make considerable intuitive sense, and probably most specialists would agree that they convey a good sense of the quality of Soviet leadership politics. However, the terminology is misleading. Rigby was describing maxims, not rules; he indicated what players must do to win at the game of politics, but not the rules by which the game is played. In fact, Rigby projected a politics largely lacking in rules—a politics based primarily on informal and impermanent personal loyalties and relatively little on formal laws and institutions. His maxims suggest an abiding collective disrespect for rules among the elite and a recruitment system that "selects" for politicians who violate rules with unusual willingness and skill.[6] Yet, although the maxims suggest, correctly enough, that there are powerful forces favoring the persistence of "ruleless" politics, it is clear even to casual observers that Soviet politics today is significantly *less* unruly than it used to be, certainly since Stalin's day, but also since the Khrushchev period.

The most obvious reason for this is that one rule in particular seems to have become well established: the rule that bars the use of violence as a normal instrument of politics. Stalin's increasing reliance on violence and terror, from the early 1930s on, lessened his need for friends and policy coalitions and, consequently, his urge to "deliver the goods" to various constituencies. By comparison, the repudiation of violence by Stalin's successors has had the effect of limiting what a top leader can do to punish rivals—thus limiting his or her ability to intimidate clients, friends, and otherwise neutral peers. Delivering the goods has again become an important element of political strategy. The ban on violence also has had the effect of distributing power resources somewhat more broadly within the leadership, mainly by expanding the amount and quality of information available to its members.[7] As a result, Soviet leadership is more "shared" than it was under Stalin, and leaders are much more constrained in the use of their power.

But are there other rules? A number of observers have suggested that members of the post-Stalin political elite gradually adopted a longer list of rules for regulating their interpersonal relations and the struggle for power.[8] Yet all agree that the rules that do exist are few in number, often only implicit, and largely unpublicized, all of which make it difficult if not impossible for those outside the leadership to verify that the rules are being observed in practice. In a word, Soviet politics still seems weakly institutionalized.[9] At the same time, whatever rules, informal conventions, or shared understandings may exist are presumed to apply only within the leadership or to the political-administrative elite as a whole. There are no obvious rules constraining the leadership from below and thereby restricting either the political process within the leadership or its exercise of power over society. Nor is there any institutional mechanism for providing formal accountability of the leaders to society, as is provided, at least in theory, by competitive elections.

Accordingly, it has seemed to many observers that both the incentives and the opportunities for virtually unlimited power aggrandizement in the hands of a single leader or tiny coalition of leaders remain huge and, therefore, that the risk of exceptionally belligerent or irresponsible leadership (or both) may be equally large, conceivably as large as in the Stalin period. Nor is it clear why this situation should soon change. Grey Hodnett wrote ambivalently of the extent to which Soviet politics has become institutionalized. "What exists is more than 'a state of nature,'" he allowed, a reflection of the great empirical uncertainties that exist and hence of the ambivalence that most specialists feel. But he was unequivocal in denying that constitutionalization had occurred, and he was skeptical that a significant move toward constitutionalization was likely in the forseeable future, given its seeming incompatibility with Soviet political culture and democratic centralism. This is also a sentiment that is widely shared.[10]

There are two key questions, however, that must be answered before one can confidently make judgments either about the measure of institutionalization thus far or about its prospects. First, while acknowledging the fact that the "shared understandings" regulating politics are for the most part informal, implicit, and even invisible in their application, one can still ask how such understandings have penetrated the broader elite and society—whether large groups outside the leadership have come to recognize them as rule equivalents; whether the leadership now secures some measure of legitimacy for the regime by behaving in accordance with these understandings; and whether an important cost in heightened popular or elite dissatisfaction and cynicism would be incurred if these understandings were violated in a particularly blatant or indefensible way. In short, one might suppose that even in the case of informal and implicit rules, the more widely they ramify and the wider acceptance they enjoy, the greater the institutional coherence and stability they lend to the system. Second, one must ask how the rulers themselves view the consequences of a weakly institutionalized political system, particularly its costs. If the elite's estimate of those costs has been rising, there may be mounting pressures in favor of strengthening the rules, thus making further institutionalization, or even constitutionalization, a more likely prospect than has been realized.

To answer these questions, we begin with the most important rule change since Stalin—the cessation, then delegitimation, of the use of physical violence against otherwise loyal political opponents and of terror against potential counterelites and other suspect groups in the population.[11] For Stalin, violence was not simply a method of discouraging opposition to Soviet power or to his own dictatorship. It was also the instrument on which he ultimately relied in order to limit conflict within the leadership and to ensure deference to his views once an issue was decided. Moreover, as remarkable as the extent of violence perpetrated under Stalin were the extraordinary confidence with which the dictator seemed to apply it and, relatedly, its seeming acceptance by his co-conspirators and victims.[12] This suggests that many others in the elite must have regarded violence and terror as perhaps distasteful but necessary and legitimate nonetheless.

Although the end of widespread political violence was signaled almost immediately after Stalin's death, it is clear that the elite's internalization of this new norm did not take place at once.[13] For example, Khrushchev claimed that shortly after the 1957 "anti-Party group" crisis was resolved, one of the leaders of the defeated conspiracy, Lazar Kaganovich, telephoned Khrushchev to plead that they "not proceed with him as they had dealt with people under Stalin." These very words, Khrushchev said, were evidence that had Kaganovich and his associates won out instead, they would have resorted to the old methods of settling accounts. But Kaganovich had been mistaken to project these assumptions onto others. "We are observing and will adhere to Leninist principles," responded Khrushchev, who promised his caller a job and the opportunity to live and work peacefully.[14] Subsequently, following Khrushchev's own forced retirement from office, a movement arose urging Stalin's full historical rehabilitation, which evidently enjoyed high-level political support but also aroused widespread anxieties at home and abroad. Khrushchev's successors equivocated but finally decided to reject the idea, and Brezhnev pledged in effect that the time for relying mainly on coercion was past and that there would be no return to the era of "administrative rule."[15]

Nor can it be said with total assurance that the resort to violence has been completely abolished, even at the highest levels, or that widespread political violence will never reappear.[16] Numerous examples from recent world history demonstrate how exceptional circumstances can result in extreme violence, even state-sanctioned terror, in what were previously thought to be relatively stable, institutionalized democracies; and a combination of the Soviet Communist Party's own revolutionary traditions and a powerful secret police perhaps makes internalized elite norms forbidding violence even more fragile than elsewhere. Nevertheless, the ongoing process of generational succession must make the likelihood of a return to mass political violence increasingly remote. One should not be surprised to find leaders who entered politics at a time when political violence was considered "normal" feeling, even decades after the formal denunciation of the practice, somewhat ambivalent at least about the utility of violence, if not about its desirability. Yet by the time Brezhnev died, several new elite generations had been inducted into politics, having been taught that violence was not a legitimate or even an effective instrument of rule under normal conditions. Those persons who were in their twenties at the time of Khrushchev's "secret speech" are now in their fifties and are increasingly the cohort running the system. It is a reasonable assumption that norms forbidding violence have been deeply etched in the minds of these men and women and that only truly exceptional provocations could result in the erosion of these norms in the forseeable future.

Authority Building

The main result of the end of terror was the return of "normal" politics and the heightened need for politicians at all levels to "deliver the goods." However, this formulation does not fully capture the ramifications of the requirement that Soviet leaders rely on persuasive methods of rule in place of the intimidation afforded by state-sanctioned violence. Particularly illuminating in this respect is George Breslauer's argument that politicians in the post-Stalin period have been led to devote increasing amounts of their scarce time and energy to expanding their personal "authority" among clients, friends, peers, rivals, and the political-intellectual elite as a whole.[17] Authority, which Breslauer defined as "legitimated power" or the willingness of an audience to acquiesce in a leader's exercise of power, is simply a more reliable means of defending one's position than is the "illegitimate" use of power in conditions in which losing is not necessarily permanent.[18] What is important is that the building of one's authority, while a form of "delivering the goods," is more than that—or rather, it means the delivery of important "public" as well as "private" goods. Breslauer maintained that contenders for leadership and leaders who have been selected must continually persuade others, both in the leadership and in the broader elite, of their competence as "problem-solvers" and as "politicians." That means, in the first instance, convincing onlookers that one has the ability to tackle successfully the "big" issues of national security, economic growth, public welfare, and so forth. It also means projecting the image of someone who will lead and solve problems without sowing so much discord in the process that the regime itself becomes threatened by paralysis or internal disorder. Although authority may initially rest on promises and reputation, eventually claims of competence are tested by reality. If the test is positive, authority is liable to be enhanced. If the test is negative and authority is eroded, leaders may choose to modify their program or style of leadership in the hope of improving their performance and credibility in the eyes of opponents. Or leaders may fall back on the more conventional instruments of patronage, manipulation, and intimidation in order to preserve their office.[19]

There are two important implications that flow from this analysis. One is that competition within the leadership, particularly that associated with successions, has become an important, even routinized, source of political and policy innovation. Competing efforts to accumulate authority seem to precipitate a collective search for novel, or simply more effective, approaches to existing problems of policy and governance. Successions, rather than occasions for political crisis as many scholars used to argue, have evidently become (perhaps in addition) a critical source of *systemic* revitalization or reequilibration and stabilization, depending on one's opinion of the defects of the preceding administration.[20]

Second, despite the absence of democratic institutions, it appears that a certain measure of accountability has now been introduced into the

Soviet political process—both accountability of individual leaders to the rest of the leadership whose members may seek to depose them should their authority diminish, and accountability of the leaders and the leadership to ever-growing numbers of the political elite and the population as a whole. Specifically, if politicians are driven to claim competence as problem-solvers and as politicians, they must eventually conform to the perceptions and biases of their audience. They will, of course, try to shape their audience's perception and understanding of affairs. This happens in all systems, although Soviet leaders may have more advantages than most in this regard. In addition, serious disagreements among the audience will make it easier for leaders to chart their own course. But the flip side of "authority" is "opinion." Not only have freer communications and the increased volume of available information made the formation of public opinion easier, but the heightened role of authority building in securing and maintaining a leader's power has also made this opinion both more important and more influential. Furthermore, although at first it may have been only the Politburo's opinion that mattered, the growing complexity of society, the narrowing ideological content of policy, and the spread of consultative norms have all had the effect of broadening this opinion and the circle of those who make it. To an increasing extent, if still indirectly, judgments about Soviet leaders' competence are shaped by policy experts, media commentators, and even ordinary citizens through their responses to public opinion polls and letters to higher authorities. Rising levels of education and the inexorable spread of information make this process irreversible.

Needless to say, the kind of accountability implied by authority building is indirect, subtle, and considerably less than the kind democratic controls are capable of providing. Moreover, although observers are right to emphasize the mutual reinforcement of power and authority—the possession of one makes it easier to acquire the other—their distinctiveness is crucial in the Soviet context. Power and authority can often serve as substitutes for one another. The more power leaders have, based on their controls of organizational resources and the size of their patronage tail, the less is their need for authority. On the other hand, the erosion of authority can often, and for prolonged periods, be compensated by a sufficiency of power, a contingency demonstrated with special force during the late Brezhnev era. Thus, when his program seemed to unravel in the mid-1970s, in the wake of successive harvest failures in 1974 and 1975, a worsening capital shortage, and the weakening of détente, Brezhnev's authority evidently eroded and his priorities, on a range of policy issues, began to be challenged cautiously but unmistakably by other members of the leadership, led by Prime Minister Aleksey Kosygin.[21] Brezhnev modified his program, in a mainly symbolic but nonetheless reassuring way. Yet it was above all his use of power—the expulsion of Nikolay Podgornyy and Kirill Mazurov from the Politburo, the diminution of Andrey Kirilenko, and the elevation of Nikolay Tikhonov and Konstantin Chernenko—that enabled the General Secretary to counter the threat. The economic situation continued to worsen, of course, although not decisively until after 1979. However, Kosygin's mortal illness finally forced his retirement in October 1980, and Brezhnev was then able to secure the position for his old friend and crony, Tikhonov, a man nearly as old as Kosygin but with only a fraction of the latter's reputation. In short, although the heightened importance of authority building has unquestionably altered the dynamics of Soviet leadership politics in crucial ways, its weaknesses remain substantial and seem to weigh heavily on the minds of Gorbachev and his fellow reformers.

Revitalizing the Party

The end of terror contributed to the institutionalization of politics in several other ways, one of the most significant being the revitalization of the Communist Party. The strengthening of the Party *qua* institution was, in the first instance, a political result dictated by Khrushchev's concerted effort to build support among regional Party secretaries and by the eventual defeat of his government-centered opposition. Yet at a deeper level, rejuvenation of the Party was probably inevitable once Stalin's successors had decided to abandon the leader cult as an important legitimating symbol. Having renounced terror and one-person rule but unwilling to repudiate Soviet power itself or the major institutions underpinning the regime, the new leaders naturally reemphasized Leninism and the principles of collective leadership.

Revitalization proceeded on several levels. Especially important was the resumption of regular meetings of the Party's most authoritative organs, the Congress and Central Committee, which had been almost completely ignored in the late Stalin period.[22] These meetings again became the locus for the transaction of important business—for example, the approval of membership changes in the Party's leading executive organs (Politburo, Secretariat), the issuance of five-year plan directives, annual reviews of the plan and budget, and so forth—and the occasion for cautious public (and more spirited private) discussions of major policy issues. Equally important were and are the opportunities these gatherings afforded mid-level Party and state officials to confer informally with members of the leadership and to consult and "network" among themselves.[23] Thus, even as it continued to serve as an agent of implementation and control, the Party reacquired its status as an instrument of collective deliberation, with an "opinion" that could be discovered, at least in its approximate form, and that must now play a role in the political calculations of those at the top.

There were other changes as well. Although there is less information available about the activities of the highest executive bodies, it is clear that the three most important executive organs—the Politburo, the Secretariat, and the Presidium of the Council of Ministers—have met on a regular, more or less weekly, basis since at least the start of the 1970s and almost certainly from much earlier.[24] Since the mid-1950s, a much higher proportion of formal Party and government decrees have been published. Although the published documents are far from the universe of decisions made, the publication of some of this material has helped to clarify the different responsibilities of these bodies, while making their exercise of power seem more legitimate.[25] In addition, even as the Party's deliberative functions were expanded, the executive responsibilities of Party officials and staff throughout the system were strengthened, particularly in supervision of the economy and within certain institutions (for example, ministries, research institutes). At the symbolic level, the 1977 constitution proclaimed the Party's "leading role" in directing society in a far more explicit and prominent way than had been done in the 1936 Stalin constitution. In the meantime, Party membership levels rose sharply—by 1981 the Party was 2.5 times the size it had been in 1955—and deliberate affirmative action recruitment policies made the Party significantly more representative, in sociological terms, of the general population. The Party today is literally a mass party—one in ten adult citizens is a member, perhaps one in four of all persons with a college degree—with deep roots in the society it leads.[26]

Perhaps the most far-reaching change associated with the Party's revitalization has been the quasi-formalization of a leadership succession procedure. When Stalin died, there were no rules for choosing a successor, nor was it clear even to insiders what position the leader should occupy—or, to reverse the question, what position carried with it the greatest power or potential authority. These uncertainties were a virtual invitation to conspiracy, unsolicited intervention by the security organs, and the use of violence. Khrushchev's subsequent emergence as *primus inter pares*—first over Lavrenty Beriya, the secret police chief who was eventually executed, then over Georgiy Malenkov, the government Premier who at first was shunted aside to a lesser but still powerful job—had all the earmarks of an entirely unexceptional, small-group power struggle. However, when the First Secretary's rivals in the leadership subsequently tried to engineer his removal in June 1957, in the famous "anti-Party group crisis," and when Khrushchev succeeded in forcing the question into the full Central Committee which supported him and threw out his opponents instead, a watershed was reached. In effect, the Central Committee asserted, or was de facto granted, the right to broker in cases of deep disagreement or deadlock at the top. When a new set of conspirators rose up against Khrushchev seven years later and presented their case before the Central Committee, this time gaining its approval with little if any dissent, it was as if the earlier precedent had been reaffirmed.

Khrushchev's victory suggested another precedent: the unambiguous supremacy of Party First Secretary over the head of government. However, this issue was immediately blurred when, a year later, Khrushchev decided to oust his former ally, Nikolay Bulganin, and take on the post of Premier in addition to his Party job. Once again, the relative power of the head of the Party seemed to be in question. These doubts were reinforced when, at the plenum ousting Khrushchev in October 1964, the Central Committee resolved never again to permit one person to hold both the top Party and government posts simultaneously. Yet, looking back at these events, the precedent now seems clearer cut. At the 1957 Plenum, full-time Party officials finally recaptured control of the Presidum (as the Politburo was then called) from full-time government officials who had long had the dominant voice, and they have never surrendered it since. The decision to prevent the Party leader from occupying the post of Premier has probably had the effect of limiting the former's formal responsibilities, hence vulnerabilities, particularly for performance of the economy, without necessarily limiting his power, especially given the Party Secretariat's capacities for oversight. At the Twenty-third Party Congress in 1966, Brezhnev's first as Party leader, the Party rules were amended in order to reinstate formally the post of General Secretary and to mandate that selection to this position be determined by vote of the Central Committee directly. These rules changes reinforced the Central Committee's formal authority governing the succession process, but they also served to elevate the special role and authority of the top leader within the leadership. Lastly, Brezhnev's eclipse of Premier Kosygin—demonstrated with stunning clarity by Brezhnev's dominant role in the Soviet-U.S. summits of 1972–1974—and more than a decade of unchallenged and widely acknowledged rule as "head of Politburo" reinforced both the fact and the perception of preponderant authority vested in the post of General Secretary.[27]

Thus, when Brezhnev finally died, what had not been obvious, let alone "legitimate" thirty years earlier, was evidently well established and accepted throughout the Party and the nation: that the Party General Secretary is the country's leading executive and that the Politburo reserves the right of nomination to this post, subject always to the Central Committee's formal assent. Such is the procedural rule implied by the events of 1957 and 1964 and followed in practice, evidently smoothly, if not entirely without conflict, during each of the three post-Brezhnev successions to date.

Although much of the day-to-day bargaining and struggle of politics remains hidden, the revitalization of the Party has lent a certain clarity and regularity to the political process, which before was conspicuously lacking. As a result, certain aspects of timing, location, and participation rights in decisionmaking have become more predictable, and perhaps symbolically legitimate, to the point where one must assume that players and spectators alike *expect* these procedures to be followed, even if the results are for the most part orchestrated behind the scenes.[28] To be sure, such procedural rules do not alone amount to a change in the structure of power. Yet such rules can nonetheless prove confining, inasmuch as they force leaders to observe schedules and information routines that, in some instances, they might greatly prefer to ignore.[29]

But how confining? Evidence suggests that at best the rules are elastic. Brezhnev's leadership in foreign policy offers a particularly striking example in this regard. During his first decade in power, Brezhnev was fastidious in his efforts to keep the Central Committee apprised of important international developments involving the Soviet Union.[30] That these efforts had some effect was suggested by a lengthy and approving reference in a speech at the Twenty-fifth Party Congress in 1976 by the Sverdlovsk province Party chief, Yakov Ryabov, who was soon to be elevated to the Central Committee Secretariat.[31] But from that point on, as Soviet-U.S. détente weakened and the relative effectiveness of Soviet foreign policy in other areas grew more ambiguous, the briefings stopped. Nor was Soviet conduct during subsequent foreign policy crises covered in the way it had been before. The intervention of Soviet armed forces in Afghanistan was reviewed only once by the full Central Committee, six months after the fact; the Polish crisis (1980–1981), in many ways a more unsettling and consequential series of events than those surrounding the Prague Spring (1968), was never formally discussed.[32]

Thus, although revitalization of the Party has clearly deepened the institutional foundations of the Soviet political process, major weaknesses persist. The rules, it is clear, matter most when the balance of power within the leadership is relatively even and when the competition for authority is most intense. To be sure, it is far from evident that the top leader, even Brezhnev toward the end of his rule, can inaugurate fundamentally new policies while ignoring accepted procedures altogether; the single plenum on Afghanistan may be instructive on this point. But it is clear that these procedures are not an important constraint on the leader who would leave policy unchanged, even when stand-pattism seems an obvious recipe for failure.

From Label Sticking to Argumentation

The end of terror also contributed to the institutionalization of politics by facilitating the recapture of science from the ideologists and the subsequent spread of empiricism and broad consultation in the discussion stages of policymaking. As in the case of Party revitalization, this development had its immediate roots in politics. Largely to win the sympathy and support of groups severely antagonized by the previous administration, both Khrushchev and Brezhnev promised renewed respect for specialists and empirical methods, the publication of more data, and the creation of new forums for the public discussion of policy. To be sure, Khrushchev talked a better game than he played. He often could not refrain from intervening in technical disputes and insisting that his own views prevail, and in this more than in any other respect, his Stalinist origins shone through. Brezhnev proved much more reliable, although the last decade of his administration witnessed a serious reversal of policy with respect to the publication of data, which was lamented and resented by much of the intelligentsia. In a broader sense, however, there were powerful objective pressures that increased the attractiveness of this strategy and would probably have driven Stalin's successors to consider it regardless of the political implications. Such pressures included the need for more information and better technical advice in an increasingly complicated world as well as the imperatives of a ruling strategy that all the successors seemed to prefer, which involved making peace with society and broadening the regime's underlying base of support.[33]

The most immediate consequence was a vast expansion over time in the sheer amount of consultation, much of it formalized, between decisionmakers and "experts" (by which I mean scholars, policy analysts, and lower-ranking administrators who have practical experience in the area in question).[34] For example, several studies have shown that policy specialists gained increasing freedom to investigate, and to debate publicly, important and contentious public issues. The specialists' ability to convey their findings and recommendations to relevant decisionmakers also increased, often thanks to formal (and routinized) channels established for precisely that purpose.[35] Under Brezhnev, it became standard practice to form large commissions, composed of a wide spectrum of institutional representatives and area experts, to prepare drafts of new laws and decrees, although always under the supervision of the Party. The penultimate drafts of new legislation were frequently published as a means of stimulating broad public debates. Even though these debates were doubtless orchestrated, with the purpose of educating the population and building consensus in support of the new laws, these debates inevitably became an important source of information for decisionmakers and, just as inevitably, an important mechanism of horizontal opinion formation within the specialist community and among the more attentive members of the mass public—opinion that must today play a growing part in the authority-building process described earlier.[36] Last but hardly least, the politicians took steps to improve their knowledge of the general public's attitudes by giving grudging, but slowly expanding approval to the sociologists to conduct applied research, much of which is simple public opinion polling, and by adopting a series of measures intended to yield a more systematic collection and analysis of the huge number of letters and complaints from disgruntled citizens that are received daily by the media, Party offices, and almost every state agency.

The impact of all this consultation is difficult to document conclusively and thus remains a source of controversy among Western observers. Yet to those who have interviewed leading specialists, whether in Soviet research institutes or in the bureaucracy, a single conclusion seems obvious and unassailable: Leading specialists have come to expect—and, indeed, regard it as entirely unexceptional—that when major decisions are to be made in their area of expertise, they will normally be afforded a chance to communicate their thoughts on the matter, which will be duly recorded if not necessarily taken into account.[37] The implication is that a norm of consultation has spread among the politicians—that politicians routinely listen to the specialists because that is what "good" policymaking requires and is what politicians "normally" do. To be sure, an expectation that legitimately interested experts and organizations will be given an opportunity to present their views on policy questions is not equivalent to an expectation that outside views will be taken into account by decisionmakers, let alone that some compromise among conflicting opinions will ordinarily be sought. A rule mandating broad consultation does not imply a bargaining rule or that logrolling and pork barreling have become conventional methods of Soviet decision-making. Nevertheless, the vast expansion of information and analysis that is available at all levels of the system has surely altered the character of political debate at the top. As Grey Hodnett has observed, there are likely to be increasing attempts to channel and otherwise manipulate this flow of information to one or another leader's advantage—that is, there is likely to be a "new politics of information channeling . . . competing with the old [and diminishing, one should add] ideological politics of scholastic exegesis." But such efforts must inevitably be selective and incomplete. Now, and in the future, high-level Soviet politics must increasingly be "a politics of argumentation rather than a politics of 'label-sticking,'" as Hodnett put it, "which is to say a politics probably of accommodation rather than one of winner-take-all."[38]

However, while Khrushchev and Brezhnev sought to improve their intelligence and to broaden their support among policy intellectuals, they also took steps to reduce the chance that expanded debate and advice-giving might lead to organized opposition or, more subtly, to the growth of intra-Party factionalism. One obvious manifestation of this effort was the harsh treatment meted out to those dissidents who organized, publicized their protests, or persisted in their activities despite warnings from police and prosecutors to stop, compared with the leniency often shown individual protestors who promptly recanted. Equally important were the severe and continuing limits placed on historiography, which prevented a serious internal examination not only of Stalin and Stalinism but also—and in many respects this was more consequential—of the fundamental policy choices adopted at the start of the 1930s (collectivization, the extreme industrialization targets of the early five-year plans) and of the great factional struggles and policy debates of the 1920s. Also falling into this category was the unwillingness of the Soviet leadership after Khrushchev to publish transcripts of Central Committee Plenums, which has likely made it more difficult to organize and mobilize existing policy "tendencies" within the elite.[39] A final manifestation that warrants mention was (and is) the curious segmentation of policy debates that one observes in the published literature, which has meant that the most empirically detailed treatments of an issue, the frankest assessments, and the most radical ideas have by and large been restricted to the most specialized (and smallest circulation) media outlets and, as a result, to the narrowest audiences.[40]

The widespread consultation currently practiced between decision-makers and policy specialists has doubtless improved the amount and quality of the information at the government's disposal and thus, potentially at least, the quality of public policy. The regime also has considerably broadened its social base, as hundreds of thousands, even millions, of the country's most educated people have been brought into the system and have become implicated in the regime's policies in a far more intimate way than mere membership in the Party would imply. This includes the vast proportion of the society's "best and brightest," who in other circumstances might be available and disposed to lead a revolutionary opposition.

Yet the leadership's persistent fear of anything that smacks of organized political competition, even within the confines of the Party, has limited the benefits of this development while adding its own special costs. The segmentation of policy discussions has prevented ideas from receiving the critical analysis they need—in particular, this practice has prevented review by specialists with different backgrounds and experience who might see inconsistencies or unwanted consequences that someone from within the field in question might not be aware of or able to appreciate.[41] As a result, many of the ideas one finds circulating in the Soviet literature are simply naive or plainly ineffective, and social learning is often slow. On the other hand, even when there are many novel ideas and considerable learning, these usually involve "small" issues or parts of problems rather than "big" issues or problems in their entirety.[42] Because of the constraints on public debate and the intolerance of factionalism, it remains extraordinarily difficult to devise a comprehensive reform program that cuts across multiple issues and constituencies. As a result, radical political-economic reform *must* be incremental and piecemeal, certainly to a far greater degree than in countries where groups, parties, or factions out of power have time to organize and work out in advance alternative programs of governance.

The limits on debate and political organization have also helped to reinforce the importance of clientelism in politics. This has its own worrisome implications for the prospects of reform because politicians who are more loyal to people than to ideas are more likely to be captured by the bureaucratic interests and perspectives of the organizations for which they work. This means that appointed administrators who are clients are likely to be less successful than ideologues or members of factions in forcing their organizations to change and almost certainly less eager than ideologues and factionalists to persist in the effort in the face of resistance from the people they are administering. In other words, the limits on public debate and the absence of even loosely organized factions must make it exceedingly difficult for someone such as Gorbachev to predict how his appointees (whether clients or friends) are likely to perform on the job—or how loyal they are likely to be in the long run, especially when it becomes clear that his policies are causing them acute, job-related discomfort. If constructing a comprehensive package of radical reforms is difficult, getting it implemented will be doubly so.

The Lessons of Brezhnevism

Our discussion so far suggests that even before Gorbachev rose to power, the institutionalization of politics had proceeded further than most observers of the Soviet scene were willing to admit. Internalized norms forbidding the use of violence in "normal" politics appear to have become widespread and deeply held, and now more than ever before, Soviet leaders are compelled to lead persuasively rather than autocratically, to deliver the goods to friends and supporters, and to build their authority among the broad elite and even the population as a whole. Soviet leaders have not ceded any of their power to determine what gets on, or what stays off, the political agenda. But they have, in practice, allowed others to take part in shaping the agenda's overall structure and contents. In the meantime, the Party and its formal bodies and procedures have become established as the arena in which politics is normally conducted. The clarification of succession procedures has probably strengthened the Party's political monopoly by further insulating the power struggle from unsolicited interventions by other organizations, such as the military. But this clarification has also led to a more inclusive kind of decisionmaking. The General Secretary and the rest of the Politburo evidently have become much more attentive to the collective views of the Central Committee, particularly when the leadership itself is divided, when competition within the leadership is intense, or when the issues involved point to a major departure from established practice. It now seems unlikely that the Politburo could install as General Secretary someone judged to be unacceptable by a clear majority of the Central Committee. More generally, the vast increase in the amount of formal consultation and the underlying spread of a consultative norm have contributed to the formation of a kind of public opinion that the leadership can neither shape as easily as in the past nor completely ignore.

To be sure, it is institutionalization, not constitutionalization, that we are describing. The "rules" of Soviet politics *are* few in number, largely informal, and difficult to verify in practice. Nor is the leader or leadership prevented from disregarding or flouting the rules when it wants. No one but the leaders has the authority to determine whether the rules are being observed or the power to punish noncompliance. Nevertheless, increasing numbers of outsiders—Central Committee members, other Party officials, bureaucrats, policy specialists, and even the more active members of the mass public—have been embraced by these "shared understandings" and, in the process, have come to expect that the latter will generally be respected. It is almost certainly the case that a large cost would have to be paid in administrative efficiency, not to mention trust and goodwill, should Soviet leaders suddenly decide that these rules no longer need be applied. By the same token, it must also be the case that increasing numbers of the leaders themselves have come to view blatant disregard for the rules as exceptional and as contrary to their own best interests. Consequently, some of the probabilities of the Soviet political process appear to have shifted. In the forseeable future and as long as normal circumstances prevail, it is virtually impossible to imagine another leader taking power who is as violent and arbitrary as Stalin. Nor is it much easier to imagine another leader as capricious and mercurial as Khrushchev.

But if a new Stalin and a new Khrushchev are difficult to imagine, a new Brezhnev is not. History suggests that each new Soviet leadership has entered office preoccupied with what it thought were the main failings of the previous administration and determined to prevent their recurrence. Khrushchev sought to delegitimize political violence and to curb the secret police. Brezhnev and Kosygin acted to strengthen collective leadership and to impose at least general limits on individual executive power. For Gorbachev, the watchword is "responsibility" or "accountability" (*otvetstvennost'*). He has argued repeatedly that the primary fault of his predecessor's leadership was its lack of responsibility—that is, its failure to acknowledge developing problems quickly enough and, then, its failure to act decisively once the character and seriousness of those problems had become clear. At the Central Committee Plenum in January 1987, Gorbachev went further and in effect ascribed this failing to the system as a whole. "It must be acknowledged directly," he declared, "that if [elected organs] had operated at full strength, both in the party and in the state, the trade unions, and other public bodies, then it would have been possible to avoid many serious errors in cadres work"—and in much else, he implied. He continued, "We need to work out and to implement measures which would secure a decisive role for collegial, elected organs. No executive organ, let alone its staff, can or has the right to substitute itself for an elected organ, to elevate itself above [the latter]. There should be created the necessary foundations— political and legal—so that elected organs may implement effective oversight over the executive staff. . . . This will be a reliable guarantee against many mistakes, including those in cadres work."[43]

There is no way of knowing for certain at this juncture whether anything practical will come of such pronouncements, not least whether something akin to constitutionalization will result, in however embryonic a form. But Gorbachev and presumably others in the leadership appear much more aware than their predecessors were of the costs of a weakly institutionalized politics, most especially of the costs arising from the huge difficulties that presently exist in holding Soviet executives, both politicians and bureaucrats, accountable for their performance in office. These costs became embodied in the accumulating policy failures of the late-Brezhnev period and, more generally, in what Gorbachev has described as the growing gap "between words and deeds," a condition the General Secretary has blamed for increasing public skepticism, passivity, and alienation. As is evident already in the new leadership's campaign for "democratization," at least some of Brezhnev's successors are determined that means be found to prevent history from repeating itself. The result is likely to be new measures aimed at strengthening executive accountability and, inevitably, at the further institutionalization of politics, Soviet political culture notwithstanding.

State Building

We have thus far sought insight into the nature of the "system" and the sources of Soviet behavior in the routines and institutions of politics. Another approach to these questions is to consider the Soviet state as an actor in its own right. One might inquire into the relative power and capacity of public institutions to fend off internal and external threats to the state's security and to achieve the developmental goals that Soviet leaders have set for themselves. The assumption is that Soviet leaders, like politicians elsewhere, are likely to emphasize the strengthening of state security, whenever the latter is seriously threatened, and to concentrate on goals that are at least partly determined (and limited) by the capacities of state institutions. Even if we leave aside the effects of domestic politics, a state experiencing severe and chronic challenges to its security or chronic "underperformance" on account of weak capabilities ought to behave quite differently than a state facing no serious challenges to its security and whose performance has generally been good.[44]

In this connection, it is useful to recall that when Stalin took control in the late 1920s, the Soviet state was relatively weak.[45] This is not to imply there were rival power centers within society that had to be dealt with; these had already been obliterated. Nor is it to question or minimize the power of the state's coercive instruments; the secret police and its system of labor camps (the Gulag) were well established and growing rapidly. Yet in terms of its other capacities and the broader context within which it had to operate, the Soviet state in the late 1920s and long thereafter was plainly vulnerable. Although most of the world was hostile to the Soviet regime throughout the Stalin period and beyond (except for a brief respite during World War II), as a military-industrial power the Soviet Union remained, at least until after the war, significantly weaker than the leading capitalist countries it counted as its main enemies and, for another twenty years, weaker than its chief rival, the United States. Nor was the regime's domestic situation, very broadly speaking, any better. The ruling Communist Party was overwhelmingly urban and working class in its composition and orientation. But an equally overwhelming proportion of the country's population were peasants (more than 80 percent as late as 1929) among whom distrust of the Bolsheviks ran wide and deep. The Soviet government, which was dedicated to rapid economic growth, initially had no ready domestic sources of capital with which to finance growth and, partly by choice, found itself barred from most of the external reservoirs of capital on which the tsarist state had depended. Apart from its ability to suppress dissent and to deter open opposition, the state's capacities for domestic governance—its presence in the countryside and the competence and reliability of its statistical, fiscal, legal, and other instruments—were by any standards extremely modest at the start of Stalin's rule and woefully deficient when measured against the dictator's immense ambitions.

Although not an explanation of Stalinism, these aspects of the state's situation almost certainly contributed to the specific form that Stalinism took. If nothing else, they powerfully reinforced the tendency of Party leaders to support any and all measures that would expand state power, irrespective of the costs. At the same time, the state's relative weakness and the lack of alternative instruments can only have strengthened the leaders' gravitation toward extremely coercive methods of rule, particularly in mobilizing capital. Finally, because of the state's limited capacities, the leaders were forced to establish clear priorities: to concentrate their energy and resources on building up the country's economic and military power and to postpone radical transformation in other, less critical sectors of society. In sum, the initial weakness of the Soviet state must be regarded as a crucial structural influence that reinforced many of the "totalitarian" features of Stalin's rule, perhaps even causing them in the sense of encouraging Stalin and his aides to opt for certain ruling methods rather than others.[46]

In some respects, the state under Khrushchev and Brezhnev bore a fairly close resemblance to its Stalinist progenitor. To be sure, leadership came to be shared, political violence largely disappeared, and the elite for the most part surrendered its utopian goals (if not necessarily the symbols) of radical social transformation. Influence over policy became more dispersed, and the Party in effect, if not in principle, relaxed its monopolies over economic and intellectual (but not coercive) resources. Yet from afar the state "looked" very much the same. On the surface, it was still an all-powerful state "administering" an extraordinarily weak and thoroughly penetrated society.[47]

Nevertheless, the situation of the Soviet state had changed, and it continued to change, in the most fundamental ways. For one thing, when Stalin died, Soviet power was considerably more secure than it had been a quarter century earlier. The external threat had substantially diminished, primarily because of World War II and Stalin's subsequent acquisition of an Eastern European empire. Although the United States remained stronger militarily, the possession of atomic, then nuclear, weapons partly lessened the USSR's comparative disadvantage. In time and as a result of large continuing outlays for the military, the discrepancy between the Soviet Union and the United States was steadily reduced, and by the end of the 1960s, a condition of approximate strategic balance had been achieved. Meanwhile, basic changes in social structure, associated mainly with industrialization, left the state's internal position similarly improved. The peasantry, although still more than half the population, was by 1953 thoroughly demoralized, rapidly shrinking, and increasingly overshadowed by a large, relatively skilled, and basically loyal working class.[48] Growth in the state's capacities for governance and problem-solving was less impressive, although the government's presence in the countryside was now much greater and capital accumulation had become considerably easier. Moreover, this was an area Khrushchev singled out for immediate attention. Statistical reporting was improved, and the data were distributed more widely and quickly. The legal system was strengthened. Moribund local governments were revitalized. New planning and control organs were created (or recreated) that increased policymakers' ability to regulate, more selectively, important details of the national economy.[49] This accumulation of state capacities continued under Brezhnev.

That Stalin built a powerful state is something few observers question and that most take for granted. Less appreciated, however, is the extent to which the expansion of state power altered the mix of pressures and constraints that impinged on Stalin's successors. Increasingly secure in their power, Soviet leaders were able to pursue goals and to enact policies that were neutral and sometimes even detrimental to state power per se. Acceptance of the principle of peaceful coexistence and the pursuit of arms control may have enhanced national security. Yet this was achieved not by increasing the Soviet state's military power but by limiting its power and that of its rivals and by attempting to institute rules of international engagement intended to further constrain, if only minimally, participant states' freedom of maneuver. Similarly, the enactment of more generous welfare policies may have strengthened the Soviet internal political order by broadening popular support for the regime. But this, too, was accomplished at a direct cost to the state by limiting the resources available for accumulation and by establishing rules allocating social burdens and risks that effectively reduced the state's power to control the economic and social behavior of its citizens. At the same time, Soviet leaders found they could pursue their aims with much less resort to coercion. The state's much enhanced strength enabled police powers to be curbed, the war being waged against the peasantry to be ended, the labor market to be deregulated, and so forth. Increasingly, material incentives and persuasion were substituted for the often harsh administrative or criminal penalties that Stalin preferred. Finally, Soviet leaders were able to pursue a larger number and broader range of goals than before, including old objectives that had been slighted under Stalin—a more progressive family policy, a more strenuous effort to reduce poverty, an increased concern for historic preservation—as well as new concerns arising out of the very successes of economic growth, such as better protection of the environment.

As before, the point here is not that changes in the relative power and capacity of the Soviet state necessarily caused these changes in the leaders' behavior. The former facilitated the latter in the sense of lowering or removing obstacles and allowing leaders to respond more easily and confidently to a broader range of pressures and incentives. The attainment of military-strategic parity did not induce Soviet leaders to seek arms control; instead, the approach of parity permitted the serious consideration of arms control as an option that strategic inferiority had previously made politically infeasible. Defeat of the peasantry did not directly cause the regime's antipeasant policies to be abandoned, but it did ensure that the adoption of policies more favorable to peasant interests would not carry the potential political danger such policies had seemed to involve in the 1920s. In short, many of the worst excesses of the Stalin period, if not directly attributable to the relative weakness and incapacity of the state, were clearly reinforced and accentuated thereby. In contrast, both at the time of Stalin's death and increasingly thereafter, these circumstances were markedly different. Insofar as the Soviet Union now had a "strong" state that before had been "weak," a critical structural underpinning of Stalinism had disappeared.

The Instruments of Coercion

It may be claimed that the "strong state" argument greatly exaggerates the break with Stalinism because it fails to take proper account of the disproportionately coercive nature of Soviet power, even under Stalin's successors. While granting that the overall power of the state has grown, critics might maintain that the power and capabilities of the primary instruments of state coercion—the military and the secret police (KGB)—have grown just as fast, if not faster. Indeed, despite the deemphasis on coercive methods, the force and intimidation exerted by the military and police were still the resources on which the regime seemed to rely most under Khrushchev and Brezhnev, both in its conduct of international affairs and in its struggle with political dissent at home. In turn, the marked increase in the stature and resources of the military and the police under Brezhnev have been taken by many observers as indicators of the rising political weight of these organs and of their disproportionate influence within the leadership.

It is true, of course, that the fortunes of the military and KGB rose sharply under Brezhnev and that coercion remained an important part of the Soviet government's foreign and domestic political strategies. For example, although the KGB suffered widespread public disparagement in connection with Khrushchev's de-Stalinization campaign, the KGB's image in the media and in artistic portrayals improved significantly following Khrushchev's ouster, especially after Yuri Andropov was named KGB chairperson in 1967. In the 1970s, the KGB's domestic role grew more visible and probably more extensive, primarily on account of the continued expansion of organized political dissent and the government's increasingly harsh attempts to stamp it out, but also as a result of the growth of Soviet contacts with the West and the anxieties this provoked among certain members of the leadership. The KGB's presence in formal decisionmaking organs also grew more prominent. In the Party Central Committee, KGB representation rose from a single candidate member in 1961 to four full members in 1981, while gains nearly as striking were registered in the leading Party organs of the union republics. In 1973, Andropov was named a full member of the Politburo, the first time a police head had sat on this body since Beriya's arrest shortly after Stalin's death. That a career in the police was no longer a barrier to high-level political office was suggested further by Geydar Aliyev's promotion to the Politburo (as candidate member in 1976) and then, in truly spectacular fashion, by Andropov's own election as Party General Secretary following Brezhnev's death.[50]

Improvements in the situation of the military were just as striking. Whereas Khrushchev had tried to hold down the growth of defense spending and to reduce conventional capabilities and manpower levels in order to pay for the expansion of Soviet strategic forces, these efforts were reversed under Brezhnev. From the mid-1960s, total defense spending rose an average 4–5 percent annually, so that by the mid-1970s, an estimated 12–14 percent of gross national product was going to the military, which was an extraordinary burden on the rest of the economy and evidence of the cost that Soviet leaders seemed willing to bear in order to increase the Soviet Union's military power. The growth of spending slowed thereafter, although it kept pace with the economy as a whole. Meanwhile, all the services survived and thrived; an independent ground forces command was reestablished (Khrushchev had eliminated it); and manpower levels were gradually returned to what they had been before Khrushchev's major cuts. Despite the attainment of strategic parity and the limitations imposed by the agreements resulting from the Strategic Arms Limitation Talks (SALT I and II), strategic modernization continued. Conventional forces also were strengthened, and the Soviet Union's much increased power projection capabilities permitted a dramatically greater involvement in various regional conflicts, sometimes far from Soviet borders.[51]

Meanwhile, although the military's presence on leading decisionmaking bodies did not significantly change under Brezhnev, the minister of defense, Andrey Grechko, a career military man, was made a full Politburo member at the same time Andropov was elevated, the first time a defense official had risen so high since Marshall Georgy Zhukov's brief four-month stint in 1957. (The Ministry of Defense retained its full membership on the Politburo until 1984.) More important, however, was the reputed success of the military in preserving its near-monopoly of detailed information about the capabilities of Soviet weapons, force structure, and strategy. According to one observer, even after the onset of formal arms talks with the United States and the leadership's increasingly explicit acceptance of strategic parity, military scientists refrained from seriously exploring the technical and strategic ramifications of arms control.[52] This self-imposed refusal to "learn" must have reinforced the military's overall conservatism on these issues and narrowed the ability of the political leadership to manage the negotiating process.

All of these facts attest to the sizable growth in the power and capabilities of the military and the KGB during the last twenty years. Yet these facts convey very little about the extent and the effectiveness of the control exerted over these institutions by the Party leadership. In fact, much of the increase in the role and stature of the security organs is best seen as having further strengthened state power but without impinging on the independence and control of the leadership. Thus, even though the KGB's presence on decisionmaking bodies was expanded, its level of representation remained miniscule compared to that of the Party and the civilian organs of government. Apart from the suppression of dissent, the only area in which the KGB seems unambiguously to have expanded its activities is in the gathering and processing of foreign intelligence, especially of a scientific or technical nature, and in the conduct of so-called active measures and disinformation aimed at manipulating foreign opinion and events.[53] To be sure, during Brezhnev's last year and with the succession struggle already under way, KGB officials apparently released information and encouraged rumors designed to discredit Brezhnev and perhaps to strengthen Andropov's position.[54] However, intelligence organizations the world over are routinely accused of doing the same, and there appears to be no evidence whatsoever of more significant attempts at intervention in high-level politics, then or at any other time since early in the Khrushchev period. Indeed, one might attribute the KGB's apparent lack of interest in domestic politics to its rising professionalism (something much remarked on by Soviet dissidents) and to the fact that with its foreign responsibilities it now has much better things with which to occupy itself.

As for the military, there is, again, more evidence of strong political control than of its weakness or absence. Although total defense spending rose steadily under Brezhnev, the defense industries were compelled to assume increased responsibilities normally consigned to the civilian economy, particularly in the production of consumer durables.[55] The military has also continued to perform important social and socialization functions (teaching Russian to ethnic minorities and encouraging "integrationist" attitudes among all ethnic groups), although fulfillment of these tasks may, at the margins, have reduced the relative efficiency and effectiveness of the military's preparedness and war-fighting capabilities.[56] The Party also moved to strengthen its formal institutional control of the military, and of defense policy generally, by giving constitutional recognition and increasing publicity to the Defense Council, headed by the General Secretary and including other key civilian leaders among its members. The Party's aggressiveness in asserting its authority surfaced in other ways as well. When Marshal Grechko died, a civilian (Dimitriy Ustinov) rather than a military professional was named as Grechko's replacement. In 1980–1981, Brezhnev engineered a series of changes in high-level military personnel in an apparently successful effort to reduce the military's pressure for armed intervention in Poland.[57] Brezhnev also was able to secure the public, if perhaps grudging, acceptance by the military of the idea that nuclear war is unwinnable, which many military leaders had long been loath to acknowledge openly. It is true, of course, that the military *has* at times resisted the Party's direction and opposed policies advanced by civilian leaders. Political control *is* reduced by the absence of a fully proficient "neutral competence" in the technical aspects of weaponry and war fighting.[58] Yet, there is no evidence that any of this has deterred the Party from imposing its choices on issues it has thought important.[59]

It is vital, therefore, to distinguish between the power and capabilities of an institution, on the one hand, and the extent of outside control over that institution, on the other. The evidence suggests that although the capabilities of the military and the KGB expanded, especially under Brezhnev, political control either did not erode or actually grew stronger. It may be that Brezhnev and his associates continued to favor coercive strategies in their pursuit of various goals because their coercive capabilities seemed greater or more reliable than the other instruments at their disposal. But that does not mean that the leaders of the military or the KGB had similarly disproportionate access to, or influence within, the councils of state. The test, of course, is how easy it is to change course, to shift resources away from the instruments of coercion in order to strengthen other state capacities. Evidence from Gorbachev's first three years in office suggests rather clearly that the civilian leadership controls the security organs and not the reverse.

The Social Contract

A strong state is not necessarily an efficient or an effective state. The Soviet state today is doubtless more secure than before and more capable in the sense of being able to do more things. But to do more things does not mean to do them well, and during Brezhnev's final years the state's performance, especially in the economic sphere, grew steadily worse. Most observers in the West, and a growing number within the Soviet Union itself, have located the causes of this national distemper in precisely those features of the system that had remained unchanged since Stalin's day: the command economy and the Party's "totalist" political monopoly. As Thane Gustafson observed, Soviet leaders continued to reject the idea that in order to retain power over outcomes, whether political or economic, it was necessary to surrender power over details. The result was that the leaders' power over *both* outcomes and details was diminished.[60]

Why was the leadership so stubborn? One possibility is that no one in power thought the alternatives were any better. Perhaps because so many Soviet politicians are engineers by training, they may simply have believed that plans, blueprints, and administrative coordination are more efficacious than chaotic markets and unregulated private exchange.[61] Another explanation would emphasize the selfish interests of the Party-state elite (the *nomenklatura*) as a whole.[62] Why would these officials, the argument runs, willingly give up their power, status, and economic benefits, as would be required by serious political-economic reform? Up to a point, both these propositions are demonstrably true. The elite *is* full of disbelievers and the purely self-interested, and this has undoubtedly strengthened the leaders' more conservative instincts. Yet, as explanations of the behavior of the leadership, neither disbelief nor selfishness is in the end sufficient.

One reason is that collective disbelief in the efficacy of alternative methods of rule was eroding long before Brezhnev died. Skepticism of the traditional methods emerged clearly in the economic reform movement that began in the late-1950s and flourished in the immediate wake of the 1965 Kosygin reform.[63] Nor did skepticism disappear when that reform was defeated. Although genuine disbelievers probably remained the majority among intellectuals, and certainly among politicians, there continued to develop an increasingly sophisticated critique of the existing political economy and an ever-widening circle of thinkers—some dissidents but many establishment figures as well—who were ready to defend such changes as would allow greater scope for market forces, unregulated individual participation in politics, and group autonomy.[64] These ideas seeped into the political elite and became at least known to those at the top, and so it would be wrong to suppose that Brezhnev and his fellow leaders stood pat simply out of ignorance of plausible alternatives. The presumption of near-uniform opposition by a self-interested elite is similarly problematic. For one thing, precisely because of their relative advantages over the rest of society, Party and state officials had the most to lose if the decline in growth persisted. At the same time, the available evidence suggests that middle-ranking members of the elite were and are divided about major reform issues and that there is a sizable minority that favors, at least in principle, far-reaching systemic changes.[65]

The question, then, is not whether there were disbelievers and self-interested politicians—there were those in abundance—but rather why these groups prevailed in the face of accumulating countervailing pressures. Part of the answer was suggested earlier. Competition within the leadership was relatively weak during the last half decade of Brezhnev's rule, at least partly because of the General Secretary's effective use of power to shore up his ebbing authority. Brezhnev must have judged, correctly, that he could survive politically without fundamentally changing course. "Let the next generation worry" was, in effect, what he decided. But that only begs the question, for we are then left to wonder why the challenge to Brezhnev's position was not more intense. The only plausible explanation is that extreme centralization and administrative methods were not simply the habits of an aging generation of leaders who did not know any better; rather, these were the elements of a comprehensive and well-understood strategy of rule. It was not obtuseness that prompted Soviet leaders to prefer bureaucratic "thumbs" to the "fingers" of the market (to use the words of Charles Lindblom); on the contrary, the defects and costs of bureaucracy were well known.[66] Nor was it selfishness, at least no more than the selfishness of leaders everywhere who want to remain in power. Instead, the regime's intolerance of autonomous groups and its refusal to surrender power over details are best explained as having been required by an overarching approach to the twin problems of economic growth and social peace, to which Khrushchev and Brezhnev, despite their many differences, both adhered. To understand this, we need to consider, first, the basic elements of the Stalinist economic growth strategy that Stalin's successors continued to employ and, second, the way in which Soviet leaders since Stalin have sought to preserve social order in the face of the significant costs the Stalinist growth model imposed on the Soviet public.

At an abstract level, any growth strategy may be conceived as a set of preferences combined with a theory prescribing the means to their attainment. In Stalin's case, the most rapid possible buildup of military-industrial power was his first priority. His "theory" presumed that massed investment was more important to growth than were factor productivity gains and that it would be more effective to mobilize and concentrate scarce and underutilized resources than to try to elicit and manipulate their proper use through incentives. The political-economic institutions comprising the command economy, erected by Stalin in the decade following his "revolution from above," may be thought of as the physical embodiment of this strategy. That much of this system then survived the dictator's death was due only in part to the skill of the bureaucrats running the system in protecting their institutions and power in the less dangerous and more predictable politics of the post-Stalin era. Almost certainly more important was the fact that many of the biases and presumptions of Stalin's growth model also persisted in the minds of Soviet policymakers. Military-industrial growth was still given priority. Directive planning, the centralized allocation of inputs, and administered pricing endured not only, or even mainly, because they were valuable and familiar to the bureaucrats but because they were and are extremely effective devices for mobilizing and concentrating scarce resources.

This strategy seemed to make sense in the context of the early years of Soviet power when there was an abundance of underutilized resources and when the technological level of the economy was low. The strategy was also effective, if not very efficient. Rapid military-industrial growth was achieved, albeit at great cost in wasted resources and human misery; the German attack in World War II was defeated; and postwar growth was impressive, at least until the early 1970s. Even though productivity growth was unusually slow in the postwar period, accumulation levels remained high and resources continued to be concentrated on the production of goods, an area in which productivity was increasing faster than in services. Soviet military power continued to increase. Growth overall was generally on a par with, or better than, what most of the developed capitalist countries recorded.[67]

Soviet performance was not so good as to prevent a growing debate about the wisdom of this strategy and the costs of the institutions required for its implementation. The weaknesses of the economy were generally recognized, and Khrushchev was able to exploit widespread anxiety about low productivity growth and the economy's especially poor technological performance in his successful attack on Malenkov's New Course in 1954–1955.[68] In the second half of the 1950s, economists and other specialists began to discuss publicly the merits of increasing enterprise autonomy and of expanding the use of "goods-money relations" (a euphemism for market forces), including a greater reliance on prof-itability as a criterion of performance. Widely known in the West as the Liberman reforms, these ideas were debated on and off until Khrushchev's fall, at which point they became the inspiration for a limited but open-ended industrial reform introduced in September 1965 by the new Prime Minister, Kosygin.[69] For a number of reasons, ranging from bureaucratic footdragging to defects in the reform program itself, the 1965 reform was hamstrung almost from the beginning, and it was finally officially repudiated in the early 1970s. Yet the underlying diagnosis of the economy's ills that had been used to justify reform in the first place remained largely unchallenged. Brezhnev, who achieved political primacy over Kosygin at least partly through his aggressive and ultimately persuasive attack on the shortcomings of his Prime Minister's economic program, nonetheless felt it necessary to combine his indictment with a demand that the reform debate continue, and as if to concede the urgency of the issue, he even promised that the Central Committee would devote a whole plenum to the question. In the event, this plenum was never held, and the cause of economic reform remained dead until Gorbachev rose to power more than a decade later.[70]

Brezhnev's unwillingness even to give serious consideration to, let alone to pay the costs of, internal reform is often ascribed to bureaucratic opposition or, more subtly, to the presumed self-interest of the *nomenklatura*. Yet, as already suggested, there had to be more to it than that. Indeed, the price of the Stalinist growth strategy included not only poor growth in productivity and lagging technological performance but also a severely depressed popular living standard and, as required for the implementation of this strategy, institutions that allowed ordinary citizens virtually no influence over the political and economic decisions that shaped their lives. Given the tremendous amount of social flux and upheaval entailed in rapid growth, the paltry material benefits that this strategy left the mass public, and the lack of opportunities for political voice, one might have expected a situation in which there was enormous potential for social disorder and political instability. The question is, How did the government manage to keep the peace?

Stalin maintained social order, although at first not very effectively, perhaps largely through violence and intimidation, but also thanks to the fantastic opportunities for upward social mobility that resulted from forced-pace industrialization, and as a result of special privileges offered to outstanding workers and to those who succeeded in entering the tiny but rapidly increasing home-grown, technical intelligentsia.[71] Why the dictator's successors felt it necessary to switch so quickly to a fundamentally new approach is still unclear and a subject deserving further study.[72] One obvious factor was the evidently widespread desire among the elite to be rid of the insecurities with which they had recently lived. There may, in addition, have been some anxiety about the popular response to Stalin's death, exemplified in the oft-noted appeal to the population not to succumb to "disorder and panic."[73] Beyond that, top leaders may also have been coming to doubt the effectiveness and durability of their coercive instruments, bolstered by the knowledge of deteriorating order within the camps of the Gulag.[74] Finally, and in the long run most importantly, the gradual slowing of upward mobility rates in the 1950s and the mounting pressures of a more complicated economy and dramatically transformed social structure undoubtedly increased the attractiveness of a more inclusive and conciliatory strategy, while elevating the costs incurred by holding firm to Stalin's approach.

Whatever the explanation, the change was almost immediate. Within six months of the dictator's death, real incomes were up sharply, the result of significant reductions both in consumer prices and in compulsory bond subscriptions, and large increases in the production of various consumer goods and services had been promised under the auspices of Malenkov's New Course. Although this program did not survive its author's political decline, it did mark a permanent shift in the government's priorities. When Stalin died, average living standards were not much higher than they had been at the start of the First Five-Year Plan, twenty-five years earlier. During the next twenty-five years, however, average living standards more than doubled, and few doubt that this was an important cause of the continuing quiescence of the Soviet public. But improved consumption by itself was not enough. Even though living standards rose steadily under Khrushchev and Brezhnev, they remained far below those in the West, and both the elite's and the public's awareness of, and impatience with, this gap grew with the simultaneous expansion of tourism and other international contacts. Meanwhile, the level of social flux remained high, which was largely the result of continued high rates of rural outmigration and urbanization, while ordinary citizens remained deprived of any significant political or economic power.

Then, in the second half of the 1950s, a more elaborate formula was worked out. The social policy introduced at this time, and for the most part sustained throughout the Brezhnev period, was relatively austere and illiberal by world standards. But it did offer the following promises: (1) to minimize the risks of continued economic growth to individuals, through high levels of job security and stable prices for most basic consumer items; (2) to share widely and relatively evenly the benefits of growth, through a steady expansion of the social wage and a generally egalitarian incomes policy; and (3) while granting no greater power over key political and economic decisions, to allow most citizens considerably greater personal freedom as workers and as consumers. In a phrase, Khrushchev developed and Brezhnev maintained an implicit "social contract" in which the government offered a series of socioeconomic guarantees in exchange for the public's compliance and support even as it continued to deny popular political rights.[75]

Although the term *social contract* and its specific contents accurately reflect the fundamentally conciliatory thrust of the domestic peacekeeping strategy of the post-Stalin regime, a number of qualifications must be interjected. In the first place, this was obviously not a true bargain because the deliberations that led to these policies were conducted on one side only. Soviet society was left with the choice of either accepting or rejecting what the state had to offer, but society played no essential role in specifying the terms. On the other hand, historical evidence suggests that relations between the state and society in the post-Stalin period have involved something like a quid pro quo, for whenever one side has shown signs of violating the implicit terms of this bargain— as in the early 1960s when Khrushchev, under severe budgetary pressure, seemed ready to renege on many of his promises—the other side has begun to behave more equivocally as well.[76]

Second, the shift to a more conciliatory strategy did not mean that coercion and intimidation were suddenly unimportant. Although mass terror ended and the amount of applied coercion declined dramatically, the state's coercive instruments were retained, used, and indeed strengthened under Brezhnev. Few doubt that state coercion and intimidation have also contributed to the maintenance of social order and popular quiescence in the post-Stalin period. But how much? By its very nature, such a question is impossible to answer with certainty. Nevertheless, it would appear that the role and overall importance of state coercion have fundamentally changed. Although repression continues to make it extremely difficult to organize open opposition to the regime, the intimidation produced by the security organs evidently has much less impact on the overall supply of would-be dissenters. This interpretation is bolstered by a limited amount of survey data collected from recent Soviet emigrants, which suggests that coercion is now applied mainly against leaders and rarely against followers; that repression tends not to work in individual cases (encouraging rather than discouraging "recidivism"); that respect for the security organs is inversely related to support for traditional practices and norms of the regime; and that social atomization—the context in which intimidation works best—is much decreased among the generations that came to maturity after the death of Stalin.[77] Such an interpretation is also supported, more circumstantially, by the relative tolerance displayed by the government for the increasingly obstreperous dissent movement during the first fifteen years of Brezhnev's rule, followed by the dramatic hardening of policy in 1979–1980.[78] This implies that the costs of public dissent (and of the failures of intimidation) were perceived by the leadership as consisting mainly in lost foreign prestige and influence and were not thought to represent a serious threat to the state's power and stability at home—that is, until the regime's domestic base of support began to shrink in the wake of a dissolving social contract.

Finally, in the case of some groups in the population, the social contract was supplemented or even replaced by other strategies of control. Officials and members of the intelligentsia were offered carefully regulated access to a wide variety of special privileges, including the much-treasured chance to travel abroad. Support from Russians was sought with blatant and constant appeals to national pride and patriotism. When it came to ethnic minorities mainly concentrated along the country's western and southern borders, the government tended to rely on a wholly conventional neocolonialism. Thus, while the center remained entirely in the hands of Russians (mainly) and Slavs (more generally), locally recruited minority elites were allowed to rule the areas in which their ethnic groups were concentrated, with few outside controls (second Party secretaries and KGB heads were usually Russian). Moscow also provided direct economic subsidies to the less-developed regions of the leading minority groups. This was done partly in compensation for the regions' acceptance of centrally determined economic priorities, such as the continuation of cotton growing in Central Asia, but also to give local elites the resources necessary to keep their political machines well oiled and under control.[79]

The social contract worked; even Gorbachev has suggested as much. In spite of the profound changes of the post-Stalin period—the death and subsequent denunciation of the infallible leader, the end of terror, and the social flux associated with continued economic growth—Soviet society experienced remarkably little internal disorder. The exceptions, as previously suggested, tended to cluster in periods in which either the leadership or the society seemed to be having second thoughts about meeting its putative obligations. However, since the mid-1970s, signs of a more substantial weakening of support for the social contract by both sides have accumulated. This time, things could not be reversed or patched up as easily as in the past.[80]

There is evidence on a broad front that the social contract was coming unraveled during the last half dozen years of Brezhnev's rule. Eroding public support was suggested by an apparent deterioration in labor and social discipline, a spreading sense of anomie and pessimism concerning the future, and an increase in open forms of protest—for example, letters of complaint, job actions, and even a few scattered attempts to form independent trade unions.[81] Gorbachev has since alluded to this period as one of "social corrosion," in which a "precrisis situation" was developing. At the same time, elite support also was eroding, as evidenced by a growing public debate in which every component of the social contract was subjected to increasingly sharp criticism.[82] Beneath these overt manifestations of decline, the social contract was losing support on numerous levels. Widespread social norms, which in the past had legitimated egalitarian distribution and a high level of economic security, were now being undermined by corruption, a flourishing black market, and a spreading perception that the actual distribution of rewards no longer measured up to any conceivable standard of "social justice." Those institutions to which had been given primary responsibility for implementing and safeguarding the social contract, such as the labor ministry and the trade unions, had in the years since grown more rigid, less responsive to their supposed constituents, and thus less able to diffuse the conflicts that policy implementation inevitably created. Finally, it was becoming apparent that most of the direct benefits of social policy—which had tended to favor blue-collar workers over white-collar professionals and employees, and persons employed in the production of goods over those in services—were flowing to constituencies that were either shrinking or, from an economic standpoint, becoming increasingly marginal. As I have written elsewhere, one could imagine "a kind of social 'de-alignment' taking shape, as the number of partisans of the old order declin[ed], relatively speaking, and the number of dissatisfied 'independents' [grew], waiting to be mobilized behind a new program."[83]

To some extent, the social contract had become yet another casualty of the economic slowdown and the diminishing resources available for consumption. The culprit fingered by most Western observers was the Stalinist growth strategy, which, as had been long predicted, was turning out to be an increasingly poor performer in conditions of a growing scarcity of resources and rapid technological change. Yet the social contract had brought with it economic costs of its own. For example, wage egalitarianism had required that the economic surplus created at relatively profitable enterprises be reallocated to less-profitable ones, but this had weakened the incentive to produce at both. The promise of security and fairness had required uniformity and a powerful, supervisory center, but that had meant severe restrictions on the flexibility and initiative of producers at the grass roots. Institutions that had been revitalized or had been newly established in order to supervise the implementation of the rules and regulations of the social contract had developed their own stake in defending the policies that mandated those rules, even when they no longer made economic sense. As a result, maintenance of the social contract took an ever-larger share of the economy's surplus. It led to increasing inefficiencies because of its inability to accommodate the growing differentiation of economy and society.

And it obstructed or prevented the kinds of economic adjustment that might have slowed the rate of decline or allowed for a smoother, less traumatic transition to a new growth strategy.

In sum, although an anachronistic growth strategy was undeniably a major cause of the deterioration in economic performance in the Brezhnev period, the contributions of an increasingly anachronistic social contract were probably equally great. This must have magnified the need for radical reform in the eyes of many in the elite, especially of the members of Gorbachev's generation and younger, who were beginning to understand that the problem of the government was not only to reverse the long-term slide in economic growth but, in addition, to rebuild the legitimacy of the Soviet state among the population at large. In other words, the "crisis" that lay on the horizon was not just economic but political. However, recognition of this also added enormously to the complexity of the government's problem. The connections between economic and social policy are numerous and complicated, and for either policy to work as intended, both must be compatible with, indeed mutually reinforcing of, each other. The choice of a new growth strategy and the fashioning of a new social contract therefore would have to proceed more or less simultaneously. That Brezhnev and most of the other members of his generation shied away from such a task is little cause for surprise.

Conclusions

Appearances can deceive, in politics as in people. When one looks beyond the structure of power in the Soviet Union to the rules of the political process, the relative strength of the state, and the nature of relations between the state and society, it is clear that the Soviet "system" today is fundamentally different than when Stalin was the leader. On the one hand, even the weak institutionalization of politics has significantly reduced Soviet leaders' freedom to pursue policies that are sharply at variance with what the larger political community prefers. Or, to put it more precisely, institutionalization has significantly raised the costs to be paid when those preferences are defied. On the other hand, the adoption of a social peacekeeping formula that includes certain limits on state power, and that emphasizes the cultivation of a broad social base of support for the state, has surely strengthened the leaders' incentives to discover, to shape to the extent possible, but ultimately to respect the preferences of the political community and, to a lesser extent, of the population as a whole. Finally, the heightened power and hence security of the state and the addition of more numerous and diverse (albeit awkward and often inefficient) state "capacities" have almost certainly weakened the pressures inducing Soviet leaders to opt for bellicose and confrontational policies both at home and abroad. This is true in part because the level of threat has fallen, but also because the leaders now have other instruments and resources at their disposal.

In short, the death of Stalin precipitated a fundamental change in the character of the Soviet regime. The social base of the new regime was considerably broader than Stalin's. This, the progressive institu-tionalization of politics, and the continued growth of state power virtually assured that Stalin's successors would pursue different goals, by different means, and with a different kind of success than the dictator had experienced. Many observers have recognized these developments and throughout the years have proposed numerous labels to characterize the post-Stalin regime, ranging from "totalitarianism without terror" to "welfare-state authoritarianism" and others. But too often the more fundamental point has been lost. If this analysis is correct, many of the structural forces that led George F. Kennan and others in the late-1940s to diagnose (probably correctly) an essentially and exceptionally bellig-erent Soviet state, and to recommend a Western policy of limited and carefully gauged "containment" in response, had by the late 1970s largely dissolved. Although containment was still practiced in one form or another, its original theoretical justification no longer applied.

This conclusion will doubtless be vigorously disputed, although pos-sibly for the wrong reasons. My argument is not that Soviet international behavior grew less belligerent in the post-Stalin era. On the contrary, in some respects Soviet behavior was clearly more belligerent or at least more aggressive. Part of the reason for this is to be found in the steady accretion of Soviet military power, which both encouraged and enabled Brezhnev in particular to look to ever-broader horizons. At the same time, the undeniably wooden character of Soviet foreign policy during most of the post-Stalin period and the regime's continuing preference for the instruments of coercion and intimidation over those of diplomacy probably should be credited to the personal conservatism and idiosyncratic biases of an unusually cohesive, solidary, and long-surviving elite gen-eration led by Brezhnev. Indeed, it is surely true in part that generational stagnation, like the locking of plates in the earth's crust, delayed and otherwise obscured the effects of numerous ongoing and far-reaching subterranean changes in society and in many of the system's institutions.[84]

Yet Kennan's original prescription for containment derived not from assumptions concerning the consequences of power and a conservative elite but rather from a diagnosis of the sources of belligerency that Kennan believed were inherent in the Soviet system itself. These were, above all, the messianic ideology of the Party; the profound insecurity of the Party's leaders, engendered by the presumed illegitimacy of the

Soviet state; and the leadership's total freedom from popular accountability.[85] It was these factors, and not power per se, that made the Soviet
state seem different from ordinary or aspiring Great Powers and that
Kennan cited as the justification for containment. This chapter has tried
to show that these same factors, whether or not they ever existed in
the extreme form Kennan and others supposed, had toward the end of
the Brezhnev period all but disappeared. Perhaps it was because containment had "worked." In any event, although possessed of awesome
military might and susceptible still to a sometimes acute if increasingly
anachronistic xenophobia, the Soviet state had in most other respects
become rather ordinary.

The preceding analysis points to a second conclusion that may also
be vigorously contested: that even before Gorbachev's rise to power,
much of the ground for radical political-economic reform had already
been prepared and, indeed, that far-reaching changes in one form or
another could scarcely be avoided. The final passing of the Brezhnev
generation is part of the explanation for this, but there are other, more
important reasons. One is that the intellectual basis of the old regime
has for the most part evaporated. Although there is wide disagreement
within the Soviet intelligentsia, broadly defined, concerning the details
of what should come next and how to get there, the central elements
both of the Stalinist economic growth strategy and of the post-Stalin
social contract have been widely and thoroughly discredited. Today one
looks in vain for serious theoretical justifications of detailed directive
planning or egalitarian wage policies, although this was already becoming
the case well before the Brezhnev leadership ended. Indeed, one of the
least-appreciated aspects of the second half of the Brezhnev period is
that especially among policy specialists the rethinking of old orthodoxies
proceeded apace, something that the conservative politics of this era
could hide but not halt. At the same time, the need for a new growth
strategy and a new social contract became rooted in inescapable objective
conditions that can now be ignored only at steadily increasing cost.
Such conditions include the requirements of continued economic growth
in conditions of advanced development, widespread resource shortage,
and accelerating technological change, and the inherent difficulties in
satisfying a population that is more educated, more affluent, more likely
than ever before to be doing white-collar and service work, and in
general more differentiated in its tastes and circumstances.

Other factors are likely to play a part as well. As argued earlier, the
current leadership seems more aware than were its predecessors of the
costs of a weakly institutionalized political process, particularly concerning the lack of accountability of leaders. This will stimulate the
search for ways to strengthen the leverage of collegial bodies over their

executives and will invite, almost inevitably, the consideration of limits on terms of office and similarly radical measures of political reform. One can even imagine the reemergence (and de facto toleration) of informal, loosely organized, but more or less permanent factions within the Party. At the same time, the current anticorruption campaign and the mounting pressure to slash nonproductive budgetary subsidies together constitute a mortal threat to the old neocolonialist approach to the management of minority ethnic groups. An increased reliance on the Russian settler communities (and on Slavic officials sent from Moscow) may suffice as a temporary expedient, but it is clearly not a long-term solution to the problems of multinational governance, particularly in conditions in which many of the minority populations are expanding at rates several times those at which the Slavic groups are growing. Here, too, some new formulae will have to be found.

Finally, there is the much enhanced power of the state. Although there may now be serious and deeply felt grievances scattered throughout Soviet society, the extreme barriers to the organization and mobilization of opposition as well as the numerous resources and instruments at the leaders' disposal make it extremely unlikely that the government could lose control over events and could find its security threatened in the near future. Awareness of this undoubtedly removes some of the pressure from the leadership, and it may weaken elite support for reform. But such awareness may also have the opposite effect. A strong, secure state tends to give its leaders a confidence that a weak, insecure state cannot—confidence that they will be able to retain control over events; to absorb the protest and turmoil that radical changes always bring; and thus to hold firm and keep the reform process on track and not to succumb to the temptation to turn back at the first sign of difficulty. Moreover, no state is secure forever, no matter how powerful or capable it may seem at present. Surely it is the prospect of reduced state security in the future, whether because of a reinvigorated United States or because of continued internal stagnation, that ultimately impels the current crop of reformers. Such threats may lie on the distant horizon, but they are easily conjured up in the minds of politicians as young and ambitious as Gorbachev.

In sum, by the start of the 1980s, sufficient forces and pressures had been assembled to make probable the institution of fundamental political-economic reforms as soon as a leadership succession was under way and the incentives for innovation and authority building had once again intensified. None of this should be interpreted as suggesting that certain reforms (market socialism or political democracy) are inevitable or that the reforms that are adopted will prove successful in rebuilding the state's legitimacy, reversing the economic slowdown, or reclaiming the country's prestige and influence internationally. Numerous outcomes are possible, including, as always, revolutionary collapse. Although I think this is extremely unlikely, it is clear that the skill and courage of leadership, and luck, will count heavily in determining which outcomes prevail, how quickly, and at what cost. However, these cautions should not obscure the larger point that powerful forces are now working to promote yet another transformation of the Soviet regime and that a historical juncture is at hand with potentially far-reaching implications for both Soviet domestic developments and world politics.

Notes

For useful comments on earlier drafts, I would like to thank all the members of the East-West Forum seminar, but especially Donna Bahry, Joe Berliner, Alexander Motyl, and our chairperson, Seweryn Bialer. Extensive criticism and helpful advice were also provided, as always, by George Breslauer and Blair Ruble. I, of course, remain solely responsible for errors of fact and grievously wrong interpretations.

1. *Pravda*, January 28, 1987; and *Materialy plenuma tsentral'nogo komiteta KPSS, 25–26 iyunya 1987 (Materials of the CPSU Central Committee Plenum, 25–26 June 1987)* (Moscow: Politizdat, 1987), pp. 6–70.

2. Peter Reddaway, "Gorbachev the Bold," *New York Review of Books* 34, no. 9 (May 28, 1987), pp. 21–25 (at 25).

3. Seweryn Bialer, *The Soviet Paradox* (New York: Knopf, 1986), p. 6.

4. T. H. Rigby, "Khrushchev and the Rules of the Soviet Political Game," in R. F. Miller and F. Fehér, eds., *Khrushchev and the Communist World* (Totowa, N.J.: Barnes & Noble, 1984), pp. 39–81.

5. This ranking is entirely my own, although a faithful summary, I think, of Rigby's own sophisticated and far less schematic discussion (see especially pp. 39–42).

6. This was an important theme of Zbigniew Brzezinski and Samuel P. Huntington's classic, *Political Power: USA/USSR* (New York: Vintage, 1965), Ch. 3.

7. Grey Hodnett, "The Pattern of Leadership Politics," in Seweryn Bialer, ed., *The Domestic Context of Soviet Foreign Policy* (Boulder, Colo.: Westview, 1981), pp. 87–118.

8. See, for example, Seweryn Bialer, *Stalin's Successors* (Cambridge: Cambridge University Press, 1980), pp. 56–57.

9. Hodnett distinguished "institutionalization" from "constitutionalization," defining the former as internalized information about roles and procedures—that is, "a shared understanding of how leaders who occupy certain specified positions . . . typically will relate—within certain limits, in certain types of situations—to occupants of other leadership and extraleadership positions." The essence of "constitutionalization," by comparison, is the idea of "juridically binding rules that 'legally' constrain the political behavior of leaders." The key

difference is that in the case of the latter, independent outside arbiters referee, whereas in the case of the former, compliance with the rules is determined (and noncompliance punished) by the rulers themselves. Hodnett, "The Pattern of Leadership Politics," pp. 106–107 and footnote 48.

10. Ibid.

11. It is worth distinguishing terror—violence applied more or less randomly and indiscriminately against large groups—from the violence applied more or less routinely against erring individuals. The former was an exceptional (although no less important) feature of Stalinist rule, the latter a constant.

12. Even when relatives of Stalin's closest associates became victims—Vyacheslav Molotov's wife was exiled, and Lazar Kaganovich's brother was reportedly driven to suicide by the threat of arrest—there seems to have been no serious interruption in these leaders' work relations. See the account in Roy Medvedev, *All Stalin's Men* (New York: Anchor Books, 1985), pp. 102–103 and 132–133.

13. Key events in the delegitimation of violence included prompt exposure of the notorious Doctors' Plot as fraudulent and the release of the surviving physicians; the June 1953 arrest of Lavrenty Beriya and other high police officials, followed by their trial and execution six months later; the simultaneous curbing of secret police powers, in particular the right to convene extrajudicial tribunals; Khrushchev's famous "secret speech" at the Twentieth Party Congress in February 1956, in which he denounced Stalin's terror, and the subsequent release or rehabilitation of thousands of surviving prisoners and deceased victims; and the 1957 "anti-Party group crisis," after which those who had led the attempted coup against Khrushchev were not killed or even arrested but were exiled to minor jobs in the provinces. For a readable and still useful history of this period, see Wolfgang Leonhard, *The Kremlin Since Stalin* (New York: Praeger, 1962).

14. This account was included in Khrushchev's closing speech to the Twenty-second Party Congress. See *Pravda*, October 29, 1961, p. 3.

15. In view of the tendency in the West to portray Brezhnev as a strong proponent of more "discipline" and therefore something of a Stalinist, it is worth quoting Brezhnev's remarks (to the December 1969 Central Committee Plenum) at length. After arguing that "a rise in labor, party, and state discipline is becoming one of the most important tasks for us," he continued with this caveat: "But by what methods will we attain it? This is an important question that requires clarity. . . . Some comrades recall bygone times and propose in essence that we return to methods of a particularly administrative sort. I think this is a poor prescription. Discipline that is wholly dependent on such methods is not the discipline we need. . . . We well understand what the . . . methods of administrative rule [*administrirovaniye*] lead to: dishonesty, expressed in concealment of the true state of affairs; attempts to cover up problems instead of posing and resolving them; prettification and false reporting. These methods also lead to over-insurance, to the loss of initiative. All this is dangerous, especially in the leadership of economic affairs. We're talking about things which are hard to calculate in monetary terms, but if we could do so, surely it would be shown that the absence of initiative, the desire not to think, timidity in raising questions, [and] red tape would cost us very dearly." L. I. Brezhnev, *Ob*

osnovnykh voprosakh ekonomicheskoy politiki KPSS na sovremennom etape (On the Basic Issues of the CPSU's Economic Policy in the Contemporary Period), 2nd ed. (Moscow: Politizdat, 1979), vol. 1, pp. 461–462. For an account of the leadership's abrupt, last-minute decision not to proceed with Stalin's rehabilitation, see Roy Medvedev, "The Stalin Question," in Stephen F. Cohen et al., eds., *The Soviet Union Since Stalin* (Bloomington: Indiana University Press, 1980), pp. 32–49 (at 46–48).

16. See, for example, the puzzling circumstances surrounding the death in October 1980 of candidate Politburo member Petr Masherov, as described by Amy W. Knight, "Pyotr Masherov and the Soviet Leadership: A Study in Kremlinology," *Survey* 26, no. 1 (1982), pp. 151–168. For a recent case of political violence practiced at the regional level, in which the long-time Party leader of the Bashkir autonomous republic engineered the arrest and imprisonment of a subordinate Party leader, see "'To Halt the Persecution,'" *Pravda*, May 6, 1987, p. 2.

17. George W. Breslauer, *Khrushchev and Brezhnev as Leaders* (London: Allen & Unwin, 1982).

18. Power is defined conventionally as the ability, whether by virtue of one's organizational position or through control of resources (including coercive resources), to impose one's preferences on another—"pulling rank," as Breslauer put it. Ibid., p. 3.

19. Although these are logically derived hypotheses, Breslauer presented a variety of data in support of the argument about leadership dynamics, taken from post-Stalin leaders' public posturing and from the policy record. Thus, particularly during succession struggles, rivals have often adopted clearly distinct positions on a variety of issues. The winners in these confrontations typically have gone on to advance comprehensive, multi-issue programs designed both to validate their leadership claims (by expanding their range of claimed competences) and to broaden their base of support (by coopting issues or solutions previously championed by the losers). The incidence of major policy shifts also seems to have been highest when, or immediately after, elite competition has been most intense.

20. This argument is made with respect to both democratic and socialist regimes in Valerie Bunce, *Do New Leaders Make a Difference?* (Princeton, N.J.: Princeton University Press, 1981).

21. That Brezhnev's position weakened in the mid-1970s now seems incontrovertible, although how seriously is unclear and was probably unclear even to participants at the time. For evidence in the case of domestic policy, see Breslauer, *Khrushchev and Brezhnev*, Chs. 13, 14; and my Ph.D. dissertation, "Managing the Soviet Labor Market: Politics and Policymaking Under Brezhnev" (University of Michigan, 1984), Ch. 5. For evidence in the realm of foreign policy, see Peter M. E. Volten, *Brezhnev's Peace Program: A Study of Soviet Domestic Political Process and Power* (Boulder, Colo.: Westview, 1982), Chs. 3, 4.

22. In the nearly eight years that elapsed between the end of the war in Europe and Stalin's death, there had been one Party congress (in 1952) and only one officially reported meeting of the Central Committee (February 1947).

During the first decade following Stalin's death, three Party congresses were held, along with twenty-seven announced Central Committee plenums. In fact, the total meeting time of congresses, Party conferences, and Central Committee plenums in 1955–1962 (information is incomplete for 1953–1954) averaged 15 days/year, as compared with 11.4 days/year in the decade before World War II. Based on *Spravochnyy tom k vos'momu izdaniyu 'KPSS v rezolyutsiyakh i resheniyakh s"yezdov, konferentsiy i plenumov TsK'* (*Index Volume to the Eighth Edition of 'The CPSU in the Resolutions and Decisions of Congresses, Conferences and Central Committee Plenums'*) (Moscow: Politizdat, 1973), pp. 28–34.

23. See, for example, Fedor Morgun's account of the December 1958 Central Committee Plenum in his memoirs, *Khleb i Lyudi* (*Grain and People*), 2nd ed. (Moscow: Politizdat, 1975), pp. 100–106. Morgun, recently named head of a new USSR State Committee for environmental protection, addressed this plenum in his capacity as a state farm chairperson from the Virgin Lands in Kazakhstan.

24. Archie Brown, "The Power of the General Secretary," in T. H. Rigby et al., eds., *Authority, Power and Policy in the USSR* (New York: St. Martin's Press, 1980), p. 140 (and footnote 23). This should be contrasted with Stalin's habit of doing business over late-night dinners and in various, ever-changing sub-committees of the leadership, as described by Khrushchev and numerous others in their memoirs.

25. The most important documentary series include the weekly *Sobraniye postanovleniy pravitel'stva SSSR* (*Collected Decrees of the USSR Government*); and the two multivolume sets, *KPSS v rezolyutsiyakh i resheniyakh s"yezdov, konferentsiy i plenumov TsK* (*The CPSU in the Resolutions and Decisions of Congresses, Conferences and Central Committee plenums*), now in its 9th edition, and *Resheniya partii i pravitel'stva po khozyaystvennym voprosam* (*Decisions of the Party and Government Concerning Economic Issues*), now in its 3rd edition.

26. These developments are conveniently surveyed in Donald R. Kelley, "The Communist Party," in Kelley, ed., *Soviet Politics in the Brezhnev Era* (New York: Praeger, 1980), pp. 27–54. Also see Jerry F. Hough and Merle Fainsod, *How the Soviet Union Is Governed* (Cambridge, Mass.: Harvard University Press, 1979), Ch. 9.

27. These developments are reviewed, although with a slightly different emphasis, in Brown, "The Power of the General Secretary."

28. Hodnett wrote as follows: "Thus we are talking about informal understandings: that business be conducted in official forums, that information will be accessible to members, that participation will be structured in certain ways, that the general secretary will take the initiative in drawing up reports, and that these reports will be collectively approved." Hodnett, "The Pattern of Leadership Politics," p. 107.

29. In a recent article on the political economy of the 1861 Emancipation Decree under Tsar Alexander II (although in fact a highly provocative discussion of problems likely to be encountered by present-day reformers), Moscow University economist Gavriil Popov underscored one of the most serious of the tsar's dilemmas—relating both to everyday governance and to efforts to introduce far-reaching changes. "But, in such a gigantic country, where simple commu-

nications between the capital and the provinces, and accordingly oversight over them, took long months, legislation [*zakonodatel'stva*] held a special significance for the state, since it represented at the grass roots the will of the Tsar and the government. Therefore, the autocratic Tsar, in Russian conditions and in the interests of his own power, had to—however strange it may seem—always be concerned about respect for the law. A special reliance on legislation was a peculiarity of the Russian autocracy. One had to deal with the laws of the empire, to observe strictly the bureaucratic procedures that were adopted. That is why the Tsar could not—not without shaking all the foundations of the bureaucratic order—simply declare a reform. It had to be prepared and discussed according to the rules established for the preparation of other laws." This, of course, is Gorbachev's dilemma as well. Popov, "The Facade and Intrigues of the 'Great' Reform," *Ekonomika i organizatsiya promyshlennogo proizvodstva*, no. 1 (1987), pp. 144–175 (at 162–163).

30. Between the Twenty-third and Twenty-fifth Party Congresses (1966–1976), foreign policy was an item on the formal agenda of no fewer than ten Central Committee plenums, and at six it was the only announced item. Three of these were devoted primarily to the unfolding situation in Czechoslovakia in 1968 (two before the Soviet invasion, one after); four followed the rise and fall of détente (the last in April 1975, shortly after the Soviet Union formally renounced the U.S.-USSR Trade Agreement). Brezhnev's own special involvement is suggested by the fact that he gave the official report at all but the last of these meetings (when the future of détente was increasingly in doubt). See Peter Hauslohner, "Prefects as Senators: Soviet Regional Politicians Look to Foreign Policy," *World Politics* 33, no. 2 (January 1981), pp. 197–233 (at 224–229).

31. Ryabov observed that foreign policy had become a central concern of the leadership and that the plenums had played "an enormous role" in developing an effective foreign policy strategy. He strongly implied that if foreign policy was the Politburo's responsibility, there was nonetheless an expectation that the Politburo would proceed with due respect for the Central Committee's collective opinion. *XXV s"yezd Kommunisticheskoy partii Sovetskogo Soyuza, 24 fevralya–5 marta 1976 goda: stenograficheskiy otchet* (*25th Congress of the Communist Party of the Soviet Union, 24 February–5 March 1976: Stenographic Report*) (Moscow: Politizdat, 1976), vol. 1, p. 223.

32. Foreign policy was last reviewed formally at the June 1980 Central Committee Plenum. See *Pravda*, June 24, 1980, p. 1.

33. The need for more information, better data, and higher quality analyses was emphasized at the Twentieth Party Congress, particularly in the speeches by Khrushchev and his ally Anastas Mikoyan. A seminal theoretical treatment of the shift to an "inclusive" political strategy was presented in Kenneth Jowitt's "Inclusion and Mobilization in European Leninist Regimes," *World Politics* 28, no. 1 (October 1975), pp. 69–96.

34. There have long existed elaborate formal rules designed to ensure collective deliberations and extensive consensus building within most institutions, and a sizable Soviet secondary literature contends that these rules, although not always observed, do have a significant impact. See Ellen Jones, "Committee Decision

Making in the Soviet Union," *World Politics* 36, no. 2 (January 1984), pp. 165–188.

35. See the especially well documented case of the criminologists by Peter H. Solomon, *Soviet Criminologists and Criminal Policy* (New York: Columbia University Press, 1978). Also see Thane Gustafson, *Reform in Soviet Politics* (Cambridge: Cambridge University Press, 1981), Chs. 3–6.

36. That the leadership was aware of and sensitive to this opinion can be shown through numerous examples. One of the more interesting instances was when Brezhnev took pains to explain why certain suggestions raised during discussion of the draft of the 1977 constitution—proposals to abolish the union republics and to pursue an even more egalitarian social policy—could not be adopted. L. I. Brezhnev, *Leninskim kursom* (*On Lenin's Path*) (Moscow: Politizdat, 1978), vol. 6, pp. 524–525.

37. Based on my own interviews with Soviet researchers and on reports from Western colleagues with similar experiences. See, in addition, Solomon, *Soviet Criminologists and Criminal Policy;* and Jerry F. Hough, *The Struggle for the Third World* (Washington, D.C.: Brookings Institution, 1986).

38. Hodnett, "The Pattern of Leadership Politics," p. 104.

39. "Tendencies" is the label that Franklyn Griffiths preferred for potential interest groups, in part to take account of the official intolerance of organized factionalism. See his "A Tendency Analysis of Soviet Policy-Making," in H. Gordon Skilling and Franklyn Griffiths, eds., *Interest Groups in Soviet Politics* (Princeton, N.J.: Princeton University Press, 1971), pp. 335–377. Khrushchev's willingness to publish plenum transcripts (but only beginning in December 1958) can be attributed partly to his preoccupation with rejuvenating the Party, but probably mostly to his interest in using the Central Committee as a means of bringing leverage to bear over the other members of the Presidium. Two plenum transcripts have been published since Khrushchev's ouster: the March 1965 session on agriculture and the June 1983 session (under Andropov) on ideological questions.

40. See, for example, Hough and Fainsod, *How the Soviet Union Is Governed,* pp. 293–297.

41. This is a central theme in Gustafson, *Reform in Soviet Politics,* esp. Ch. 6.

42. In labor policy, for example, there have been some notable advances in specialists' understanding of labor turnover and the causes of poor labor discipline. But there still is surprisingly little awareness of even the existence, let alone the associated advantages and disadvantages, of broadly different strategies for managing the labor market, which give different weights to the roles played by wage policy, training, job placement, and various forms of direct state intervention. See Hauslohner, "Managing the Soviet Labor Market."

43. *Pravda,* January 28, 1987.

44. The "state" is inherently a fuzzy concept. Martin Carnoy defined it as simply "the public sector." By comparison, Dietrich Rueschemeyer and Peter Evans described it as "a set of organizations invested with the authority to make binding decisions for people and organizations juridically located in a

particular territory and to implement these decisions using, if necessary, force."
While wanting to avoid a prolonged discussion, I would nonetheless prefer a
somewhat broader definition than the last: the entire set of public institutions
and legal norms, whose decisions and obligations are considered by those
formally charged with executing public authority to be binding on all the state's
citizens, against whom coercion will normally be applied in the case of noncompliance. See Martin Carnoy, *The State and Political Theory* (Princeton, N.J.:
Princeton University Press, 1984), p. 3; and Peter B. Evans et al., eds., *Bringing
the State Back In* (Cambridge: Cambridge University Press, 1985), pp. 46–47.

"State" should be distinguished from political "regime," a concept perhaps
only slightly more precise. Drawing from the work of David Easton and the
current group of "international regime" theorists, I define regime as a particular
configuration of institutions and norms, both legal and informal, that may or
may not transcend an individual leadership or government. A regime is more
than a particular kind of state, insofar as it implies of a set of widely shared
norms and expectations concerning the way in which public authority will be
exercised, the goals and values for which that authority will be exercised, and
the outcomes that should ordinarily obtain. I define government in the more or
less conventional manner as the set of officials (or roles) charged with executing
public authority, that is, with making and implementing publicly binding decisions.
My central argument in this chapter is that the Soviet regime changed in the
1950s, following Stalin's death, and is in the process of changing again under
Gorbachev. On regimes, see David Easton, *A Systems Analysis of Political Life*
(New York: John Wiley & Sons, 1965); and Stephen D. Krasner, ed., *International
Regimes* (Ithaca, N.Y.: Cornell University Press, 1983).

45. Much of the following discussion is motivated by Theda Skocpol's
pioneering work, *States and Social Revolutions* (Cambridge: Cambridge University
Press, 1979); and by the efforts of those wanting to "bring the state back into"
contemporary political analysis (Evans et al., ibid.).

46. Western historians of the Stalin period have begun to make essentially
the same point. See, in particular, J. Arch Getty's extremely compelling argument
that the Great Purges of 1937–1938 were at least partly an outgrowth of the
central leadership's mounting frustration about its inability to control events
(and officials) at the grass roots. Getty, *Origins of the Great Purges* (Cambridge:
Cambridge University Press, 1985). Also see Moshe Lewin's account of the state's
response to the social upheavals that accompanied the First Five-Year Plan,
"Society, State, and Ideology During the First Five-Year Plan," in Sheila Fitzpatrick,
ed., *Cultural Revolution in Russia, 1928–1931* (Bloomington: Indiana University
Press, 1978), pp. 41–77.

47. The reference is to Allen Kassof's influential article, "The Administered
Society: Totalitarianism Without Terror," *World Politics* 16, no. 4 (July 1964), pp.
558–575.

48. Of course, these accomplishments were not without their costs. The state's
enormous and growing military power was purchased at such a price in deferred
consumption as to leave Soviet living standards well below those in the West.
Furthermore, although national security may have been enhanced by this

expansion of military power and by empire in Eastern Europe, the result was to intensify fear and hostility toward the Soviet Union throughout Europe and elsewhere. Domestically, defeat of the peasantry left a perhaps permanently deformed rural sector, which in the future would prove to be an ever-mounting economic burden.

49. As one example, the reestablishment in 1955 of a government labor ministry, which was then placed in charge of designing and implementing a radically reformed national wage policy, enabled the regime to pursue a substantially more generous and egalitarian social policy than Stalin had allowed, while at the same time affording the government more effective control of unplanned wage drift, which had been a serious problem since the First Five-Year Plan. See Hauslohner, "Managing the Soviet Labor Market"; and Alastair McAuley, *Economic Welfare in the Soviet Union* (Madison: University of Wisconsin Press, 1979), Ch. 8.

50. For these and related developments, see Amy W. Knight, "The Powers of the Soviet KGB," *Survey* 25, no. 3 (1980), pp. 138–155. Aliyev was Party leader in Azerbaijan when he was named a candidate Politburo member (in 1982 he was promoted to full member and the post of First Deputy Premier), but before his election as republic Party First Secretary in 1969, Aliyev had been a career officer in the NKVD/KGB.

51. For an overview of the military's role and growing power, see David Holloway, *The Soviet Union and the Arms Race* (New Haven, Conn.: Yale University Press, 1983). On Soviet power projection, see Stephen S. Kaplan et al., *Diplomacy of Power* (Washington, D.C.: Brookings Institution, 1981).

52. Edward L. Warner, III, *The Military in Contemporary Soviet Politics* (New York: Praeger, 1977), p. 229ff.

53. This emerges clearly in William R. Corson and Robert T. Crowley, *The New KGB: Engine of Soviet Power* (New York: William Morrow, 1986).

54. See the events described in Sidney I. Ploss, "Soviet Succession: Signs of Struggle," *Problems of Communism* 31, no. 5 (1982), pp. 41–52.

55. Holloway, *The Soviet Union and the Arms Race*, pp. 118–119.

56. See, especially, the richly detailed study by Ellen Jones, *Red Army and Society* (Boston, Mass.: Allen & Unwin, 1985).

57. Richard D. Anderson, Jr., "Soviet Decision-Making and Poland," *Problems of Communism* 31, no. 2 (1982), pp. 22–36.

58. This felicitous phrase comes from Hugh Heclo, "OMB and the Presidency—the Problem of 'Neutral Competence,'" *The Public Interest*, no. 38 (Winter 1975), pp. 80–98.

59. See Condoleezza Rice, "The Party, the Military, and Decision Authority in the Soviet Union," *World Politics* 40, no. 1 (October 1987), pp. 55–81; and, more generally, Timothy J. Colton, *Commissars, Commanders, and Civilian Authority* (Cambridge, Mass.: Harvard University Press, 1979).

60. Gustafson, *Reform in Soviet Politics*.

61. Cf. Charles E. Lindblom, *Politics and Markets* (New York: Basic Books, 1977).

62. M. S. Voslensky, *Nomenklatura: The Soviet Ruling Class* (Garden City, N.Y.: Doubleday, 1984).

63. On both the economic and the political dimensions of this movement, see Moshe Lewin, *Political Undercurrents in Soviet Economic Debates* (Princeton, N.J.: Princeton University Press, 1974).

64. Particularly influential in this respect were the early writings of Tat'yana Zaslavskaya, the Novosibirsk-based sociologist, who has become an extremely important public exponent of radical political-economic reform under Gorbachev. For one especially eloquent and candid example of her views, see T. I. Zaslavskaya, "On the Role of Sociological Research on Labor Resources," in A. Z. Maykov, ed., *Problemy ratsional'nogo ispol'zovaniya trudovykh resursov* (*Problems of the Rational Utilization of Labor Resources*) (Moscow: Ekonomika, 1973), pp. 82–98.

65. For Soviet data on this question, based on a survey of Georgian republic officials, see T. M. Dzhafarli et al., "A Few Aspects of the Acceleration of Scientific-Technological Progress," *Sotsiologicheskiye issledovaniya*, No. 2 (1983), pp. 58–63. Also see Mark R. Beissinger, "In Search of Generations in Soviet Politics," *World Politics* 38, no. 2 (1986), pp. 288–314.

66. Lindblom, op. cit.

67. See U.S. Congress Joint Economic Committee, *USSR: Measures of Economic Growth and Development, 1950–1980* (Washington, D.C.: U.S. Government Printing Office, 1982); and Frederic L. Pryor, "Growth and Fluctuations of Production in O.E.C.D. and East European Countries," *World Politics* 37, no. 2 (January 1985), pp. 204–237.

68. The New Course, elaborated in the summer of 1953 when Malenkov was the dominant Soviet leader, prescribed a much greater emphasis than before on raising living standards, to be achieved in part by limiting investment in heavy industry and the growth of defense expenditure. See the discussions in Leonhard, *The Kremlin Since Stalin*; and Breslauer, *Khrushchev and Brezhnev*. For evidence of the role that widespread anxiety about lagging technological performance played in the subsequent repudiation of this program, see especially the speech by Nikolay Bulganin, Malenkov's successor as Prime Minister, to the Central Committee Plenum in July 1955, as reported in *Pravda*, July 17, 1955, pp. 1–6.

69. These ideas are most often associated with the Khar'kov economist Yevsey Liberman, who popularized them in a series of articles beginning in 1955. For a good discussion of the debates preceding the Kosygin reform and a brief account of the immediate aftermath, see Abraham Katz, *The Politics of Economic Reform in the Soviet Union* (New York: Praeger, 1972). There is a sizable Western literature on the mixed-to-disappointing results and subsequent politics of this reform. For references and discussion, see Bruce Parrott, *Politics and Technology in the Soviet Union* (Cambridge, Mass.: MIT Press, 1983), Chs. 5, 6; and Hauslohner, "Managing the Soviet Labor Market," Chs. 3, 4.

70. Brezhnev's attack on the 1965 reform began in a speech to the Central Committee Plenum in December 1969 and ended with a speech to the same body three years later (December 1972). His suggestions that the debate should continue were offered indirectly in his December 1972 speech and plainly in a speech at the December 1973 Plenum. Brezhnev made at least two public references to a plenum on the economy in the course of 1972–1973. See Brezhnev,

Ob osnovnykh, vol. 1, p. 454, and vol. 2, pp. 116ff and 198ff; and Brezhnev, *Leninskim kursom,* vol. 3, p. 476, and vol. 4, p. 218. At the Twenty-fourth Party Congress, Brezhnev did introduce an important modification of the traditional growth strategy (in fact harking back to the First Five-Year Plan) that seemed to offer a means of raising the economy's technological level but without the costs of internal reform—that is, a selective relaxation of autarky and increased reliance on imported technology under the cover of East-West détente. See Volten, *Brezhnev's Peace Program;* and Parrott, *Politics and Technology,* Ch. 6. But when this new policy failed, the arguments favoring internal reforms grew more strident.

71. As a result of efforts to reconstruct the social history of Stalinism, the positive aspects of this formula (Stalin's "carrots") have begun to receive increased attention. See, for example, Sheila Fitzpatrick, "Stalin and the Making of a New Elite, 1928–1937," *Slavic Review* 38, no. 3 (1979), pp. 377–402; and Vera Dunham, *In Stalin's Time* (Cambridge: Cambridge University Press, 1976).

72. For a useful, but now forgotten discussion of this issue, see the symposium "Toward a 'Communist Welfare State'?" *Problems of Communism* 9, no. 1 (1960), pp. 1–22, and no. 3, pp. 44–51.

73. *Pravda,* March 7, 1953, p. 1.

74. The erosion of order in the labor camps, which apparently began even before Stalin's death and accelerated thereafter, is treated at length by Aleksandr I. Solzhenitsyn, *The Gulag Archipelago, 1918–1956,* trans. Harry Willetts (New York: Harper & Row, 1976), vol. 3, part 5.

75. At times, Khrushchev appeared interested in expanding opportunities for meaningful popular participation and voice in local government and enterprise management. But the First Secretary's behavior was equivocal, and nothing lasting came of it.

76. Thus, the riot at Novocherkassk in June 1962, prompted by a combination of sudden increases in food prices and output norms, was only the most serious (and best known) of a series of events that marked a dramatic increase in the level of popular unrest and worker militancy during Khrushchev's final years in office. For an account of the Novocherkassk incident, see Solzhenitsyn, *The Gulag Archipelago,* vol. 3, part 7 (Ch. 3). For some statistical evidence on the upsurge in worker unrest in the early 1960s, see Alex Pravda, "Spontaneous Workers' Activities in the Soviet Union," in Arcadius Kahan and Blair Ruble, eds., *Industrial Labor in the U.S.S.R.* (New York: Pergamon, 1979), pp. 333–366 (at 349). These data suggest that the level of unrest fell sharply in the second half of the 1960s and then rose again in the early 1970s, although not becoming as serious as in the earlier period. For additional evidence on both sides' equivocation during the 1960–1964 period, see Hauslohner, "Managing the Soviet Labor Market," pp. 144–158.

77. Donna Bahry and Brian D. Silver, "Intimidation and the Symbolic Uses of Terror in the USSR," *American Political Science Review* 81, no. 4 (December 1987), pp. 1065–1098. The results of this survey suggest, however, that intimidation continues to provide some "general deterrence" to dissent.

78. See Peter Reddaway, "Dissent in the Soviet Union," *Problems of Communism* 32, no. 6 (1983), pp. 1–15.

79. On the importance of patronage and other aspects of political machine operations in Uzbekistan, see Nancy Lubin, *Labour and Nationality in Soviet Central Asia* (Princeton, N.J.: Princeton University Press, 1984).

80. The following paragraphs draw heavily on my article, "Gorbachev's Social Contract," *Soviet Economy* 3, no. 1 (1987), pp. 54–89.

81. On the rise in worker militancy, see Betsy Gidwitz, "Labor Unrest in the Soviet Union," *Problems of Communism* 31, no. 6 (1982), pp. 25–42.

82. For some of the details, see Hauslohner, "Managing the Soviet Labor Market," pp. 425–445.

83. Hauslohner, "Gorbachev's Social Contract," pp. 62–63.

84. For a broadly similar, albeit more cautiously stated proposition concerning the impact of generational solidarity, see Bialer, *Stalin's Successors*, p. 61. In addition, there is a variety of empirical evidence, apart from the aging of the Brezhnev leadership and its implicit reluctance to admit younger members, that is at least consistent with the hypothesis of an unusually solidary elite generation. See, in particular, Jerry F. Hough, "The Generation Gap and the Brezhnev Succession," *Problems of Communism* 28, no. 4 (1979), pp. 1–16; George W. Breslauer, "Is There a Generation Gap in the Soviet Political Establishment?" *Soviet Studies* 36, no. 1 (1984), pp. 1–25; and Beissinger, "In Search of Generations in Soviet Politics."

85. X [George F. Kennan], "The Sources of Soviet Conduct," *Foreign Affairs* 25, no. 4 (July 1947), pp. 566–582.

3

The Yeltsin Affair: The Dilemma of the Left in Gorbachev's Revolution

Seweryn Bialer

On November 11, 1987, in the presence of Mikhail Gorbachev, the Moscow Party Committee, sitting in a plenary session, fired its First Secretary, Boris Yeltsin. Several days later, it was announced that Yeltsin had been appointed to the far less important post of First Deputy Chairman of the state committee responsible for the construction of civilian housing. He subsequently lost his position as a candidate member of the all-powerful Politburo. Thus ended the saga of Boris Yeltsin, one of the most colorful and intriguing figures of Soviet politics in the first stage of the Gorbachev era.[1]

The Yeltsin affair may in the future be seen as a minor episode in Gorbachev's quest to modernize Russia, but it was the first major domestic political crisis of the Gorbachev era. It raises a number of important questions about Gorbachev's power and the constellation of forces in the Politburo; about the danger to *perestroika* (restructuring) not only from the conservative Right but also from the liberal Left; about the General Secretary's capacities as a leader in a time of stress; and not least about the limits of *glasnost'* (openness) as Gorbachev understands them.

The factual account of the Yeltsin affair that follows is based on many sources: discussions with officials, aides, and experts in many branches of the Soviet Party and state; conversations with Western and Communist diplomats in Moscow; and the published Soviet record. The reliability of the many Soviet sources is uneven. I have reason to believe that many were participants or close observers of the events that made up the Yeltsin affair. Nevertheless, judgment, experience, and instinct guided me in deciding what to accept or reject from the mass of available information.

The Facts of the Yeltsin Affair

The fifty-six-year-old Yeltsin graduated in 1955 at the age of twenty-two from the Ural Polytechnical Institute in Sverdlovsk as a construction engineer. His entire career was connected with the city of Sverdlovsk in the Urals. Yeltsin joined the Party comparatively late, at the age of thirty in 1961. This was during the peak of Nikita Khrushchev's anti-Stalin campaign. For eighteen years, Yeltsin was an engineer and the manager of housing construction in Sverdlovsk. His last managerial job, in 1968, was as the director of a very large housing construction organization in Sverdlovsk. In 1968, he was recruited into the Communist Party apparatus, the powerful professional party bureaucracy. His first job was as the Secretary of the Construction Department of the Sverdlovsk Provincial Party Committee, which he held for eight years. His career took off in 1975 when he became the Secretary for Industry of the Sverdlovsk Provincial Party Committee, and most unusually, just a year later the first Party Secretary of the Sverdlovsk province. He spent nine years in this position and as is usual for provincial party secretaries became a deputy of the Supreme Soviet (in 1978) and a full member of the Party Central Committee in 1981. Only in 1985 did he start his career in Moscow. A month after Gorbachev took over, in April 1985, Yeltsin was appointed the chief of the Construction Department of the Central Committee, and in July 1985, he was promoted to the position of Central Committee Secretary for Construction. In January 1986, he took over the key position of the First Secretary, that is, the head of the Moscow city Party Committee, and in March 1986, at the Twenty-seventh Party Congress, was coopted to candidate membership in the ruling Politburo.

The Yeltsin affair started at the October 21, 1987, Plenum of the Central Committee, where a dramatic confrontation between Yeltsin and the Politburo took place. The October meeting was convened in the Kremlin ten days before the festivities marking the seventieth anniversary of the Russian Revolution were to begin. The meeting of the Central Committee and its agenda were planned considerably ahead of time. It started at 10 AM. It was attended by more than three hundred full members and many of the one hundred sixty candidate (nonvoting) members of the Central Committee. The meeting was to be very brief.

According to plan, only two items of business were to be considered, one of marginal importance, the second of cardinal importance. The first was the removal from the Politburo of the Azerbaijani Geydar Aliyev, the First Deputy Prime Minister, whose political decline was well known and whose removal from the top leadership was widely expected. Aliyev was brought to his high office in Moscow by Yuri Andropov in 1983. As the former chief of KGB in Azerbaijan, Aliyev had been Andropov's subordinate and was assigned to the government post to fight corruption and slackness. He was not, however, the type of official who would fit into the untraditional style of leadership required by Gorbachev's *perestroika* and was not among the General Secretary's confidants or loyalists. Moreover, after Aliyev became a First Deputy Prime Minister, it was discovered that he had been deeply corrupt when he occupied the positions of the KGB chief and later First Party Secretary of Azerbaijan. His retirement from the Politburo and Central Committee was accomplished routinely at the end of the Central Committee's meeting.

The plenum's important item of business was to be Gorbachev's report about his planned speech to a November 2 meeting of the Central Committee that would include members of the Supreme Soviet and many foreign guests. This meeting would commemorate the seventieth anniversary of the October 1917 Revolution. Fifteen pages of theses for this crucial speech were distributed well ahead of time to all members of the Central Committee. Gorbachev's speech, the first comprehensive critical review of Soviet history and discussion of *perestroika* in light of that history, was of major importance. It required, therefore, in a period when the democratization of the Party was proclaimed, an approval of the Central Committee, the collective ruling body of the Party.

At the meeting, the members of the Central Committee were sitting in a hall facing the Presidium, which was composed of full members of the Politburo that sat on the dais. The candidate members of the Politburo and the secretaries of the Central Committees occupied the first row of the seats in the hall. This solemn meeting started with Gorbachev's discussion of the key points of his intended anniversary proclamation. One cannot stress enough the importance of the planned anniversary speech and the solemnity of the occasion of its consideration by the Central Committee. The top Party leadership attached major significance to it.[2]

To underscore the unity of the Party leadership and the political elite regarding the rather difficult and controversial questions of the revisions of Soviet history and of the ideology of *perestroika* and domestic and foreign policy, the Politburo adopted an important decision. The choice was made that the members of the Central Committee, when they received the comprehensive theses of the November 2 speech, could send to the General Secretary their suggestions, but that Gorbachev's speech at the October 21 Plenum would only be voted on and not discussed. I stress the unusual, solemn, and symbolically important nature of the October 21 meeting because Yeltsin's action was a major breach of Party etiquette and confidence not simply because of what he said but because he said it at this particular occasion. As one official remarked, "There was not much new for me in what Yeltsin said. I was aware for some time how he felt about some things in the Party work. But this was categorically not the place and the time to bring up his favorite critical themes."

After Gorbachev finished his two-hour presentation, he asked whether there were any questions. Apparently nobody at the meeting asked for recognition. Gorbachev started to leave the podium, when Boris Nikolaevich Yeltsin raised his hand. The General Secretary recognized Yeltsin and asked whether he had any remarks on Gorbachev's presentation. Yeltsin answered that he had none and that he fully supported it. He wanted, however, to make a statement about a number of important matters that had accumulated during his work within the Politburo and in his post as the First Secretary of the Moscow Party organization. This was entirely unexpected to Gorbachev, the Presidium, and the members of the Central Committee. After a short pause, Gorbachev said that this request was highly unusual and asked whether there were any objections from the participants. Hearing none, he said that if Yeltsin wanted to speak, he should be given the opportunity. Gorbachev left the podium for Yeltsin, taking his place at the chair in the middle of the Presidium table.

Yeltsin's Speech

Yeltsin spoke in a highly emotional voice and with visible nervousness that persisted throughout his speech, which lasted about ten minutes and was not interrupted by the audience. He first informed the plenum that he had sent to the General Secretary a letter of resignation from his position as candidate member of the Politburo and his post as the First Secretary of the Moscow city Party Committee. He then said that he was unable any longer to avoid discussing the seriousness of the domestic problems and of the situation within the leadership. He touched on three themes: the implementation of the reforms; the behavior of Politburo member and Central Committee Secretary Yegor Ligachev; and the attitude of the leadership to the Party's rank-and-file membership and to the people.

Perestroika, Yeltsin said, was moving far too slowly. The leadership of the Party was not pushing hard enough or decisively enough to overcome resistance to *perestroika*. What reformers wanted to achieve, he said, was a truly revolutionary transformation. But the Party leadership lacked the necessary "revolutionary determination and exercise[d] insufficient revolutionary pressure" to achieve this goal. He had been forced continually to make major personnel changes in the Moscow Party apparatus and the local government but had seen no measurable progress and was extremely frustrated.

Then, continued Yeltsin, there was one man in the top leadership with whom he could not work anymore and indeed would refuse to work anymore. This man, Ligachev, was an intriguer. He still adhered to the old, condemned style of leadership. He compiled secret dossiers on all members of the leadership. He put obstacles in the path to *perestroika*. He repeatedly sabotaged his, Yeltsin's, efforts to improve the living conditions in Moscow. According to Yeltsin, Ligachev should be censured by the Central Committee.

Furthermore, accused Yeltsin, the Party leadership was not telling the people the whole truth about the difficult domestic situation. The achievements of *perestroika* were marginal and very limited. The conditions of people's lives had changed very little. The Party was promising much, but it could not in the existing situation keep its promises. For example, the Party leadership claimed that in the next two to three years there would be major economic improvements, but this was unlikely.

Finally, almost as an afterthought and in passing, he also said that he wondered whether in the Politburo there was a tendency "to be too nice to each other" at a time when the situation with the reforms was so difficult. The members of the leadership, he added, often said "too many nice words about the General Secretary when they should press him harder." (Yeltsin used the Russian phrase *slovo slavit*, which in direct translation means, using words of praise.)

Yeltsin said that his work within the Politburo as a candidate member was not going well. It was quite possible, he said, that he lacked the necessary experience for such a high position. But it was also probable that he did not receive from his Politburo comrades the necessary support for pushing *perestroika* with greater force. In this situation, he concluded, he saw no alternative but to send his letter of resignation.

The Central Committee's Response

Yeltsin's statement was met with stunned silence and astonishment. After he finished and returned to his seat in the first row of the hall, Gorbachev got up and asked whether any of the comrades at the meeting wanted to take the floor. There was a prolonged silence and Gorbachev repeated his question. After another prolonged silence, Ligachev asked to be heard. Altogether, aside from Yeltsin and Gorbachev, twenty-three members of the Central Committee took the floor. The discussion, which lasted almost three hours (and was interrupted for a short lunch break), rejected unanimously the main points of Yeltsin's statement. The discussants spoke sometimes in sadness for what they considered Yeltsin's folly and sometimes in anger.

Ligachev started his brief speech by saying that he could not accept Yeltsin's charges that he had obstructed the Moscow leader's efforts to implement *perestroika*. Yeltsin had made many mistakes and had been criticized for them by the leadership. If conditions in Moscow were not good, this was Yeltsin's responsibility. The leadership of the Party today, Ligachev continued, was truly collective. He, Ligachev, worked within this collective and with full loyalty to it. Yeltsin's remark about excessive praise for Gorbachev was a disgusting, politically harmful, and untrue insinuation. "We respect greatly the General Secretary and give him the respect that is very clearly his due for his immense work and wise stewardship."

Another discussant remarked that he did not consider himself an angel and he made mistakes, but he did not consider Yeltsin an angel either. The picture that Yeltsin painted—that only he was in step with the needs of *perestroika* and all others were out of step—had little to do with reality and indicated a lack of critical judgment and an immense arrogance.

Some of the speakers were clearly baffled by the vehemence of Yeltsin's statement and by the decision to make it at this particular meeting. One party intellectual praised Yeltsin as an honest man and commended the personal and political courage that was required to make his statement but disagreed entirely with its substance. "That Yeltsin made his speech," he said, "is a clear sign of our democratization, but it is a shame that he made such a bad use of democratization."

Yeltsin's former colleague from Sverdlovsk, Prime Minister Nikolai Ryzhkov, spoke with anger. "What Yeltsin displayed," Ryzhkov argued, "is not at all courage. What kind of a courage is it to blame one's own failures on others when things are difficult? What kind of a courage is it to offer to quit in the middle of a gigantic battle for the future of our country? This is not the courage of a communist; this is sheer cowardliness." A colleague of Yeltsin's from the Moscow city Party leadership spoke about "the nervousness, almost neurosis" in Yeltsin's style of work, his inability to bring order and deliberate procedures into the work of the Moscow Party organization and municipal institutions. This colleague criticized what he called Yeltsin's search for cheap popularity, his inclination to demagoguery, and his unhealthy ambitions.

Many speakers, including Politburo members, accused Yeltsin of being a panic-monger, a man who because of his own ambitions and weaknesses of character could not resist grandstanding despite the obvious potential danger that this would create for Party unity at such a crucial moment in Soviet history. Many Central Committee members expressed their astonishment that Yeltsin had dismissed everything being achieved in the process of *perestroika*. Was it true, they asked, that their work had accomplished nothing?

One Politburo member said that Yeltsin regularly attended the weekly meetings of the Politburo. Given that, why had he not made his feelings known at any of these meetings? The only answer to this question was that Yeltsin suspected or knew that his comrades in the Politburo would disagree with his views. His present action counterpoised the Politburo's positions to those of the Central Committee and made clear that in appealing to the Central Committee over the heads of his Politburo comrades, Yeltsin wanted to split the Party leadership. But he should have known, and he would learn, that such tactics would not work. It was especially vexing, this member continued, that Yeltsin had felt it necessary to voice his dissatisfactions at this very important and solemn meeting on the eve of the celebration of the anniversary of the revolution. Yeltsin wanted to exploit the opportunity created by the meeting; he wanted to catch the Party leadership unprepared for his attack. Yeltsin showed immense arrogance and personal ambition by putting his own personal concerns above the interests of the Party.

Yeltsin on the Defensive

After twenty-three speakers had taken the floor, Gorbachev proposed that the discussion should be closed. He turned then to Yeltsin and told him that before he, Gorbachev, summed up the discussion, Yeltsin would have the opportunity to react to what the Central Committee comrades had said about his statement. During the discussion, Yeltsin had taken copious notes and had shaken his head many times in disagreement with the speakers. He proceeded to the speaker's podium, pale with the top button of his shirt open and the tie askew, but in control of his feelings and his voice. His response to the discussion, lasting about fifteen minutes, was entirely defensive. Nevertheless, he did not take back any of what he had said.

He started by saying that many comrades misrepresented the motives that made him speak up at this meeting and misunderstood many of the things he said. He spoke because he had the good of the Party at heart. He said that two accusations that were made against him were especially painful: that he had offended and attacked the General Secretary and that he was breaking the unity of the Party leadership. With regard to the first, he wanted his comrades to know that he deeply respected the General Secretary and supported his program unconditionally. He absolutely rejected the idea that he had accused the Politburo, let alone the General Secretary, of creating a new cult of personality. Yet the General Secretary, in order to lead, had to be told the truth. *Paradnost'* (false optimism) and *ochkovtiratel'stvo* (false reporting) had to be eradicated. As for the accusation that he was violating the unity of the Party leadership, that he also totally rejected. Unity, Yeltsin said, was absolutely necessary, but it had to be based on principles of honesty and not achieved by hiding differences of opinion and judgment. Yeltsin considered it his duty to bring the disagreements between himself and Ligachev to the attention of the Central Committee.

Some comrades, continued Yeltsin, asked how his work as the First Party Secretary of Moscow was being sabotaged and thereby frustrated in the task of improving the living conditions for Muscovites. He offered two examples. He considered it necessary to prevent further growth of Moscow's population until the infrastructure of the city was expanded and housing conditions improved. Yet every year, the numerous ministries and state committees that were located in Moscow had the right to bring to Moscow from outside about seventy thousand new employees. He requested the Secretariat of the Central Committee to abolish altogether, or radically reduce, the number of those *limitchiki* (from the word limit—the yearly quota of permissible hiring from outside Moscow). Ligachev, however, opposed this. The continuation of this practice was contributing to the poor living conditions in Moscow.

Another example involved visitors (tourists, but mainly "temporary" workers and shoppers from outside the capital) to Moscow. Their number was very large. By his estimates, about seven hundred thousand people visited the city, day after day, throughout the year. These visitors, for all practical purposes, were permanent residents of Moscow. He requested the Secretariat of the Central Committee to increase the supplies of food and consumer goods allocated for Moscow in order to take into account these "permanent visitors." Again, Ligachev prevented a positive response. In consequence, citizens of Moscow were being treated unjustly. They had to pay for the visitors with food and consumer goods shortages that were unjustified.

"I, too, am no angel and make mistakes," continued Yeltsin. "I can be justly blamed for at least part of the difficult situation that exists in Moscow. But Comrade Ligachev's responsibility for this state of affairs is very great, and he does not admit any of his own wrongdoings." "He hopes," added Yeltsin, "that the General Secretary will understand his motives, and he is sure that the Party line on *perestroika* will continue and will achieve an historical victory." (It should be mentioned that Yeltsin's statements did not raise any criticism about the Party's international policy.)

At some point during Yeltsin's closing remarks, Gorbachev interrupted him and appealed, "Boris Nikolaevich, withdraw your resignation and let us try to work together." With a stony face, Yeltsin responded, "I sent my letter [of resignation] and I stand behind it." In reply, someone from the audience cried out, *"Kak vam ne stydno?"* ("Aren't you ashamed of yourself?"). Otherwise, Yeltsin's speech was not interrupted. Then Gorbachev took the floor and spoke for more than a half hour from notes that he had evidently prepared during the discussion of Yeltsin's remarks. The General Secretary spoke with an even voice, although at some points with clearly restrained anger and bitterness and occasionally with sorrow. His speech was interrupted a number of times by applause that started either in the Presidium or in the audience itself.

Gorbachev's Response

Gorbachev began by saying that Yeltsin's declaration was a surprise to everyone, and a bitter one at that. Gorbachev called the unanimity of all members of the Central Committee who had spoken gratifying. The Central Committee, he said, was the collective institution that represented the will of the Party as a whole, and it had rejected as unfounded and unsustainable the assertions of Yeltsin. It was clear that with his declaration of resignation Yeltsin put himself above the Party and against the Party. It was too bad that in his closing remarks Yeltsin had not found it possible to accept the critique of his comrades openly and courageously.

His opening declaration and his closing remarks were a vote of no confidence in the collective leadership of the Party, Gorbachev said.

> Yeltsin mentioned in his closing remarks his personal respect for me as the General Secretary of the Party. I reject his respect. I do not want it. I still hoped that after the critique without exception from all members of the Central Committee who spoke honestly and emotionally of the groundlessness of Yeltsin's views, he would recognize the wrongheadedness of those views and express his respect for the collective leadership, the Politburo, the Secretariat, and the Central Committee itself. But he did not do it. He did not withdraw his resignation. He put himself above the Party.

"I find it necessary," continued Gorbachev, "to inform the members of the Central Committee that Yeltsin's declaration of resignation from this post, which amounts to nothing less than desertion during a battle, has its prehistory." When Gorbachev was in the Crimea during August, Yeltsin sent him a letter in which he expressed his desire to resign. But Gorbachev telephoned Yeltsin and persuaded him to wait and then discuss the issues that bothered him after the celebration of the seventieth anniversary of the revolution. After returning from the Crimea, said Gorbachev, he had a personal, one-on-one discussion with Yeltsin, and they agreed that this was not the time for discussion and that they would meet and talk at length about the questions Yeltsin had raised after the celebration of the seventieth anniversary of the revolution. Nevertheless, Yeltsin, in contravention of Party ethics and the simple rules of comradeship and decency, had put this question directly before the Central Committee without having it discussed on the Politburo.

Why could not Yeltsin stick to his agreement, Gorbachev asked, and instead found it necessary to make his unexpected statement and introduce a dissonant note in this solemn and immensely important proceedings? Perhaps he calculated that he would catch the plenum by surprise, and it would therefore be unprepared to give a resounding response to his attack on the collective leadership of the Party. Or, perhaps he could not contain anymore his panicky mood and felt compelled to expose himself. What made Yeltsin disrupt the proceeding, Gorbachev asserted, was personal, uncontrollable ambition. Yeltsin's contention that everybody in the leadership except himself was out of step with *perestroika* was simply an illusion of grandeur.

Even though Yeltsin had declared that the Party leadership lacked "the revolutionary determination to press forward with necessary speed the course of *perestroika,*" he could not and did not offer any alternative program of *perestroika* or strategy for achieving it. Yeltsin showed himself to be totally helpless and ignorant in matters of theory and political strategy. His call to press for a quickening of *perestroika* was tantamount to unprincipled political adventurism, to skipping the necessary stages of a planned process. From the theoretical point of view, Yeltsin's declaration should be evaluated by the Central Committee as a "petit-bourgeois outburst" by a man who had lost his way among the intricacies of a complex period and who evidently lacked Party *zakalka* (tempering).

Gorbachev continued by stressing the difficulties of the process of revolutionary transformation, which Yeltsin had said he encountered in his own work. Gorbachev added that all members of the leadership probably underestimated at the beginning how difficult the task would be, but he stressed that the Party was telling the truth to the people and was not making rash promises that it could not keep. The Party leadership always stressed that progress and improvement would first of all depend upon the people themselves and on how hard they worked. With regard to the two to three years that Yeltsin mentioned, he had badly misunderstood what the Party leadership was saying.

According to Gorbachev, the Party was not saying that in two to three years the economic situation would change radically. Rather, the

Party simply contended that the next two to three years would be critical to the progress of *perestroika*. The foundations of the new economic system had to be put in place. The new managerial style had to take hold in practice. Material and spiritual incentives for better and harder work had to be made available. In short, conditions had to be created for a take-off in the process of modernization.

Again in this case, said Gorbachev, Comrade Yeltsin showed himself unbelievably helpless and naive in matters of theory and strategy. He did not recognize in fact that in the process of *perestroika*, the Party had to combine long- and middle-range tasks and that success in the middle-range tasks would be necessary for the achievement of longer-range tasks. The immediate Party goal would be exactly such a crucial middle-range task of creating material, organizational, and psychological conditions necessary for future success in economic modernization. This task had nothing to do with Yeltsin's big words about the lack of "necessary revolutionary pressure" from which the Party leadership allegedly suffered.

Gorbachev then went on to describe Yeltsin's style of work, which had been criticized by the leadership in January 1987, and finished by saying that the plenary meeting of the Central Committee had been conducted in the spirit of openness and democratization, that everybody, including Yeltsin, had a full opportunity to say what was on his mind. Gorbachev remarked that the Central Committee, in a free discussion without any pressure, had demonstrated its maturity in a very unusual and difficult situation, had rejected calls for steps that would lead to political adventurism, and had supported the collective leadership of the Party.

Gorbachev asked the participants in the plenum to adopt a short two-point resolution. The first point was that the plenum considered the declaration of Yeltsin politically mistaken. The second point was that the plenum empowered the Politburo of the Central Committee, together with the Moscow city Party Committee, to consider Yeltsin's request to resign from his position and take cognizance of the views expressed at this plenum.

Gorbachev then asked whether anybody wanted to make any remarks about the proposed resolution. A construction foreman, who was a member of the Central Committee and a hero of socialist labor, raised his hand and was permitted to go to the podium, where he said,

> I am not against the proposed resolution of the Central Committee. I will vote for it. But I simply want to ask Comrade Yeltsin a question. How could it happen, that you, such a big leader, are not thinking about our country, about our Party, but became preoccupied with your own career

[*zaboleli kareerizmom*], tried to get even with some people, settle private scores, forgetting about the difficult tasks that we set out to accomplish. Is this permissible? No, it is not.

The question was, of course, rhetorical. Yeltsin did not answer. The Central Committee voted and unanimously adopted the resolution proposed by Gorbachev, with Yeltsin abstaining.

The Aftermath

Two days after the November 7 celebration of the seventieth anniversary of the Bolshevik Revolution, a meeting of the Politburo took place with Yeltsin present where the events of the October 21 Plenum were discussed and the sources and consequences of Yeltsin's behavior analyzed. At this meeting, the decision was taken to ask the Central Committee to expel Yeltsin from his position as candidate member of the Politburo and fire him from his job as the First Secretary of the Moscow Party organization. A Secretary of the Central Committee, Lev Zaykov, the former Party Secretary of Leningrad who was responsible in the Secretariat for the military industry, was appointed in Yeltsin's place. According to reports, it was at this meeting that Yeltsin was psychologically broken and made ready to engage in harsh self-criticism—that is, to "confess" his sins.

The bill of Yeltsin's faults agreed upon and formulated by Gorbachev and others at the November 9 Politburo meeting can be summed up in six specific items. First, Yeltsin was described as an ambitious power-seeker who put his ambitions above the interests of the Party and was unable to work well within the context of collective leadership.

Second, Yeltsin was a showoff who was good at using grand words and seeking easy popularity by criticizing obvious shortcomings. He visited, for example, the workers' cafeteria in the giant Moscow automobile factory and after testing the food exploded in indignation. He demanded to see the district Party Secretary and berated him in the presence of the workers. But afterward, Yeltsin did nothing about the situation; the factory cafeteria continued to serve the same bad food. He visited a subway station and bitterly condemned its crowding and running behind schedule. But nothing changed afterward.

Third, Yeltsin demonstrated an inability to introduce major innovations into the functioning of the consumer supply system for Muscovites even when such innovations were suggested to him. A major example cited was the case of produce supply to Moscow. The bulk of the produce was delivered to enormous wholesale centers that in turn distributed it to district centers, where retail stores picked it up. In the process, more than one-third of the produce rotted. A proposal was approved by the Bureau of the Moscow Party Committee to deliver the produce in special containers directly to the retail stores as well as to the district centers. But this proposal did not receive Yeltsin's attention and was never implemented.

Fourth, although Yeltsin did spend much of his time meeting with rank-and-file Muscovites and making speeches, he could not find time to meet regularly with his subordinates in the Party-state administration or oversee their work in a reasonable fashion. For example, the man in charge of the Moscow Agricultural-Industrial Administration tried unsuccessfully for three months to get an audience with Yeltsin. This man was forced to write Yeltsin a letter with specific intermediate-range suggestions for improving the effectiveness of the organization, but even then the administration head received no answer. On the other hand, Yeltsin inspected an official who was on his job for only two months and gave him one week to improve his work radically. After the week passed, he was dismissed. Yeltsin apparently was interested only in the types of improvement that could bring immediate results; he neglected to pay attention to potential improvements that would require a longer time to prove themselves realistic and successful.

Fifth, Yeltsin showed bad judgment on a number of occasions by opting for cheap, showy "democratization" when more patience and good sense were required. One case mentioned was that of *Novy Mir*, a major literary monthly in the forefront of the *glasnost'* campaign. The editor in chief of the magazine, Sergey Zalygin, was not a Party member. A well-known Party member on the magazine's editorial board proposed that each month a different member of the board act as editor in chief. Otherwise, he threatened that he would resign from the board. The permanent editor in chief replied that he had been appointed to his job and did not agree to the proposed "democratization." But Yeltsin backed this critic, and only the intervention of a Politburo member prevented disruption of the journal's work.

Another case concerned the sensitive issue of the privileges of high bureaucrats and was not brought up publicly in the discussion of Yeltsin's transgressions. Immediately after becoming the First Secretary of Moscow, Yeltsin declared war on the number of "black cars" with chauffeurs, the most visible status symbols of officialdom. He tried and initially succeeded in reducing the number of such cars assigned to individuals. But in 1987, he continued the campaign beyond what Party leaders considered reasonable limits, in their eyes seeking cheap popularity by doing so and unwittingly encouraging acts of youth hooliganism against official cars. (Yeltsin also declared war on the special stores where the privileged could buy goods unavailable on the market. These stores were characterized by yellow curtains that kept people from looking inside them. The measure of Yeltsin's failure on this issue was that shortly before his dismissal he discovered that in the very building of the Moscow Party Committee where he has his office, such a "yellow curtains" store still existed and was engaged in business as usual.)

Sixth, and beyond any doubt the key indictment against Yeltsin raised by the Party leadership, was his alleged impatience and volatility, which found its prime expression in his personnel policy. Moscow Party and municipal officials lived in constant fear of being fired by Yeltsin at the drop of a hat and without the opportunity to defend themselves. The first wave of wholesale firing took place in 1986, and the second commenced in the late spring and early summer of 1987. In the almost two years of Yeltsin's stewardship, the core of the Moscow apparatus was changed twice. One leader expressed dissatisfaction with Yeltsin's cadre policy as follows:

> Before firing an official who is not accused of corruption, you have to give him at least some chance to show a willingness and ability to improve his performance. Most importantly, you fire an official only if you have a replacement whom you are reasonably convinced that he will be better than his predecessor. Moreover, the constant fear of being fired has a paralyzing effect on the cadres. They become afraid to take any risks and simply wait for the ax to fall.

In addition, Yeltsin was apparently bringing many of his loyalists from Sverdlovsk to Moscow, thereby creating factions in the apparatus of the Soviet capital.

In the meeting of the Politburo, Gorbachev also reviewed in some detail his, the Politburo's, and the Secretariat's experience in dealing with Yeltsin and his alleged shortcomings. According to Gorbachev, by December 1986, it had become apparent to him and his comrades that Yeltsin's stewardship in Moscow was not going well. At one of the meetings of the Politburo in January 1987, Yeltsin was warned that the rate of replacement of Moscow Party and state officials was indefensibly high and could not continue. That is to say, Yeltsin was simply told that if by the word "shake-up," which he used in the Politburo meeting with regard to the Moscow apparatus, he was considering a second round of wholesale personnel changes, the Politburo would not support him. Yeltsin was reported to have reacted to this warning in a positive way. He allegedly said, "I am a young member of the Politburo without much experience. I received today a good lesson. I needed this lesson. It is not too late. I will find in me the strength necessary to draw the right conclusions from this lesson."

Gorbachev concluded by saying that Yeltsin did not heed the warnings from the leadership either then or later when the General Secretary himself had a number of face-to-face meetings with Yeltsin to help him settle down in his job. Yeltsin was for *perestroika*, but the way in which he wanted to implement it was almost entirely by the old "administrative" methods. By doing so, he was in fact compromising the goals of *perestroika*. This, and Yeltsin's "petit-bourgeois," panicky, and disloyal outburst at the October 21st Central Committee Plenum, disqualified him from Party leadership positions.

Yeltsin's Disgrace Made Public

On November 11, in accordance with the decision of the Politburo, a meeting of the Moscow city Party Committee (about two hundred fifty full and candidate members) devoted to the Yeltsin affair took place. The meeting was attended by the General Secretary and other members of the Politburo and Central Committee Secretariat. The meeting started with a long report by Gorbachev that lasted more than an hour. His speech had three themes. The first was a very harsh and much more detailed critique of Yeltsin's views and of his performance as First Party Secretary of Moscow. The second was the rejection as baseless and simply ridiculous of Yeltsin's accusations that the Central Committee Secretariat had sabotaged his efforts to improve the economic situation in Moscow. Gorbachev reassured the Moscow Party organization that improvement in the living conditions of the Muscovites was one of the Party leadership's highest priorities. The third was the conclusion that should be drawn from Yeltsin's behavior and his performance as First Party Secretary of Moscow. Yeltsin had clearly shown that he lacked organizational skills and was unable to treat his subordinates in a "comradely" fashion.

In his speech, Gorbachev also stressed that Yeltsin was not being criticized simply because he dared to make critical remarks about the work of the Politburo and some individual leaders. There was nothing untoward in this criticism as such. What was wrong was when and how he made his criticism, particularly his ultimatum to the Party, "Accept it or I will resign."

In the ensuing discussion, Yeltsin's subordinates in the Moscow Party and state bureaucracy denounced him in the harshest terms, repeating in various ways the accusations raised in the General Secretary's speech. Almost none of Yeltsin's subordinates defended him, although a few admitted in a more than perfunctory way their own "contribution" to the failure of Yeltsin's leadership. There were also some speeches that criticized Yeltsin but showed signs of personal compassion and regrets for the unfulfilled hopes of his leadership. In a comment on the meeting, one participant concluded, "As a rule, those who were totally subservient to Yeltsin when he was in power now took their revenge and attacked him with venom. Many others, especially outside of the Party apparatus, were measured in their criticism and sympathetic to Yeltsin's misfortune."

At the end of the discussion, Yeltsin was given the floor to reply to his accusers. His was the speech of a psychologically broken man who was left with no alternative but to accept his full defeat and engage in a ritual of abject "self-criticism." As one participant described it, "It was very difficult to listen to Yeltsin. He spoke slowly, he seemed to be lost, and I had the impression that he was ashamed." Yeltsin agreed that his work in Moscow had been unsuccessful. He described his threat to resign as a "tactical mistake" and the source of his behavior as "personal ambition." Only during a few moments of his speech could one glimpse the old Yeltsin, when he spoke about his hopes when he took over the leadership of the Moscow Party and about his continuing commitment to *perestroika*.

After a short closing speech by Gorbachev that dismissed with contempt Yeltsin's promises to do better, a resolution was adopted officially firing Yeltsin from his post of First Secretary, which he had already lost de facto. On the next day, November 12, a meeting of the Moscow Party activists, with the city Party committee, took place to inform them about the Yeltsin affair. On November 13, meetings of the same kind took place in the Moscow district Party committees. Thus ended the phase of *perestroika* in the Moscow city Party organization that had begun with great hopes in January 1986 with the firing of the corrupt Victor Grishin and the appointment of the young and dynamic Boris Yeltsin. But the repercussions of the affair were, and are, far from over.

Yeltsin's Leadership Style

Before the serious repercussions of the Yeltsin affair can be considered, however, one has to look more closely at Yeltsin's personality and style of leadership in order to explain his extraordinary behavior. This is necessary to separate the issues of Yeltsin as a man and as a leader from the problems of Gorbachev, his supporters, and *perestroika*. In the West, and among the Soviet intelligentsia, Boris Yeltsin was a highly visible symbol of *perestroika*. In the West, this was in part the result of the very successful CBS documentary in which he emerged as a highly attractive man with a colorful personality. But aside from that, the reasons for his popularity, both in the West and in the Soviet Union, are not too difficult to fathom. As even his harsh critics admit, as the Party boss of Moscow he showed himself to be a man of personal integrity, honesty, and incorruptibility. He was an extrovert who made numerous speeches and gladly granted interviews. He met often with rank-and-file Muscovites at their places of work and in public. He was a man of grand, populist, and popular gestures, such as traveling to work by means of public transportation. He was dynamic and untiring, fully devoted to his job and the public welfare. He was particularly effective, and courageous, in criticizing the dark sides of the Soviet past and the country's present shortcomings. He was devastating in his continuing attacks against the thoughtlessness, dogmatism, corruption, and privileges of the Soviet bureaucracy. These traits alone would explain the venom with which his downfall was greeted by the Moscow Party and municipal bureaucracy and the shock and alarm that his public disgrace created among the Soviet creative intelligentsia.

Yeltsin's personality and style of leadership contained, however, other traits that revealed him to be a much more complicated figure. His shortcomings, of course, were freely discussed by his former colleagues after his downfall, which was in keeping with the ugly Soviet tradition of the past. Nevertheless, some of his shortcomings have been confirmed independently and have a ring of truth. To sum them up, Yeltsin's behavior as a leader was at times truly dictatorial, impatient, chaotic, and inattentive to the implementation of decisions. Yeltsin was not a good manager and, to say the least, not easy to work with. He knew the construction business very well and was leader of Sverdlovsk at a time when the expectations of accomplishment and growth were rather low. He was probably unprepared to direct the largest and most complex Soviet city, Moscow, in one of the most stormy and unconventional periods of its history, when the measurements of success had escalated sharply.

Yeltsin's leadership of the Party in Sverdlovsk was clearly a success. It provided a trampoline for advancement to Moscow and a rapid career, which eventually received the support of the General Secretary. Accounts of Yeltsin's style of leadership in Sverdlovsk agree, however, that he was incorruptible as well as high-handed, authoritarian, impatient, and individualistic.

During the late Brezhnev era, or even in the first years after his death (in 1982), such a leadership style in the Soviet provinces and republics was far from unusual. But it was one thing to use this style in a large city far from the capital during a period of limited control from above and passivity from below. It was an entirely different matter to attempt this kind of leadership in Moscow during a stormy period of *glasnost'* and *perestroika*. In the immensely centralized Soviet Party-state, Moscow's city Party organization included many dozens of ministries and state committees and thousands upon thousands of high Party, state, military, police, cultural, and other officials with their own kingdoms, patrons, privileges, and interconnections. What was done in Sverdlovsk could not be done, at least by the same methods, in Moscow. Moreover, in Sverdlovsk, Yeltsin was in a city where he grew up, where he had made his career, and where he had built his own political machine. In Moscow, he was a newcomer, an outsider whose independence was inevitably curtailed by the closeness of the watchful Politburo and Central Committee Secretariat. It is not surprising, therefore, although ironic, that a Soviet source could pronounce this epitaph for Yeltsin: "He was a man who was deeply committed to *perestroika*, but wanted to achieve it by using old methods of leadership."

However, it is difficult to explain Yeltsin's response to the development of *glasnost'* in the Moscow theaters. There is no doubt that theaters in general, and Moscow theaters in particular, were, and are, the main beneficiary of *glasnost'*. Quite simply, the official censorship of plays and the supervision of their production by the Mininstry of Culture has been entirely abolished. Yeltsin might have been expected to support such a policy wholeheartedly. Yet a Party official told me that Yeltsin opposed this policy strongly. This Party official called him "obscurantist" in this respect.

Dubious about this claim, I talked with two leading figures of the Moscow theater, a playwright and a director, whose credentials and support of *glasnost'* were impeccable. They fully confirmed this allegation. Moreover, they told me that the ultrareactionary and anti-Semitic organization Pamyat' (Memory) openly supported Yeltsin in this policy as it supports him now, describing his downfall as a purge of a "true Russian." The only explanation I myself, and my colleagues from the Moscow theater world, can offer is that Yeltsin probably was eager to keep control of the theaters in "his" city for himself.

Finally, Yeltsin's personal relations with Gorbachev have to be considered. As unlikely as it may seem now, some Soviet sources insist that Yeltsin was brought to Moscow in 1985 initially on the initiative and under the patronage of Yegor Ligachev, his future nemesis. In due time, Gorbachev himself was impressed by Yeltsin's vigor, his enthusiasm for *perestroika*, and his populism. It seems, however, that Yeltsin was never Gorbachev's friend but rather was a man for whom Gorbachev had sympathy and hope.

Yeltsin, on his part, was devoted primarily to the reform program, rather than to Gorbachev himself. It seems that starting in the late fall of 1986, Gorbachev had an increasingly troubled relationship with Yeltsin. Gorbachev was bombarded with complaints about the Moscow leader's high-handed treatment of powerful Party and state officials. Yet at the same time, Gorbachev recognized Yeltsin's genuine commitment to *per-*

estroika and felt he needed such a man in Moscow and as a potential counterweight to Ligachev in the Politburo. Gorbachev's refusal to accept Yeltsin's resignation in August 1987 showed this clearly. Gorbachev tried to moderate, to temper Yeltsin's impetuousness by explaining to him the difficulties that he was creating for the leader. In this effort, Gorbachev ultimately failed.

Both in the Soviet Union and in the West, Yeltsin was most often characterized as a "populist." But populism comes in many varieties and may represent and incorporate quite divergent tendencies. It is reconcilable, for example, with nationalism and authoritarianism. Yeltsin's populism was authentic in his fight against the economic privileges of the powerful. But it was nonliberal and nondemocratic in the style of leadership that it presented, in its overreliance on administrative methods in promoting change.

Yeltsin's outburst at the October Plenum was the result of (1) deep frustration with his Politburo colleagues, particularly Ligachev, and with his subordinates and (2) physical and emotional exhaustion that verged on a nervous breakdown. Yeltsin was realistic enough to recognize that during his almost two years of leadership, no significant material improvements had occurred in the Soviet capital. The rank-and-file Muscovite was not treated better or with greater respect and attention by the local bureaucrats. The performance of the service establishment—restaurants, stores, repair shops, transportation—had not improved in any visible way.

Yeltsin's state of mind can be glimpsed from his Moscow meetings with some Western and Asian ambassadors in the month preceding the October Plenum. In a virtually unprecedented way, he openly shared with them the deep frustration of his job and displayed a despondent mood. "I have already twice changed the personnel of the Moscow Party district committees and of the district municipal authorities, but I can see no real improvements in their work." To one ambassador, he added in private, "I do not know any more what to do."

Yeltsin also was probably preoccupied with a rapidly approaching event that might prove personally embarrassing and, in the new mood of *glasnost'*, politically very harmful. In January 1986, at the Conference of the Moscow Party Organization that elected delegates to the Twenty-seventh Party Congress, Yeltsin, less than two months in his job, gave his first comprehensive report of the state of affairs in Moscow, which lasted almost three hours. Gorbachev and members of the Politburo were present with about two thousand Moscow officials and Party activists. Grishin, the former Party boss of Moscow, was forced to come to this meeting and sit facing the audience while Yeltsin spoke about the catastrophic results of his predecessor's long rule in almost every sphere of endeavor.[3]

Yeltsin's speech was brilliant, biting, and uncompromising. The speech more than anything else established him at the beginning of his tenure in office as a hero of *perestroika*. The Moscow newspaper in which a much-shortened version of his speech appeared became a valued possession for Muscovites and for intelligentsia in other Soviet cities. In summing up, however, Yeltsin apparently made a rash promise that in his report to the next conference of the Moscow Party organization he would preserve the structure of this speech and would record the improvements that had taken place under his leadership. He would also assume responsibility for any grave faults that had remained uncorrected. Some Yeltsin associates said he looked with dread to this approaching date (late spring 1988) knowing full well how little accomplishments he would have to report.

A Soviet source in whose commitment to radical reforms I have all reasons to believe, and who spoke about Yeltsin as an honest and well-meaning man, characterized the dilemma between Yeltsin's personality and the current needs of *perestroika* in the following manner:

> *Perestroika* is not a demagogic slogan, and the support of it should not consist of demagogy. *Perestroika* is a colossal task that requires unceasing, difficult work. It is not enough to speak of existing faults and to unmask wrongdoings. One has to show untiringly and patiently how to work better, how to improve things. The first act of *perestroika* is over; the second has begun. Grandiose declarations and criticism do not suffice anymore; the time has arrived for the hard, arduous, and consistent labor of each of us. Not to work hard, not to have the strength of character never to give up, to display panic and hysteria when the going is difficult, is to betray the cause of *perestroika*. And this is what Yeltsin did, regardless of his intentions.

Repercussions for *Perestroika*

The repercussions of the Yeltsin affair for the process of reform were entirely negative. They encouraged the conservatives in Moscow and on the periphery of the country to resist changes, particularly criticism from below, and honest, investigative reporting.

Before the Yeltsin affair, the only enemies of *perestroika* identified by the General Secretary were the forces of inertia, bureaucratization, and defense of vested interests. Now a new, parallel enemy was added—the forces of "political adventurism" and those who wanted "to jump through stages." In short, this enemy consisted of those who wanted a stronger push for reforms; who wanted to go beyond the pace established by the top leadership; and who were particularly set to purge the inherited apparatus. The Yeltsin affair sent a strong cautionary signal to those within the power structure who were wholeheartedly committed to Gorbachev's course. It discouraged from commitment those of the intelligentsia who were still cautiously waiting on the sidelines trying to decide whether to support actively the General Secretary's program and policies.

This much was admitted by Gorbachev himself on January 8, 1988, at a meeting with top Soviet newspaper and magazine editors. Although he did not refer to Yeltsin by name in his talk to the editors, Gorbachev acknowledged publicly for the first time that the events surrounding the dismissal had caused wide anxiety and doubt about the leadership's commitment to change. "We shall not conceal the fact that the Party's rebuff was viewed by a certain part of the intelligentsia, especially young people, as a blow to *perestroika*."[4]

The Yeltsin affair was the first major political crisis of Gorbachev's administration. The General Secretary's handling of the affair is, in my opinion, open to some criticism. It seems that the decision not to publish Yeltsin's plenum declarations in full in newspapers (or at least for inner party circulation) has proven to be a political error. According to the rules adopted by the Party leadership under Gorbachev, only the report delivered by a party leader at the beginning of a plenum of the Central Committee and the closing speech usually made by the General Secretary are published; the discussion is not. The concealment of the full texts of Yeltsin's speeches was therefore true to the existing rules.

Yet it seems to me that this course of action was politically wrong for at least two reasons. The rumor mills that eventually and inevitably "reproduced" Yeltsin's declaration, and that commanded credibility, were sensationalistic and much more harmful than Yeltsin's accusations had been. Moreover, by prohibiting their publication, Gorbachev called into question his policy of *glasnost'* and reinforced the doubts and hesitations of many among the intelligentsia about the seriousness of the principles of *perestroika*. The publication of Yeltsin's remarks could have neutralized, in a large part, the negative repercussions of the Yeltsin affair while offering a powerful example of *glasnost'* in action.

Gorbachev and his close associates may recognize by now that the political calculus of their decision was rather faulty. Gorbachev and his loyalists in the leadership have started in *perestroika* a process that cannot been entirely controlled and directed. Actions that reinforce *perestroika* will inevitably be accompanied by unintended consequences that will not be to the liking of the leadership core. In the long run, if Gorbachev is genuinely committed to *perestroika*, which seems unquestionable, retreat

from the principle of *glasnost'* in dealing with those unintended consequences will harm the reforms without avoiding these consequences.

The convening of the Moscow city Party Committee on November
11 to discuss the Yeltsin affair and remove him from his position of
leadership was unavoidable. Political logic and the cause of *perestroika*
required that Yeltsin be fired and disgraced. This course of action was
needed to serve as a warning that the General Secretary could not be
crossed by any power figure either on the Left or, especially, on the
Right without swift and decisive retribution. That after his disgrace
Yeltsin was appointed to the important position of First Deputy Chairman
of the state Construction Committee and was not expelled from the
Party Central Committee was in itself a bow to the newly proclaimed
style of leadership and to the process of democratization. An official
supporter of Gorbachev spoke with anger about the harm done by
Yeltsin and remarked, "If I were to follow my emotions I would like
to see Yeltsin sent far away from Moscow as a manager of a construction
enterprise where with hard work he will atone in at least a small degree
for the harm that he caused to the party. But politically it was necessary
to retain him in a position of high managerial responsibility in Moscow
itself."

The meeting of the Moscow city Party Committee and the public
firing of Yeltsin were necessary. Yet the way in which the meeting did
proceed in dealing with Yeltsin did not help *perestroika*. The proceedings
of the meeting brought back memories of public confessions and vicious
attempts at "character assassination." Although Gorbachev's speech at
the meeting was rather measured and dignified, the spectacle of most
of Yeltsin's associates and subordinates harshly and one-sidedly criticizing
his behavior during his entire tenure in office and attacking him personally
was disgusting. Only a few weeks before, those same people were
kowtowing to Yeltsin and keeping silent about their dislike of him. The
old, disgraced Soviet tradition dominated the proceedings, and the new
principles of *perestroika* were mostly absent. The course of the meeting,
from which large excerpts were published in *Pravda*, again discouraged
the supporters of *perestroika* and increased the doubts of the uncommitted.

Some sources in Moscow asserted that Gorbachev was dismayed by
the fact that so many of the Moscow city Party and government
functionaries behaved at the meeting in a "nonconstructive way." Certainly, by attacking Yeltsin they did what was expected of them. But
Gorbachev allegedly was appalled by their inability to recognize their
own responsibility for the state of affairs in Moscow and by their lack
of constructive thinking about how to improve the situation. Moreover,
according to this source, it was a mistake to leave the selection of parts
of the proceedings of the Moscow meeting for publication in *Pravda* to

its editor, Yuriy Afanas'ev, which compounded the error. The selection was biased in stressing those parts of the speeches that were motivated by the desire of the Moscow Party functionaries to distance themselves from Yeltsin and settle their scores with him.

An indication that this assessment may be correct was contained in an article written by a worker, a member of the Central Committee, in *Sovetskaya Rossiya* on November 24. (This article was clearly instigated by the top leadership.) The whole tone of the article was serious and balanced, the critique of Yeltsin comradely, the writer's affection, compassion, and respect for Yeltsin very clear. Toward the end of this article the author openly criticized the meeting of the Moscow city Party committee.

> What was lacking at this meeting was the recognition of the collective responsibility [of the Moscow Party Committee] for the way in which the Moscow Party Organization worked and for the Party reputation of Boris Yeltsin. I will say it straight. The Secretaries of the City Party Committee and the members of its bureau did not present themselves in the best light. At the Moscow Party Plenum they harshly criticized Yeltsin. But one should not forget that these same comrades to a large degree did hide and cultivate the undemocratic style of work in our Party organization. They lacked the courage and Party consciousness to express their disagreements with the prevailing style of leadership. This same can be said about the district party secretaries. This is unconscionable.[5]

Repercussions for Gorbachev

It is generally accepted in the West and in the Soviet Union that the Yeltsin affair constituted a setback for Gorbachev and his loyalists in the leadership. However, the seriousness of this setback has been exaggerated. The setback for Gorbachev should be considered from a dual perspective—what it did to his political power and how it influenced his program of *perestroika*.

When analyzing Gorbachev's power, one should distinguish among its three interrelated but nevertheless distinct aspects. The first concerns his security in office, the extent of any danger to his position as the General Secretary. The second pertains to his ability to determine the policies emanating from the top leadership institutions—the Politburo, the Central Committee Secretariat, the Presidium of the Council of Ministers, and eventually the Central Committee of the Party. The third relates to his ability to push through the implementation of his program by the vast army of party and state officials, the party activists, the professional strata, and his rank-and-file supporters.

Gorbachev's Security in Office

With regard to Gorbachev's security in office, the Yeltsin affair did not change anything. The General Secretary was not before, is not now, and for the foreseeable future will remain in no danger of losing his official position. The sensationalist Western writers who predicted that "today was Yeltsin's turn; tomorrow it will be Gorbachev" were simply ignorant of the realities of power in the Soviet Union. After the election of the General Secretary and his initial consolidation of power (which Gorbachev achieved long ago), the flow of power in the Party hierarchy is vertical—from the Secretary General and his loyalists down to the Politburo and the Secretariat, from the Politburo and Secretariat in turn to the Central Committee, and so on.

Of course, without mass terror and unlimited personal dictatorship, such as Iosif Stalin's, and particularly in periods of major change, this vertical flow of power is not perfect. It has constraints and can produce surprises. Nikita Khrushchev learned that lesson twice: in 1957, when he barely survived the attempt to oust him by a coalition of enemies, the so-called anti-Party group, which mustered a majority in the Politburo; and in 1964, when virtually the entire Politburo, most of them individuals appointed by Khrushchev himself, successfully engineered a coup that ousted him. The position of the General Secretary now and in the foreseeable future is very different.

There is no danger of an anti-Party group, a coalition of "old guard" leaders, or Stalinists forming in the Politburo. The remnants of the old guard in the leadership are a tiny minority in positions primarily of symbolic and not real power (Andrei Gromyko, Mikhail Solomentsev). The majority of the Politburo and an overwhelming majority of the Secretariat are composed of men whom Gorbachev brought into the leadership. They seem to be personally loyal to him. Khrushchev was ousted in 1964 because he wanted to rule without the Politburo, which without mass terror was impossible. He alienated all its members by his combination of ambition, primitiveness, capriciousness, and volatility.

Gorbachev is a stable, sophisticated, genuinely charismatic leader who has forged a coalition of core supporters within the leadership, men with whom he works very closely. Of course, if by the end, let us say, of 1990, positive results of his *perestroika* are lacking while its negative, destabilizing unintended consequences are looming, his security in office may be in danger. Yet even then, one should remember, it will probably be Gorbachev and his core associates who will define what success means, or they may change their policies in order to remain in power.

Gorbachev's Ability to Determine Policy

With regard to the General Secretary's ability to determine the policies emanating from the top Soviet leadership institutions, the Yeltsin affair has had a negative, and in some respects, possibly lasting impact. The Yeltsin challenge made the Soviet top leadership acutely aware of the danger that they faced from the Left, but this does not constitute a direct challenge to their power because the top Soviet power institutions are packed by personally loyal and disciplined Gorbachev supporters. Boris Yeltsin was a singular exception in the leadership rather than a forerunner of frustrated radical reformists in the General Secretary's entourage. Let us remember also that not a single Central Committee member supported Yeltsin.

The challenge from the Left comes from the supporters of Gorbachev's *perestroika* among the intelligentsia, the writers and directors, the media, economists, academics, some trade unionists, and probably also officials of the non-Russian republics. The danger they pose is that they are apt to provide ammunition for the rightist opponents of Gorbachev, who are the prime enemies of *perestroika,* and stiffen the resistance to reform of the vested bureaucratic interests. The leftist pressure for much more *glasnost'*, democratization, and personnel changes than Gorbachev feels are feasible at the present phase of *perestroika* will push him to policies that are more cautious, more centrist than he would like. This is the dilemma of the Left in Gorbachev's revolution and the dilemma of the General Secretary himself. He needs the Left to push the reforms, but he wants the Left to be restrained and controlled. Without Gorbachev's commitment to *perestroika,* the Left has no chance whatsoever to realize its goals. But by trying to accelerate the tempo and radicalize the nature of reforms, the Left strengthens the enemies of reform and draws Gorbachev away from the more radical visions of *perestroika.*

The question of Gorbachev's power after the Yeltsin affair to determine top level policies turns inevitably to speculations about his relations, and differences, with Yegor Kuzmich Ligachev. The sixty-eight-year-old Ligachev is a very powerful Politburo member and Secretary of the Central Committee who is, both at home and abroad, a symbol within the top Soviet hierarchy if not of opposition to *perestroika* then certainly the radical substance of Gorbachev's reforms and the methods by which they are to be implemented.

Ligachev never publicly argues against *perestroika* as such. But he almost always introduces into his speeches and in closed meetings with Party officials the need to be very cautious about changes, to slow their speed and make them less radical. He warns against the danger of

spontaneity in the process of *perestroika* and emphasizes the necessity
of a grass-roots democratization by the inviolate rule of the hegemony
of the Party. He urges administrative rather than economic methods of
modernizing the USSR, and he stresses the limits rather than the promise
of social, political, and particularly cultural reforms. He also warns
against too critical a view of the Soviet past.

Yeltsin's challenge to the Party leadership and his inevitable ouster
played perfectly, it would seem, into Ligachev's hands. Ligachev's stature
in the post-Yeltsin period has clearly grown. This can be partly seen
in the greater visibility afforded Ligachev inside the Soviet Union.
Ligachev's newly acquired confidence can also be glimpsed from the
interview that he granted on his visit to France in December 1987,
where far from building up the General Secretary's authority, he stressed
the central role that he, Ligachev, occupied within the Secretariat of the
Central Committee.

Is Ligachev's challenge to Gorbachev's position, stature, and power
truly dangerous to the General Secretary? In my opinion, by granting
self-serving and boastful interviews as he did in *Le Monde,* Ligachev is
making a political mistake. As a Soviet official remarked, aside from its
immediate negative consequences for the *perestroika,* the Yeltsin affair
has also shown clearly that "one does not make jokes with the General
Secretary." Yeltsin's challenge to Gorbachev from the Left has momentarily
helped and strengthened Ligachev on the Right of the Politburo. Yet in
the longer run, the challenge has surely demonstrated to Gorbachev that
given the danger to his program from the Left, he cannot afford and
tolerate for long a strong voice from the Right in the Politburo. Sooner
rather than later Ligachev will have to go, most probably by being
kicked upstairs to a position of symbolic but not executive power (for
example, by retiring Gromyko from the position of the Chairperson of
the Supreme Soviet and appointing Ligachev). Indeed, the incremental
erosion of Ligachev's power has already taken place. Ligachev lost the
portfolio for ideology at the Party conference in June 1988.

It is generally agreed in Moscow that even if Gorbachev is forced
out, Ligachev will not become Gorbachev's successor. Ligachev's support
within the Politburo is not strong. Moreover, Ligachev may, as he boasted
in the French interview, chair the Secretariat's meetings, but his institutional power within the top hierarchy of the Party apparatus has
already been curtailed. His control over personnel has been circumscribed
by Georgii Petrovich Razumovsky, who is a Gorbachev loyalist, a newly
elected candidate member of the Politburo, and a Secretary of the Central
Committee.

Ligachev's position as the key ideologist of the Party is being strongly
and successfully challenged by Gorbachev's close friend and protégé,

Alexander Nikolaevich Yakovlev, the Politburo member and Secretary of the Central Committee in charge of domestic and foreign propaganda, press, culture—in one word, *glasnost'*. Incidentally, with Yeltsin gone, Yakovlev is becoming the lightning rod for the conservatives' resistance to *perestroika*. But Yakovlev, although identified now as the strongest voice among Gorbachev's associates for radical transformation, is not a Yeltsin. He is a tried-and-true party politician, highly intelligent and knowledgeable, balanced, cautious, and resourceful. With Gorbachev's full support and trust, it is Yakovlev whom the odds favor to become the major supporting power for Gorbachev, with Ligachev on the sidelines.

Gorbachev's Power to Secure Implementation

With regard to the General Secretary's power vis-à-vis his ability to secure the implementation of his program, the Yeltsin affair temporarily reinforced an already existing negative trend. There can be no doubt that resistance to the progress of the *perestroika*, to its implementation in practice, has increased in parallel with Gorbachev's consolidation of his power position. From the political point of view, this is not illogical. In 1986, Gorbachev was speaking about changes in a very general way, and everybody could agree that there should be changes. But in 1987, he took major and very concrete steps to expand *glasnost'* and democratization and to reorganize the economy. These actions directly affected those who wanted to preserve their own privileges and power within the bureaucracy. It is not surprising, therefore, that resistance to the reforms is growing. At the same time, there is no evidence of a meaningful *organized* opposition to Gorbachev's program. The main obstacle to Gorbachev's power is not organized opposition at any level. Rather, resistance takes the form of social inertia and bureaucratic resistance by those who are for *perestroika* in words but not in deeds.

This resistance can be broken only step by step through a combination of personnel changes, incentives and disincentives, and persuasion. By the end of 1990, Gorbachev hopes to achieve what can be called a "revolutionary breakthrough," where the principles of *perestroika* will take hold in practice in the activities of the bureaucracies, managers, and workers. To achieve this, Gorbachev will seek to combine steady pressure from above that utilizes the advantages of the highly centralized political system with pressure from below that will be created by *glasnost'* and democratization.

In his efforts to implement *perestroika* and mobilize the party and the masses, Gorbachev does not rely on the support of any particular power structure (for example, the Party apparatus), as was the case with every past top Soviet leader. Rather, he is trying to forge an unorthodox and heterogeneous coalition. This coalition includes high and low Party, government, and economic officials and managers; liberals, in the Western meaning of the term, from among the intelligentsia; "pure" Leninists who believe that Lenin's vision of socialism was betrayed by all his successors; military men who see Gorbachev's program of modernization as the only way to ensure Soviet international security; Russian patriots who want to make the USSR great again and increase its international influence; intelligence officials who know Soviet weaknesses better than anybody else; anti-Stalinists who participated in Khrushchev's campaigns and now see the opportunity to resume what was interrupted twenty years ago; Soviet "yuppies" who want to hitch their wagons to a rising star; political and cultural leaders in the non-Russian republics who see in *perestroika* a chance to defend the cultural heritage of their nations and increase their degree of autonomy from Moscow; dissidents such as Andrei Sakharov who are concerned about world peace and believe that Gorbachev is moving in the right direction; and many, many others.

The Yeltsin affair probably encouraged the centrists in this "rainbow coalition" who want to modernize the Soviet Union but are wary of *glasnost'* and democratization. The affair discouraged the leftists in the coalition who consider the instruments of modernization, such as *glasnost'* and democratization, as important as economic modernization itself. But neither the centrists nor the leftists in the coalition had any choice, any alternative, but to support Gorbachev's own vision of *perestroika*. Whether this rainbow coalition will be strong enough to implement Gorbachev's reforms remains, of course, an open question.

The most deleterious effect of the Yeltsin affair was the loss of momentum in the reform. It would be dangerous to Gorbachev's reform program, and maybe even for his own position, to ease the pressure for *perestroika,* to acquiesce to its loss of momentum. Gorbachev must, and probably will, bring even stronger pressure for implementation and for radicalization of his reforms, particularly in the economic sphere.

Gorbachev is a determined reformer. But politics, even in the Soviet Union, is the art of the possible. His policy was, is, and will remain a zigzag one, with a general push for comprehensive reforms being followed by periods of consolidation, to be again replaced by periods of all-out offensive similar to the one that took place in the Soviet Union between January and June 1987. There is nothing abnormal about a process in which long-term strategy is realized by different tactics at specific periods.

Notes

Due to the political sensitivity of this chapter's focus, my sources must remain confidential, and references have been kept to a minimum.

1. For an informative view of Yeltsin, see Timothy J. Colton, "Moscow Politics and the El'tsin Affair," *The Harriman Institute Forum* 1, no. 6 (June 1988), pp. 1–8.

2. For Gorbachev's anniversary speech of November 2, 1987, see Mikhail Gorbachev, *October and Perestroika: The Revolution Continues* (Moscow: Novosti, 1987).

3. For Yeltsin's speech, see *Moskovskaya pravda*, January 26, 1986, p. 1.

4. *Pravda*, January 13, 1988, p. 1.

5. *Sovetskaya Rossiya*, November 24, 1987, p. 2.

4

State and Society: Toward the Emergence of Civil Society in the Soviet Union

Gail W. Lapidus

There is a difference between reform and quasi-reform. If quasi-reform is a reorganization at the top, purely a reorganization of the apparatus, reform is a more serious matter. Reform vitally changes the organizational relationships between the state apparatus and members of the society, collectively and individually, and this is what its main substance lies in.[1]

—B. P. Kurashvili

Western analyses of the contemporary Soviet scene frequently portray Mikhail Gorbachev as but the latest in a long line of reforming tsar-autocrats, from Peter the Great to Iosif Stalin, who have sought to impose radical and coercive programs of modernization on a passive, backward, and recalcitrant society. Although this analogy is not entirely off the mark, it fails to capture the extent to which the process of reform now under way in the Soviet Union is also a long-delayed response by the leadership to fundamental social changes that are altering the relationship of state and society. The current attempt at reform is only in part a renewed effort at mobilization from above; this process of reform is also a far-reaching and highly controversial effort to adapt a set of anachronistic economic and political arrangements to the needs of an increasingly complex modern society.

The Roots of Gorbachev's Reforms

Gorbachev's initial reform strategy was animated by the need for serious and comprehensive economic reform to arrest the deterioration of Soviet economic performance that jeopardized both domestic stability and international power. But Gorbachev and his associates increasingly came to recognize that economic stagnation had its roots in deeper social and political problems and that far-reaching changes were necessary if these problems were to be successfully addressed. Gorbachev's sweeping attack, made at the January 1987 Plenum of the Communist Party's Central Committee, on the cumulative effects of economic stagnation, social corrosion, political conservatism and inertia, the spread of apathy and cynicism, and the absence of legal and political accountability (an analysis remarkably similar to that of many Western Sovietologists in the late 1970s and early 1980s) demonstrated a clear recognition that sociopolitical change was a prerequisite for successful economic reform. His remarks expressed a realization that in the environment of the 1980s the "human factor" had become decisive.[2]

This growing recognition of the social sources of stagnation was in turn reflected in the evolution of Gorbachev's conception of *perestroika* (restructuring). From a narrower focus on economic acceleration it expanded to encompass, in Gorbachev's words, "not only the economy but all other sides of social life: social relations, the political system, the spiritual and ideological sphere, the style and work methods of the Party and of all our cadres. Restructuring is a capacious word. I would equate restructuring with revolution . . . a genuine revolution in the minds and hearts of people."[3]

To accomplish this revolution, in Gorbachev's view, it is essential to stimulate the initiative and the creativity of the Soviet population by attacking the institutions and social norms that have long stifled it. As Nikita Khrushchev had done some thirty years earlier, Gorbachev has sought to mobilize popular support to carry out structural and policy changes, to curb the powers of officialdom, and to bring abuses of power under public scrutiny. But the novelty and significance of Gorbachev's strategy lie in its realization that Soviet society has reached a level of maturity that requires a new approach to its governance; and that the Soviet people, and above all the educated middle classes, can no longer be treated as the objects of official policy but must be treated as genuine subjects.

Khrushchev had launched this process of inclusion—a shift, however erratic, from the centralized, coercive statism of the Stalinist system to a more conciliatory and flexible approach to social forces.[4] Gorbachev has sought to extend the process of inclusion further. By contrast with Khrushchev's focus on the working class and peasantry, Gorbachev's strategy aims at incorporating the new social strata and values that are a product of the Soviet scientific-technological revolution as well as appealing to the skilled, the energetic and the creative in every walk of Soviet life. His efforts seek to overcome the alienation of key segments of the Soviet population—from Andrei Sakharov to avant-garde writers and artists, from the entrepreneurs of the unofficial "second economy" to disaffected workers, peasants, and youth—and to enlist their talents and energies in the revitalization of the Soviet system.

Gorbachev's reforms involve a redefinition of socialism itself in an effort to tap the sources of vitality, dynamism, and innovation that have increasingly developed outside the framework of official institutions. By widening the boundaries of legitimate economic, social, political, and cultural behavior, the reforms seek to draw back within these boundaries individuals and activities that had deserted them or been excluded. In short, Gorbachev's reforms are an effort to substitute "voice" for "exit" in Soviet sociopolitical life.[5]

In broadening the boundaries of legitimate social activity, Gorbachev's strategy draws on many of the ideas of leading Soviet intellectuals who in the 1960s and 1970s were considered dissidents. Some twenty years ago, three distinguished members of the Soviet intelligentsia—Andrei Sakharov, Roy Medvedev, and Valery Turchin—addressed a letter to the Soviet leadership appealing for a gradual democratization of the Soviet system and outlining a series of measures for reform. Sakharov, Medvedev, and Turchin compared the Soviet economy to an urban traffic intersection, observing that when only a few cars were present, traffic police could easily cope with their task, but when the stream of traffic increased, fining the drivers and replacing the police no longer guaranteed a smooth flow of traffic. "The only solution," these three intellectuals argued, "is to widen the intersection. The obstacles hindering the development of our economy lie outside it, in the social and political sphere, and all measures that do not remove these obstacles are doomed to ineffectiveness."[6] Gorbachev's policies not only echo many of these recommendations; the policies stem from a similar understanding that economic development and the growing maturity of Soviet society demand fundamentally new approaches to its management.

The thrust of Gorbachev's strategy is to alter the basic premise of the Stalinist system from "all that is not permitted is prohibited" to the principle that "all that is not prohibited is permitted."[7] But an expansion of the public arena that broadens the scope of legitimate activities and permits a greater degree of social self-regulation involves a significant redefinition of the role of the Party-state. In political and economic life as in culture, expansion of the public arena would diminish the role of central controls and expand the role of market forces, offer increased autonomy and resources as well as responsibility to a wide range of organizations and individuals, and introduce a degree of "socialist Darwinism" in promoting greater reliance on competition and self-regulation rather than on state-sponsored protection. In short, this expansion would give new impetus, and lend official support, to the emergence of an embryonic civil society.

But these changes confront Soviet reformers with an acute dilemma: the tension between the need to increase social initiative to revitalize the Soviet system and the fear that increased social autonomy will threaten central control. By simultaneously encouraging greater discipline as well as greater autonomy, and more effective central control as well as wider democratization, the current process of reform has set in motion contradictory pressures and opportunities in Soviet social life and policies, and contributes to major cleavages within the political elite.

In this exploration of the social dimensions of the process of reform, I will focus on three broad issues: the way in which broader changes in Soviet social structure and values made reform both urgent and possible; the new perspectives on Soviet society that inform the reformist program; and how societal reactions affect the prospects for a fundamental transformation of the Soviet system.

The Political Impact of Social Change

Seventy years after the victory of the Bolshevik Revolution, Mikhail Gorbachev asserts that the Soviet system stands at a crossroads, confronted by a set of choices that will determine whether the Soviet Union will enter the twenty-first century "in a manner worthy of a great power." That such an issue can even be raised is not only a measure of the gravity with which an important part of the Soviet leadership views the present situation; it also reflects a virtual revolution in consciousness within the Soviet elite. The growing conviction that domestic stability as well as international security was increasingly jeopardized by the economic stagnation, social corrosion, and political immobility of the Brezhnev era, and that only radical departures from the prevailing policies and norms would serve to avert further deterioration, reflects profound discord within the Soviet political establishment about the urgency of mounting problems, their causes, and the measures required to address them.

By the late 1970s, the erosion of confidence in the Soviet regime within the broader society, and in Leonid Brezhnev's political leadership within the broader elite, was apparent to Soviet citizens and foreign observers alike. This erosion was the product of two mutually reinforcing trends: an objective deterioration in the performance of the Soviet economy, which brought with it a mounting array of social and political problems, and a growing sense of demoralization within the Soviet elite, which reflected a shift in perceptions of regime performance.

The deteriorating performance of the Soviet economy was the key catalyst in the growing perception of failure, both in and of itself and because economic failure compounded other sociopolitical problems. But the economic slowdown and diminished international competitiveness might not have generated a sense of urgency had their presence not coincided with and contributed to a change in attitudes: an increasingly negative assessment of regime performance, which reflected a change in the criteria used to evaluate it; a growing sense of failure; and heightened pessimism about the future—in effect, a crisis of confidence within the Soviet elite. By the early 1980s, not only Western observers but key Soviet officials were in a fashion unprecedented since the early 1920s, beginning to speak of a "crisis" in order to convey the urgency of the situation.[8]

In this respect, the Soviet case resembles that of a number of authoritarian regimes that, beginning in the 1970s, underwent a series of transitions from authoritarian rule. The critical catalyst in many such cases was a deterioration of regime performance. This deterioration contributed to a loss of confidence within the ruling elite and to the development of major cleavages within it, often combined with the alienation of a growing segment of the population. In Latin America, Spain, Portugal, and Greece, authoritarian systems evolved (in however erratic and uncertain a fashion) in the direction of liberalization if not always democratization, redefining and extending the rights of individuals and groups and providing them increased protection from arbitrary state action. In the Soviet case, however, the totalitarian legacy of the Stalin era, as well as the weak development of liberalism and constitutionalism in the Russian political tradition, placed distinctive constraints on the potential for economic and political liberalization.[9] To what extent these can be overcome in the years ahead is the fundamental question of Soviet politics.

The inauguration of the process of reform in the USSR was in large measure a function of elite politics and cleavages, in which leadership succession served as a major catalyst. But the impetus for reform and the direction it is taking are a product not only of a deteriorating Soviet international position, but of fundamental changes in Soviet social structure and values in the post-Stalin period that altered the aspirations, resources, and behavior of key social groups. By undermining traditional forms of social control and motivation, these changes helped to delegitimize traditional policies and political formulas, and to provide a rationale for fresh approaches.

The social and demographic changes from the mid-1950s to the mid-1980s transformed the passive and inarticulate peasant society of the era of Stalin into an urban industrial society with a highly differentiated social structure and an increasingly articulate and assertive middle class. The society over which Khrushchev ruled in the 1950s was still predominantly rural. By the mid-1980s, by contrast, two-thirds of the Soviet population lived in cities, and a growing percentage had been born in them. In 1959, only three Soviet cities had populations larger than 1 million; by 1985, that figure had reached twenty-two. Modernization was transforming the quality of urban life as well, while the spread of television brought urban lifestyles and values to the remotest corners of Soviet territory. When Khrushchev was dismissed in 1964, fewer than one in three Soviet families owned television sets. By 1988, television was almost universal and had not only brought a vast new universe of events and images into the Soviet household, but had rendered obsolete the system of agitation and propaganda through which the Party had for decades conveyed its message to the Soviet people.

Rapid urbanization was accompanied by a dramatic increase in the educational levels attained by the Soviet population. In 1959, two-thirds of the Soviet population over the age of ten had no more than a primary education; by 1986, almost two-thirds had completed secondary education. The combined effects of urbanization and rising levels of educational attainment transformed the Soviet working class from a relatively homogeneous body only recently drawn from the countryside to a differentiated one whose working-class membership was now increasingly becoming hereditary. Moreover, rising educational and skill levels among younger cohorts of the working class increasingly distinguished them from older generations of workers who were relegated to the ranks of the less skilled and enjoyed correspondingly lower status and pay. Younger workers also displayed a different set of orientations and values from their predecessors: a declining interest in work itself and a growing focus on family and leisure activities, including increased absorption in consumption, in the amenities made possible by the shift from communal and dormitory housing to private apartments, and by the greater range and availability of leisure activities.

Expanded educational opportunities have also sharply increased the percentage of the Soviet population with higher education. In 1959, only 5.5 million Soviet citizens had higher education; by 1986, the figure had reached 24 million. The growth in the number of "scientific workers" was particularly dramatic: from 1.5 million in 1950 to 15 million in 1986.[10] In short, not only was an increasing percentage of the Soviet working class becoming better educated; by the mid-1980s, a large urban middle class, including a substantial professional, scientific-technical and cultural intelligentsia with new cultural as well as material requirements, had emerged as a major actor on the Soviet scene.

This urban middle class, moreover, occupied an increasingly important place in both the membership and the leadership of the Communist Party itself. More than one-third of all urban males with higher education were Party members, and higher education had become the norm rather than the exception within the upper ranks of the Party, and even the Politburo itself.

The revival of Soviet sociology in the 1960s and 1970s brought the tools of social science to the study of these changes and of their likely impact on the aspirations, attitudes, and behavior of the Soviet population. Inhibited as they were by ideological and bureaucratic constraints, primitive methodological approaches, simplistic formulas about social reality, and the absence of adequate data, these sociological studies were nonetheless able to capture what was becoming a major source of social strain: the increasing tendency of the rising aspirations of the Soviet population for improved material well-being, upward social mobility, and occupational satisfaction and autonomy to outstrip the realistic possibilities for their fulfillment.[11]

For some, the demand for better and more varied food, consumer goods and services, and for higher quality education and health care, found outlets in the burgeoning second economy. For others, material dissatisfaction and frustration at limited opportunities for upward social mobility were expressed in low labor productivity, high turnover and absenteeism, rising alcoholism, and other social pathologies. The "double shift" of the female labor force, burdened by heavy household duties as well as full-time employment, took its own toll in declining birthrates. For others, disaffection took the form of emigration. Although tacit official acquiescence in these various forms of "exit" during the Brezhnev era afforded a safety valve, it offered no serious promise of future improvements.

A wide range of Soviet sources, from sociological studies to Soviet films and fiction, offered evidence that a significant shift in values was taking place in the Brezhnev era: growing pessimism about the Soviet future, increasing disillusionment with official values, and an accompanying decline in civic morale. The sources of alienation differed for different social groups and individuals, but their common thrust was a shift in the standards by which the regime's performance was evaluated. Traditional explanations of failure—the survival of capitalist remnants, growing pains, the aftermath of war, the machinations of unseen enemies—had lost their persuasiveness to a generation reared in the expectation that the Soviet Union was about to overtake the West and disillusioned by the chasm that separated myth from reality.

Indeed, it was precisely among the younger and best-educated segments of the Soviet population, including the inhabitants of its largest and most developed cities, that dissatisfaction appeared to be highest and the rejection of official norms most pronounced. This shift was a striking and new development, for these groups had traditionally provided the staunchest support for the Soviet system. By the 1980s, however, it was among young people and the better educated that new attitudes and values were taking root, and these included a more critical view of state control over economic life, greater openness to private economic activity, and greater commitment to personal freedom and individual rights.[12]

The evidence of alienation from official norms was not confined to the social science writings; it was equally apparent in Soviet cultural life. The most widely read novelists and poets and the most popular artists among the intelligentsia were not those favored by the Party and cultural establishment, but those who addressed universal moral concerns, such as the meaning of truth, the nature of good and evil, the significance of memory, and issues of national history and identity, both Russian and non-Russian. It was these themes that provoked intense discussions in Soviet literary and cultural journals and were an expression of the erosion of traditional ideological commitments and the search for new values and sources of meaning within the Soviet educated elite.

Other currents, less hospitable to tolerance or liberalization but equally alienated from the ethos of the Brezhnev era, also commanded some support in this urban milieu. One was a technocratic orientation that sought to solve current problems by applying new scientific and technological tools and managerial techniques and that saw the military economy as a possible model for emulation. Another was, if anything, antitechnological, identified with a romantic nationalism that found its symbolism in the Russian past and protested the ravages inflicted on nature and culture by the unbridled pursuit of industrialism and material progress. Even more extreme forms of nationalism and chauvinism—both Russian and non-Russian—flourished in the comparative laxity of the time, although they did not receive public expression until the era of *glasnost'*.

The spiritual alienation of important segments of the intelligentsia was further compounded by its growing exposure to the outside world. As Khrushchev's son-in-law Aleksei Adzhubei recalled recently, "When Khrushchev went to the exposition in Brussels in 1957, he decided that all the writers, managers, journalists, actors should visit the exhibit. When he visited the United States, representatives of all the professions went too."[13]

Détente extended this exposure. Scientists and scholars, students and professionals, writers and dancers and journalists took part in the expanding network of exchanges and came into contact with new ideas and approaches, alternative ways of looking at the world or of organizing professional life, and different standards of achievement. The desire for international recognition and status among professional peers, as well as the expansion of communication on issues of mutual interest, created a sense of community that transcended differing political and social systems and acknowledged that Western standards of excellence were of universal significance. Foreign radio broadcasts and letters from émigrés to friends and relatives in the USSR further pierced the Iron Curtain, bringing new sources of information about the outside world. Even in Soviet enterprises, the growing presence of Western technologies and machinery operating alongside domestic products encouraged direct comparisons with what the Soviets would later call "world standards of excellence."

These experiences provided new criteria for evaluating Soviet achievements and shortcomings. Judged by these standards, Soviet performance was increasingly found wanting, and earlier official explanations of failure were no longer convincing. Greater contact with the outside world thus contributed to the pessimism and demoralization of an influential scientific-technical and cultural intelligentsia resentful of, and frustrated by, an authoritarian, patronizing, and exclusionary pattern of political rule. This mood provided an important impetus for reform.

This transformation of Soviet attitudes had its counterpart in Soviet behavior as well. Growing alienation and a decline in civic morale contributed to a shift in expectations and energies from the public to the private realm and to the emergence of an intellectual and moral rationale for the increasing privatization of life. "Exit" became an increasingly important option for a small but significant segment of Soviet society, whether in the burgeoning "second economy"; in a blossoming popular culture; or in the emergence of a rich array of informal and unofficial groups pursuing a broad range of cultural as well as sociopolitical activities, from rock music to the preservation of historical monuments. These activities were facilitated by newly available technologies, from automobiles to videotape recorders, not readily amenable to governmental control. Ossified official norms and institutions were thus progressively supplanted by new forms of largely autonomous expression that responded to the preferences of consumers rather than officials. These trends were exemplified by the decline of the Komsomol, the official Soviet youth organization, along with the emergence of a rich and complex youth culture. But the most extreme and dramatic form of "exit" was undoubtedly the emigration of leading writers, artists, and cultural figures from the Soviet Union to escape a stifling cultural orthodoxy or political repression. This "exit" served to accelerate both the erosion of cultural vitality and the growing demoralization of those who remained behind.

What all these trends reflect is the government's decreasing ability to channel and shape the direction of social change. The very image of "revolution from above," with all its connotations of state domination of a passive society, no longer corresponds to a reality where social forces have achieved a degree of autonomy and indeed actively impinge on the political system in unprecedented ways. The erosion of political control of important sectors of Soviet life is abundantly illustrated by the evolution of the "second economy," the very existence of which epitomizes the subversion of centrally established priorities and challenges centralized control of prices, distribution of income, and the allocation of capital and labor. The spread of corruption, particularly within the political elite, threatens the organizational integrity and political legitimacy of the Party and feeds both the resentment of those excluded from patronage and the hostility of those who are critical of it.

A parallel development is visible in the escape of important dimensions of social behavior from official control. People marry, reproduce, and divorce without reference to official demographic policy; they migrate from north and east to south and west in defiance of planners' preferences; and their devotion to religious beliefs and practices resists all efforts to invigorate atheistic propaganda. A whole spectrum of social pathologies, from alcoholism and drug addiction to crime, exemplifies the limits of political control.

This entire trend has complex and contradictory implications, encompassing as it does a whole range of activities and behaviors with varying consequences. The enhanced space for autonomous social behavior allows for increased autonomy as well as corruption in Central Asia. It permits both historical preservationism and nationalistic xenophobia, Christian orthodoxy, and punk rock in Moscow. Its manifestations evoke an equally ambivalent reaction within the Soviet elite, where it is welcomed by some as an opportunity for greater social initiative and deplored by others as acquiescence in the weakening of discipline. The tension between these contradictory assessments was reflected in conflicting approaches to the process of reform itself.

Toward Socialist Pluralism:
The Social Strategy of the Reformers

Gorbachev's reform strategy involves a significantly new conception of socialism based on a novel set of assumptions about the nature of Soviet society and its relation to the political order. Although the translation of new approaches into policy remains embryonic and somewhat contradictory, support for socialist pluralism, political democratization, and legal reform reflect new ways of thinking about the Soviet system of rule and embrace a new model of socialism.

The point of departure of this new strategy is the view that Soviet development has created an increasingly differentiated, complex and modern society that remains largely unknown to the Soviet leadership and that it has been trying to govern by methods that are no longer appropriate. The "fictions" of the Stalin era have for too long been accepted as social reality, stereotypes have been a substitute for genuine social research, and unbending dogmatism has stood in the way of necessary policy reassessments. Even the tools required for effective policy-making remain inadequate and undeveloped because of Stalin's mutilation of the social sciences and the ideological and bureaucratic impediments to their revival. The primitive level of economics, not to mention sociology, demography, ethnography, psychology, and the study of public opinion, and the paucity of economic and social statistics have deprived not only policymakers but society as a whole of the self-knowledge that is a prerequisite to genuine progress. The first requirement, in the striking words of Alexander Yakovlev, is that "present-day socialism must become acquainted with itself."[14]

The changes under way in the ideological and cultural sphere and the renewal of selective de-Stalinization express a recognition that the delegitimation of key features of the Stalinist ethos—and above all its continuing legacy in the Soviet mindset—is a necessary first step in clearing the way for new approaches toward society. It has been essential to attack the equation of Stalinism with socialism and to portray Stalinism as a response to specific conditions at a particular historical moment rather than a universally valid approach to economic, social, or political dilemmas.

The renewal of public discussion of the crimes as well as the errors of the Stalin era and the presentation, in Gorbachev's speech on the occasion of the seventieth anniversary of the October Revolution, of a revised framework for the interpretation of Soviet history—one that emphasized those features of the Lenin and later periods that provide doctrinal support for *perestroika*—are an effort to gain enhanced freedom of action for new approaches.[15] The effort at delegitimization focuses on several features of the Stalinist legacy that constitute particular obstacles to sociopolitical reform: ideological dogmatism, lack of trust in Soviet society, the denial of social diversity, and an arbitrary and exclusionary pattern of centralized rule that violates fundamental norms of socialist democracy.

The delegitimation of these deeply entrenched features of Soviet ideology and practice has been accompanied by an attempt to encourage "new political thinking" in a number of areas of domestic as well as foreign policy. These new departures are obviously neither entirely novel nor completely unprecedented; in most cases they involve official endorsement of views and perspectives developed within the scholarly community and cultural intelligentsia during the Khrushchev and Brezhnev eras. In many cases these views had been sharply criticized and explicitly repudiated earlier, and their advocates treated as dissidents and expelled from their positions.[16]

Perhaps the most far-reaching feature of the reformist program is the shift from the notion of a "single truth" to a recognition of the legitimacy and indeed the necessity of divergent opinions. The entire Leninist conception of a vanguard party was premised on the need for Party tutelage over backward masses. Although the post-Stalin era was marked by a considerable broadening of the boundaries of permissible discussion on a wide range of issues, Gorbachev's call for "socialist pluralism," his insistence that open discussion was a prerequisite of scientific progress as well as of cultural vitality and should extend from technical to political issues, directly challenged the traditional claims of Party ideology.

The notion of socialist pluralism acknowledged the diversity of groups and interests as well as of ideas. The underlying assumption of socialist pluralism was clearly expressed in Gorbachev's address on the seventieth anniversary of the October Revolution when he declared: "We start from the fact that socialism is a society of growing diversity in opinions, relations, and activities of people."[17] This view of Soviet society also prompted Gorbachev's explicit call for a fundamental reassessment of socialist ideology. At the January 1987 Central Committee Plenum he criticized what he called the "schematic and dogmatic approach" to Party ideology that had prevailed in the past. He attacked the persistence of theoretical concepts that remained at the level of the 1930s and 1940s while the country's needs had fundamentally changed. He deplored the disappearance of vigorous debates and creative ideas and the absolutizing of particular authors and points of view that, Gorbachev implied, ought to have been treated as contingent and context dependent. Above all, he explicitly repudiated portrayals of Soviet social structure that denied the presence of contradictions and therefore of social dynamism, rather than presenting Soviet society as embodying diverse interests.

This view has been further elaborated and forcefully advocated by Politburo member Aleksander Yakovlev, the Party Secretary responsible for ideology. Yakovlev has repeatedly singled out dogmatism as the key obstacle to reform because "by its very nature [it] denies development." Dogmatic thinking, Yakovlev has argued, "is an inability or unwillingness to comprehend phenomena of the objective world in all their fullness and dynamism and in the contradictory nature of their development. It presents the surrounding world as an ossified formation, and science as a set of infallible 'truths' and propositions. . . . From this viewpoint, it is legitimate to describe dogmatism as authoritarian thinking elevated to a political, moral and intellectual principle."[18]

The call for socialist pluralism echoed a memorable article that had appeared in late 1986 in *Izvestiya* calling for greater debate and controversy on major issues of the day. "We must get used to the idea that a multiplicity of voices is a natural part of openness," its author had argued.

> We must treat diversity normally, as the natural state of the world; not with clenched teeth, as in the past, but normally as an immutable feature of social life. . . . We need in the economy and other areas of Soviet life a situation where multiple variants and alternative solutions are in and of themselves developmental tools and preconditions for obtaining optimal results, and where the coexistence of two opposing points of view on a single subject is most fruitful.

Reminding his audience of the high price paid in the past for intolerance toward other opinions, he concludes, "We must learn to live under democratic conditions."[19]

Official acquiescence in the necessity for, and indeed the desirability of, divergent opinions has not only widened the arena of public discussion; it has also served to legitimize the very notion of debates in Soviet public life. At a meeting with social scientists in spring 1987, Yakovlev proclaimed that "science can develop only in a process of constructive debates, in a clash of opinions. . . . We must realize that no one has a monopoly on truth, either in posing new questions or in providing answers."[20] Nor have words remained divorced from deeds. The most visible evidence of this new outlook was the dramatic transformation of the Party's theoretical journal, *Kommunist*, under the editorship of Ivan Frolov and then Nail Bikkenin, from a dreary and sterile custodian of ideological purity to a forum for lively debate on major policy issues.[21]

Formal debate has even found its way to Soviet television. Programs that present diametrically opposed positions on major issues of the day—including a debate about reform itself—and that conclude without an authoritative and final resolution of the issue are a novel departure from long-standing practices.

At the same time, the expression of multiple views is not unlimited in scope, nor does it enshrine full freedom of expression. As Gorbachev himself has affirmed, freedom extends only to those views that serve the cause of socialism. In practice, however, the limits of tolerance remain ill-defined and its boundaries fluid and hotly contested, as the controversy over the Nina Andreyeva letter in the spring of 1988 reaffirmed. But the effort to shed what some Soviets have labeled the "unanimity complex" in favor of socialist pluralism has far-reaching consequences for Soviet society and politics.

The endorsement of *glasnost'* (public disclosure), with its simultaneous connotation of both candor and publicity, constitutes a second major departure in regime-society relations. *Glasnost'* is, needless to say, a policy of preemption intended to reduce the reliance of the Soviet population on foreign and unofficial sources of information—from foreign television and radio broadcasts to gossip—to fill the voids created by Soviet silence. The Chernobyl experience gave enormous impetus to this effort. The fact that the Soviet people first learned of a major domestic catastrophe with far-reaching implications for their own health and welfare from foreign broadcasts, and that the news was initially denied by their own government, was a major political embarrassment. It dramatized as never before the high costs of traditional Soviet secretiveness, both domestically and internationally, and strengthened Gorbachev's determination to expand the flow of information and communication in order to enhance the credibility of the leadership among its citizens.[22]

Glasnost' is also a symbol of trust. It reflects a recognition by the Soviet leadership of the maturity of the Soviet population and a partial repudiation of the patronizing notion that only a small elite can be entrusted with truth. The call for greater openness in place of secrecy, for realism rather than varnishing, is thus a movement toward the normalization of Soviet public life and the potential emergence of a public sphere.

Glasnost' is equally an expression of confidence in the legitimacy of the Soviet system and its leadership, and a recognition that the pretense of infallibility is no longer necessary to command popular allegiance and support. Indeed, greater publicity for shortcomings and problems— whether the shoddy construction of nuclear power plants or the spread of drug addiction—is an indispensable precondition for successfully addressing them.

The case for *glasnost'* and its intimate connection to the prospects for reform was most eloquently put by Tat'yana Zaslavskaya, the reformist sociologist, who argued in a remarkable article in *Pravda*, "If we continue to keep from the people information about the conditions under which they live, say, the degree of environmental pollution, the number of industrial accidents, or the extent of crime, we cannot expect them to assume a more active role in economic or in political life. People will trust and support you only if you trust them."[23] *Glasnost'* is therefore indispensable for genuine feedback and for creating a mechanism for two-way communication between government and society.

Dramatic new departures in Soviet cultural policy—the most far-reaching and tangible of the changes thus far—are another expression of the new orientation toward inclusion and trust.[24] The publication of long-suppressed novels and poems and the screening of controversial films long kept from public view are not only a form of reconciliation with the intelligentsia but also an expression of a more tolerant and inclusive approach to Soviet culture, past and present. The reappraisal of the contributions of such writers and poets as Mikhail Bulgakov, Boris Pasternak, Marina Tsvetaeva, and Anna Akhmatova, once scorned for their deviation from "socialist realism," and the repudiation of measures taken against some of them, extends the boundaries of permissible literature to figures previously outside it. The process of reintegration even extends to selected figures in the emigration, which holds out the prospect of ultimately reuniting the "two streams" of Russian culture at home and abroad.

Finally and of potential significance for the future, *glasnost'* is linked to accountability. An expanded and more independent role for the media—including serious investigative reporting—is an important instrument for exposing abuses of power and position and for holding officials accountable for their actions. Needless to say, it also offers a convenient weapon for use against political opponents. It is nonetheless of great importance that *glasnost'* has extended, in however tentative a manner, to the first cautious exposés of abuses by the police and the KGB.

Even military and security affairs, traditionally forbidden territory, have begun to be opened, however tentatively, to public discussion and criticism. In a round-table discussion reported in *Literaturnaia gazeta*, a group of scientists questioned the conscription of university students, arguing "our society does not need soldiers more than it needs . . . physicists, biologists, engineers and social scientists."[25] The morality of nuclear weapons has been openly challenged in the Soviet press. A well-known Belorussian writer, Ales' Adamovich, for example, publicly argued that "for me there are no military men more courageous and worthy than those who . . . give their military expertise to the antiwar movement."[26] Even sensitive foreign and security policy issues—from Stalin's contribution to the rise of fascism, to the impact of SS-20 deployments in Europe, to the decision to intervene in Afghanistan, to the size of the Soviet military budget—have begun to be aired. Indeed, Soviet journalists and diplomats have complained publicly that excessive security hinders their work and have called on Soviet defense authorities to provide more information about the country's defense budget and military capabilities so journalists and diplomats will not have to rely exclusively on Western data.[27]

A further novel feature of the reformist program is its explicit recognition of the differentiation and complexity of Soviet society. The
fiction of an essentially solidary society (consisting, in Stalinist orthodoxy,
of two classes—workers and peasants—and one stratum, the intelligentsia)
had already begun to dissolve in the post-Stalin era. But this fiction
could not be directly challenged as long as Khrushchev's vision of
communism, with its apotheosis of equality, homogeneity, and community,
held sway.

With the revival of sociological research in the 1960s and 1970s, a
more complex portrait of Soviet social structure began to emerge.[28] It
was a portrait that recognized the evolution of a complex pattern of
stratification in the Soviet Union; provided evidence of differences in
earnings, status, and educational attainments among various social groups;
and suggested that new forms of social differentiation might be structurally
reproduced in a socialist society. The structure of power and its impact
on social stratification remained a closed subject. Nor was it yet possible
to acknowledge that different strata and groups might have fundamentally
different social interests and that these interests might be a source of
serious social antagonisms and conflict. The role of bureaucracy was
equally off limits, as was any critical examination of Soviet ideology as
an expression of special social interests.

The obstacles to a serious examination of these issues were illuminated
by a major debate about the nature of social contradictions under socialism
that erupted in the early 1980s. Prompted by the crisis in Poland and
the anxieties it provoked about the potential for social instability in the
Soviet Union itself, the debate engaged key philosophical journals,
extended to the Party journal *Kommunist* and ultimately engaged General
Secretary Yuri Andropov himself. A number of participants, most prom-
inently Anatoliy Butenko, head of a sector in the Academy of Sciences
Institute of the Economy of the World Socialist System, asserted that
socialism did not automatically preclude the possibility of antagonistic
contradictions and that they were not only possible but highly likely.[29]
Butenko went on to argue that they were not merely the result of
capitalist remnants but were generated by the development of socialism
itself; that these contradictions represented not merely individual de-
viations but had a systemic character; and that they could be provoked
by conflicting individual as well as group interests, such as a situation
in which "managers" attempt to satisfy their own selfish interests at
the expense of the "managed."

The proponents of this view were forced to retreat, and *Voprosy filosofii*
(in an October 1984 editorial) was obliged to admit that serious ideological
errors had been committed. But the Gorbachev era, with its new approach
to Soviet society, has vindicated the Butenkos by giving explicit en-

dorsement to precisely the views that were earlier criticized. Butenko himself, in a recent article in the same journal, pointedly criticized the erroneous understanding of socialism that had prevailed until Gorbachev's Political Report to the Twenty-seventh Party Congress. Butenko argued that the "theoretical dogmas, errors and prejudices that took root in the 1960s and 1970s" represented, in effect, an "ideological defense of extreme, bureaucratic centralism," which expressed the professional and social aspirations of the Soviet bureaucracy; he called for an expansion of self-government as an antidote.[30] In an interview, he asserted that Lenin's warnings of the dangers of bureaucratism and the need for public self-government had been ignored and replaced by Stalin's apotheosis of the state. Butenko concluded, "As long as a state exists whose functions are performed by special agencies and the people working in them, the possibility exists that they will become divorced from the masses and will act in their own selfish interests."[31]

The view that Soviet society encompasses diverse and potentially conflicting social interests, a view long held by Tat'yana Zaslavskaya, among others, and circulated in confidential memoranda and reports in the 1970s, has been not only legitimized but given prominence by its publication in *Kommunist*.[32] But the debate has since gone considerably further in focusing on the development of bureaucracy as the key to the emergence of the Stalinist system, and its defense of its ideological and political interests as the main obstacle to economic and political reform, thereby rekindling a debate that Leon Trotsky had launched more than a half century ago.[33]

This new approach to Soviet society is of enormous potential significance as a point of departure for the management of social and political affairs. By explicitly acknowledging the presence of conflicting interests (including bureaucratic interests), rather than obscuring and suppressing them, it not only takes another step toward the legitimation of diversity, it creates the necessary foundation for developing mechanisms for conflict management. It even acknowledges the need for some political expression of diverse views, although not of politically autonomous expression. In an unpublished talk with Soviet writers, Gorbachev himself reportedly acknowledged the need for a functional equivalent of a party opposition,[34] although other Soviet leaders clearly do not share this view. But the recognition of the need for greater political expression of social diversity provides a basis for reformers' efforts to revitalize the system of soviets, introduce competitive elections of officials, reduce the role of the Party, and, above all, of its apparatus in Soviet economic, social, and political life while sanctioning the emergence of a wide range of unofficial and nonparty organizations.

Indeed, the proliferation of informal groups and unofficial organizations concerned with a broad array of cultural, social and political issues is the most dramatic new departure on the Soviet political landscape. An officially sanctioned conference of unofficial groups in August 1987 brought together the representatives of some forty-seven such groups and generated proposals encompassing a variety of sociopolitical problems, like providing assistance to invalids and the aged, democratizing the Soviet electoral system, and building a monument to the victims of Stalinism—a proposal adopted a year later following the Nineteenth Party Conference. By 1988, the Soviet press reported that some 30,000 grassroots associations were in existence, provoking major debates about how they should be handled. By the time of the Party Conference in June 1988, a considerable number of unofficial groups and clubs had emerged with distinct political programs of their own, and some were engaged in organizing public demonstrations on environmental and political issues. Proposals were even under discussion to allow selected informal organizations to nominate candidates in local Soviet elections, posing a direct challenge to the existing *nomenklatura* system.[35]

The shift from an emphasis on social homogeneity to a recognition of social diversity and potential for social conflict, and the emergence of increasingly active unofficial organizations in defense of group interests, is especially apparent in the area of nationality problems. Khrushchev's assertion, at the Twenty-second Party Congress in 1961, that "the Party has solved one of the most complex of problems, which has plagued mankind for ages and remains acute in the world of capitalism to this day—the problem of relations between nations,"[36] marked the high tide of Soviet optimism about the achievements of Soviet nationality policy. In subsequent years the speeches of successive Soviet leaders took an increasingly sober tone. At the Twenty-sixth Party Congress in 1981 Brezhnev acknowledged that although the various nations of the Soviet Union were more united than ever before, "this does not imply that all the problems of the relations among nationalities have been resolved. The dynamics of the development of a large multinational state like ours gives rise to many problems requiring the Party's tactful attention."[37]

This sober reassessment was reaffirmed in even stronger terms by Yuri Andropov in December 1982. Using the occasion of the sixtieth anniversary of the creation of the Soviet multinational system to deliver a major address on the subject, he reminded his audience, "Soviet successes in solving the nationalities question certainly do not mean that all the problems engendered by the very fact of the life and work of numerous nations and nationalities in the framework of a single state have disappeared. This is hardly possible as long as nations exist, as long as there are national distinctions. And they will exist for a long time, much longer than class distinctions."[38]

A growing recognition by the Soviet leadership that successful management of national relations was critical to the stability of the system and demanded patient and delicate social engineering in turn generated increased encouragement and support for empirical social research on ethnic processes. Indeed, Andropov inadvertently testified to the previous shortcomings of such efforts when he called for the formulation of a "well-thought out, scientifically substantiated nationalities policy."[39]

The need for such a policy became painfully urgent following Gorbachev's accession to power. The new pressures and expectations generated by the reform process, as well as the new opportunities and diminished risks for expression of grievances that *glasnost'* appeared to sanction, brought to the surface long-simmering resentments among Russians and non-Russians alike that exploded with stunning force from Alma Ata to the Baltic to Armenia and Azerbaijan. While expressing the usual criticism of national chauvinism and narrow mindedness, Gorbachev's response also acknowledged past mistakes in nationality policy, criticized social scientists for excessively optimistic accounts of Soviet achievements, and explored new approaches for dealing with grievances.[40] Recognizing that national tensions could jeopardize his entire reform program, and ultimately his leadership as well, Gorbachev has called for a Central Committee plenum to be devoted to nationality policy. The seriousness of the issue was further underscored by the Nineteenth Party Conference, which devoted one of six final resolutions to inter-ethnic relations and called for the creation of new institutions to deal with nationality policy.

The central thrust of these emerging perspectives on national and social problems is a gradual retreat from utopia and a growing realization of the limits of social engineering. The Khrushchev era represented the height of the optimism and millenialism inspired by the Bolshevik Revolution and revived again during the era of the First Five-Year Plan. It again stimulated optimistic expectations about the future, the perfectibility of socialism, the malleability of human nature, the merging of nations, and the imminence of full communism.

That optimism has steadily receded in the post-Khrushchev era, and Gorbachev's accession dealt it a final blow.[41] The recognition that capitalism has by no means exhausted its potential—and that indeed the gap that Khrushchev so confidently expected to narrow has actually widened in the intervening period—involves a more sober assessment of international as well as domestic realities. The decision to remove from the Party program all concrete targets and explicit goals is a repudiation of a long tradition of exaggerated and unrealistic promises, just as the shift in terminology from "developed socialism" to "developing socialism" extends the time horizon for the achievement of full communism into a remote and indistinct future. Even discussions of the fate of the Soviet multinational system are more likely to emphasize the positive contribution of cultural and national diversity to Soviet life than the aspiration to create a homogeneous Soviet people.

This trend toward greater realism, and indeed outright pessimism, is accompanied by a growing realization that a wide range of social problems may well be structurally rooted in and reproduced under socialism. Where a wide variety of social pathologies—from chauvinism to corruption, from drug addiction and prostitution to crime—were once barely acknowledged and treated as "relics of the past," a phrase that implied a vast chasm would separate the socialist society of the future from its capitalist ancestry, current discussions of a wide range of social problems increasingly accept their universality in all social systems, explore why and how such behaviors are socially reproduced, and focus more on "managing" social problems than on "solving" them.

Moreover, recognizing the limited capacity and resources of the state to address a variety of social needs, and the rigidity and bureaucratization that central control entails, new thinking about social problems is directed to the potential role of voluntary associations and private initiatives in addressing them. Indeed, to the extent that *glasnost'* has focused public attention on a broad range of previously invisible and unacknowledged social problems—from unemployment to homelessness, from abandoned children to the absence of day-care centers for the aged—it has also opened the door to public discussion of how to address them. Terms like "altruism" and "charity" have reappeared in the Soviet lexicon. The campaign for democratization seeks to endow local Soviets with enhanced powers and resources that could permit new initiatives in social policy. The emergence of a wide variety of unofficial organizations creates additional frameworks for private initiatives in the name of compassion and charity. Even the Russian Orthodox Church has begun to press for the right to engage in volunteer activities such as nursing. In short, the reforms under way will both require and permit a pattern of provision for social welfare that joins public and private initiatives in novel ways.

All these trends have far-reaching implications for social science as well as for Soviet policy in the Gorbachev era. They involve the admission that Soviet social science is as yet incapable of contributing to a serious understanding of social reality or of helping to generate a suitable strategy for managing a process of reform, particularly one that demands a "civilized" rather than a forcible resolution of contradictions.

The deplorable state of the social sciences has been recognized at the highest level of the leadership. The Politburo itself met in May 1988 to discuss the need to develop serious social research and training, and a subsequent Central Committee decree spelled out a whole range of measures intended to promote serious research and training in sociology on a nationwide scale.[42]

It has become essential to the reform effort to have and to publish accurate economic and social statistics, as well as information about the needs, interests, values, and behavior of diverse social groups and the possible effects of their behavior on social processes.[43] With this objective in mind, a whole series of additional initiatives have been undertaken to give impetus to the development of the social sciences. Following a series of well-publicized criticisms of official economic and social statistics, the Central Statistical Administration was replaced by a new State Committee for Statistics, charged with "increasing the reliability of information, expanding the purview of *glasnost'*, and deepening the analysis of processes of economic and social development in the country."[44] New textbooks in social studies are being prepared and annual school examinations in history and social studies had to be cancelled in 1988. Political science as a discipline has made further strides toward institutionalization in the past few years, and its growing legitimation was symbolized by the creation, in the summer of 1988, of a new Center for Political Science Research.[45] Sociology has been given even greater prominence under Gorbachev. Not only will formal training and research be expanded in existing universities and institutes; two new institutes for sociological research have recently been established outside the framework of the Academy of Sciences. An All-Union Center for the Study of Public Opinion, under the leadership of Zaslavskaya herself, will conduct surveys designed to assist the leadership in assessing popular reactions to the reform program while the second will focus on socio-economic aspects of *perestroika*.[46]

Ultimately, the capacity of the Soviet system to develop new mechanisms for the expression of social diversity and for the management of conflict will depend on the successful implementation of political and legal reforms. Political changes that would reduce the concentration of power in the hands of the central ministerial and Party apparatus, and movement toward establishment of the rule of law backed by a judiciary with some degree of independence, are essential to any effort to institutionalize the reform process and to provide some guarantee of its irreversibility. Both within the political leadership and among reform-minded scholars, specialists and journalists, serious attention is now being devoted to these issues; and the Nineteenth Party Conference provided some impetus to the process.[47] It is the fate of these efforts that will hold the key to the prospects of Gorbachev's reforms more broadly.

The Social Impact of the Reforms

For the first time since the October Revolution, Soviet society has emerged as a major, though not a unitary, actor on the Soviet political stage. Both its importance and its diversity have been impressed on the consciousness of the political leadership in unprecedented ways. Amorphous yet dynamic, it remains an uncertain weight on the scales of the Soviet future.

Clearly Gorbachev's reforms have been most warmly welcomed among segments of the intelligentsia. The most palpable result of these reforms has been in the cultural sphere, where they have given the cultural intelligentsia considerably enhanced autonomy and have enriched the cultural fare available to consumers of contemporary Soviet culture and the media. A dramatic rise of public interest in political affairs is perhaps the single most visible manifestation of the impact of *glasnost'* and *perestroika*. This is reflected in the soaring circulation of leading newspapers and journals during the past two years, especially those of reformist orientation.[48]

The new atmosphere has also created a degree of trust and perceived reciprocity between the intelligentsia and the regime that had heretofore been missing. Gorbachev's emphasis on the power of ideas and the call for "new thinking" in virtually every domain of Soviet life sets out an agenda that is unprecedentedly dependent on the inputs of specialists and professionals and is more responsive than in the past to their concerns as professionals. Their status and visibility have been correspondingly increased, as have their opportunities for travel abroad. Even within this group, support for the reforms is by no means universal; indeed, the intelligentsia provides leadership for antireformist currents as well. But insofar as we may take Andrei Sakharov as a bellwether of the once dissident, liberal intelligentsia, his supportive stance may be taken as an indication of the relative success of the Gorbachev regime in eliciting "voice" within this milieu.

The benefits of Gorbachev's reform program for other social and occupational groups have been far less apparent. Although the reforms hold out the long-term prospect of improvements in the supply and quality of consumer goods and services, in the short run it has raised expectations that are unlikely to be met. Indeed, the initial impact of the reforms on the economy has been sufficiently disruptive to output and wages to justify the widespread anxieties of Soviet workers. Moreover, discussion of the need for a price reform and the prospect of job insecurity threaten to jeopardize traditional and valued entitlements, whereas the promise of greater workplace democracy is unlikely to offset a real and feared decline in the standard of living. Decades of economic mythmaking have shaped popular expectations in ways that will be politically costly to undo. The simultaneous demand for low prices and abundant supplies of goods and services at those low prices is but one example of the dilemma. For the population at large even *glasnost'* must appear as a mixed blessing because the media no longer offer the comfortable assurance of success and certainty.

The process of reform is at least equally unsettling to important segments of Soviet officialdom and the many millions of state and Party bureaucrats whose role and status under the new arrangements are highly uncertain and whose power is apt to be sharply circumscribed. The widespread skepticism, anxiety, and resistance encountered even at this early stage of reform—and the relatively limited response to the new opportunities it offers for economic initiative—raise troublesome questions about how successfully the process of implementation will proceed.

Fundamental constraints on far-reaching liberalization are also imposed by the structure of the Soviet system itself. The monopoly of political power by the Party could well be maintained even with new electoral arrangements that require a greater degree of responsiveness to societal forces. Public ownership and the limited development of private property rights limits the resources that can be mobilized by independent social actors. These structural features of the Soviet system highlight the far greater obstacles to a transition from authoritarianism in the Soviet case compared to the situations prevailing in Latin America and Latin Europe.

Gorbachev's program confronts additional impediments that stem from the built-in tensions and contradictions of the reform process itself. The urgent need to overcome stagnation and social alienation by stimulating initiative conflicts with the fear of losing control. The acknowledged need for greater diversity of opinions is widely seen as threatening to the principles of socialism itself. Greater permissiveness and tolerance of various forms of social nonconformity and political protest leave unclear the boundaries of "anti-Soviet" behavior. Finally, while the reformers have come to view political democratization as a condition of economic reform, there are also obvious tensions between the two. Whether within the workplace or at a national level, a substantial expansion of political participation could well create greater constraints on the reform process.

Attitudinal constraints, deeply rooted in Soviet political culture, are a further inhibiting factor. Although neither pervasive nor unchangeable, the widespread attitude toward change appears to reflect an instinctive calculus that the danger of losses outweighs the hope of gains. Moreover, there are remnants of an anticommercial ethos long reinforced by Party ideology that inclines at least a part of the population to be suspicious of private entrepreneurship. There is also a deeply engrained tendency to equate egalitarianism with social justice, which serves as an obstacle to efforts to link rewards to performance.

What is especially striking in the Soviet case is the general poverty of sociopolitical thought, a poverty that extends even to the Soviet emigration. In the absence of more comprehensive sociopolitical programs that would offer viable alternatives to the status quo, vague sentiments that range from romantic nationalism to extreme chauvinism risk to fill the void.

A final set of constraints on potential liberalization is the depth of social and national cleavages. The chasm of mutual distrust between the Russian working class and intellilgentsia was mirrored even in the distance between the dissident intellectuals and the attempts at a free trade-union movement, although in some non-Russian republics, from the Baltic to Armenia, the force of nationalism provides precisely such a bond. Ironically but not surprisingly, the extension of *glasnost'* and "democratization" has brought national tensions and antagonisms to the surface. The Gorbachev leadership may well be persuaded that allowing the expression of grievances is a necessary first step in successfully addressing them; but new political and legal mechanisms for conflict management remain to be developed.

Notes

1. B. P. Kurashvili, in *Sovetskoe gosudarstvo i pravo*, no. 10 (1983).

2. *Pravda*, January 31, 1987. Gorbachev's remarks virtually echo the diagnoses of Soviet political, economic, and social problems in the chapters by Seweryn Bialer, Robert Campbell, and Gail Lapidus in Robert Byrnes, ed., *After Brezhnev: The Sources of Soviet Conduct in the 1980s* (Bloomington: Indiana University Press, 1983). Gorbachev's views are strikingly congruent with the those of the reformist Soviet economic sociologist, Tat'yana Zaslavskaya.

3. *Pravda*, August 2, 1986.

4. See Kenneth Jowitt, "Inclusion and Mobilization in Marxist-Leninist Political Systems," *World Politics* (October 1975), pp. 69–97, for an insightful discussion of this issue.

5. Albert Hirschman introduced these terms to describe the options available to a customer faced by deteriorating performance of a firm: to stop buying its products and turn to competitors or to express dissatisfaction to management in an effort to alter its behavior. *Exit, Voice and Loyalty* (Cambridge, Mass.: Harvard University Press, 1970), p. 59.

6. "Appeal for a Gradual Democratization," in George Saunders, ed., *Samizdat: Voices of the Soviet Opposition* (New York: Monad Press, 1974), p. 405.

7. This principle has been advocated by leading Soviet public figures, including academician V. N. Kudryavtsev, director of the Academy of Sciences Institute of State and Law. See *Voprosy filosofii*, 1 (January 1987).

8. See, for example, Konstantin Chernenko, in *Kommunist*, no. 13 (1981), pp. 10–11.

9. For a useful overview drawn from Latin American experiences, see Guillermo O'Donnell et al., *Transitions from Authoritarian Rule: Comparative Perspectives* (Baltimore: Johns Hopkins University Press, 1986).

10. Tsentral'noe statisticheskoe upravlenie, *Narodnoe khoziaistvo SSSR* (Moscow: Finansy i Statistika, 1987), pp. 523, 647.

11. These trends are discussed in some detail in Gail W. Lapidus, "Social Trends," in Byrnes, *After Brezhnev.*

12. Brian Silver, "Political Beliefs of the Soviet Citizen: Sources of Support for Regime Norms," in James Millar, ed., *Politics, Work and Daily Life in the USSR* (Cambridge: Cambridge University Press, 1987). Similar trends by age cohort were revealed in a poll of Muscovites conducted at the Institute of Sociological Research of the Soviet Academy of Sciences for the *New York Times* and CBS News in May 1988. See *New York Times*, May 27, 1988, p. A7. By contrast, among the refugees from World War II interviewed in the Harvard Project of the 1950s, regime support was greater among younger age cohorts and increased with level of education. Raymond Bauer and Alex Inkeles, *The Soviet Citizen* (Cambridge, Mass.: Harvard University Press, 1959). Support for regime norms was higher among those respondents who reported high levels of material satisfaction, but "satisfaction" was highly dependent on subjective perceptions. Recent Soviet research, for example, found that residents of Moscow and Leningrad were in fact less satisfied with the quality of life they enjoyed than were respondents from seventeen other cities because the former's higher expectations created a wider gap between aspirations and real possibilities. See also Oleg Bozhkov and Valeri Golofast, "Otsenka naseleniem uslovii zhizni v krupnykh gorodakh," *Sotsiologicheskie issledovaniia*, no. 3 (1985).

13. *New York Times*, November 4, 1987.

14. *Pravda*, April 18, 1987. Yakovlev's views are more fully developed in his "Dostizhenie kachestvenno novogo sostoianiia sovetskogo obshchestva i obshchestvennye nauki," *Kommunist*, no. 8 (1987).

15. Films such as Abuladze's *Repentance* and novels such as Anatoli Rybakov's *Children of the Arbat* helped reopen the Stalin question. Gorbachev's seventieth anniversary speech reaffirmed elements of the prevailing orthodoxy regarding Lenin and Stalin but was unflinching in referring to Stalin's "unpardonable crimes," broke new ground in defending Lenin's New Economic Policy and his essay "On Cooperation" as precedents for Gorbachev's own reforms. He also presented both Bukharin and Khrushchev in a more positive vein than has been customary. A number of articles have since appeared in the Soviet press offering a favorable appraisal of Khrushchev's contributions.

16. Indeed, a recent article explicitly blames Leonid Brezhnev and his Politburo colleague and Party ideologist Mikhail Suslov for the emergence of a Soviet dissident movement because they destroyed the key vehicle for criticism of Stalinism, namely Aleksandr Tvardovsky's journal, *Novyi mir.* Yuri Burtin as cited in Julia Wishnevsky, "A Guide to Some Major Soviet Journals," Radio Liberty Research Bulletin, RL Supplement 2/88 (July 20, 1988).

17. *Pravda*, November 3, 1987.

18. Yakovlev in *Pravda*, April 18, 1987.

19. *Izvestiya*, October 28, 1986.

20. *Pravda*, April 18, 1987.

21. See, for instance, the debates over the meaning of social justice, in *Kommunist*, no. 13 (1986). A wide array of Soviet journals now provide an unprecedented forum for discussion and debate on major issues of domestic development.

22. The argument is more fully developed in Gail W. Lapidus, "KAL and Chernobyl: The Soviet Management of Crises," *Survival* (May/June 1987).

23. *Pravda*, February 6, 1987.

24. An editorial in *Kommunist* in October 1987 defended this new orientation, contrasting Lenin's tolerant approach to culture and to the intelligentsia with Stalin's arbitrary effort to impose "bureaucratic regulation."

25. *Literaturnaia gazeta*, May 13, 1987.

26. Ibid., May 13 and June 8, 1987.

27. See, for example, V. Dashichev, in *Literaturnaia gazeta*, May 18, 1988; A. Bovin, in *Izvestiya*, June 16, 1988; V. Berezhkov, in *Sovetskaia molodezh*, August 20, 1987; and A. Bovin, in *Literaturnaia gazeta*, March 16, 1988.

28. See Murray Yanowitch, *The Social Structure of the USSR* (Armonk, N.Y.: M. E. Sharpe, 1986) for a useful collection of translations of important Soviet articles.

29. The debate was launched by academician Petr Fedoseyev in *Problemy mira i sotsializma*, 9 (September 1981), and was taken up by the journal *Voprosy filosofii* in articles by Vadim Semenov (9 [September 1982]) and Anatoliy Butenko (10 [October 1982] and 2 [1984]). Their views were attacked in a series of articles in *Pravda* and in *Kommunist*.

30. *Voprosy filosofii*, 2 (February 1987).

31. *Moskovskaya pravda*, May 7, 1987, p. 3, as quoted in *Current Digest of the Soviet Press* 39, no. 18 (June 3, 1987), p. 3.

32. *Kommunist*, no. 13 (1986). Zaslavskaya's long-standing advocacy of an "interest group" approach to the Soviet political economy is reflected in her editorship of a journal on economic sociology, which focuses on "the analysis of the development of the economy as a social process representing the specific behavior and interaction of classes, strata and groups in Soviet society." T. I. Zaslavskaya and R. V. Ryvkina, *Izvestiia sibirskogo otdeleniia akademii nauk SSSR: seriia ekonomiki i prikladnoi sotsiologii*, no. 1 (January 1984).

33. When Tat'yana Zaslavskaya first referred to entrenched bureaucratic opposition to reform (*Ekonomika i organizatsiia promyshlennogo proizvodstva*, 7 [1985], pp. 3–22), it was a striking statement. The discussion of bureaucracy and its interests has now become a staple of the Soviet media. See, for example, Vladimir Shubkin, *Znamya*, April 1987, pp. 162–186, and the roundtable on *Ogonyok*, March 12, 1988.

34. Samizdat Archive, "Beseda chlenov soiuza pisatelei SSSR s M. S. Gorbachevym," AS no. 5785 (June 19, 1986).

35. A sharp exchange over the desirability of allowing informal associations to nominate candidates to stand in new Soviet elections was carried in *Izvestiya*, March 20, 1988, p. 3.

36. *Pravda*, October 18, 1961, p. 1. For a more extensive discussion of the evolution of Soviet views, see Gail W. Lapidus, "Ethnonationalism and Political Stability: The Soviet Case," *World Politics* 36 (July 1984).

37. *Pravda*, February 24, 1981.

38. *Pravda*, December 22, 1982.

39. Ibid.

40. The new elements in the present approach involve an unprecedented acknowledgment of past errors in nationality policy, including the treatment of the Baltic states; a fresh approach to bilingualism, which offers more scope for teaching and using national languages; and a search for new procedures and mechanisms for addressing national grievances. See *Kommunist*, no. 3 and no. 13 (1987).

41. For two important treatments of this broad theme, see John Bushnell, "The 'New Soviet Man' Turns Pessimist," in Stephen Cohen et al., eds., *The Soviet Union Since Stalin* (Bloomington: Indiana University Press, 1980), pp. 179–199; and Alexander Dallin, "Retreat from Optimism," in Seweryn Bialer and Sophie Sluzar, eds., *Radicalism in the Contemporary Age*, III (Boulder, CO: Westview, 1977), pp. 117–157.

42. *Pravda*, May 13, 1988; *Izvestiya*, June 12, 1988.

43. Zaslavskaya has sharply criticized the suppression of economic and social statistics and has charged that the Soviet Union is in last place among developed countries in the level of publicly available social statistics, a criticism echoed by Gorbachev himself. (*Pravda*, February 6, 1987.)

44. *Pravda*, August 7, 1987.

45. For a useful discussion, see Archie Brown in Alexander Dallin and Bertrand Patenaude, eds., *Soviet Scholarship Under Gorbachev* (Stanford: Stanford University Press, 1988).

46. *Pravda*, March 18, 1988.

47. The need for a socialist *Rechtsstaat* (*sotsialisticheskoe pravovoe gosudarstvo*) was endorsed by the Nineteenth Party Conference, discussed on the front page of *Pravda*, August 2, 1988, and elaborated in *Kommunist* no. 11 (1988). The inadequacy of Soviet political institutions, and the need for a socialist "theory of checks and balances," was a major theme of the 1987 annual conference of the Soviet Association of Political Sciences (Archie Brown, in Dallin and Patenaude, *Soviet Scholarship Under Gorbachev*).

48. Total subscriptions have increased over 18 million in the past year alone, while the number of subscribers to *Ogonyok* doubled, from 561,415 to 1,313,349. *Novyi mir* reached a record 1,150,000 in January 1988 (*Moscow News*, no. 8 [1988], Wishnevsky, "A Guide to Some Major Soviet Journals"). The letters editor of *Ogonyok* reported that the volume of mail from readers had also increased dramatically, from 15,000 letters in 1986 to 50,000 in 1987 to 20,000 in the first three months of 1988 (*New York Times*, April 24, 1988).

5

The Sobering of Gorbachev: Nationality, Restructuring, and the West

Alexander J. Motyl

The massive nationalist demonstrations that erupted in Soviet Armenia in February 1988 surely surprised Mikhail Sergeyevich Gorbachev as much as they perturbed him. For seven decades, the Armenians had all the makings of a model Soviet nationality. Materially satisfied and politically loyal, they had not been a major policy concern since the early 1920s, when they opposed the Red Army's takeover of their independent state. Literally overnight, the demonstrations changed the image the Armenians presented to the rest of the world. A watershed in the development of the republic, the demonstrations transformed Armenia from an exotic backwater into a paragon of popular mobilization.[1]

If as many as 1 million Armenian demonstrators were manifestly infected by nationalism, then it is likely that the virus is much more virulent than Soviet officials have been willing to admit. As disturbing as this fact must be for the Kremlin, it would be a gross error for Western observers to conclude that the Armenian events herald an incipient nationalist rebellion or an impending civil war. Rather, the importance of the demonstrations lies in what they hold for Gorbachev's program of restructuring (*perestroika*) the Soviet system. The demonstrations are a foretaste of the side effects of *perestroika* and suggest that the "national question" of the Soviet Union may prove to be the rock on which Gorbachev's reforms may founder. As Gorbachev has haltingly come to realize, he confronts a dilemma: On the one hand, *perestroika* is necessary to revive the system; on the other, it is likely to aggravate the national problem and, in the long run, to threaten Soviet stability.

The Non-Russians and Central Authority

Western policymakers, scholars, and journalists have often treated the Soviet national question as a peripheral concern. Moscow in general, and the Kremlin in particular, are perceived as "where the action is," with the result that non-Russians are reduced to nonissues. This perception is not only erroneous, but also pernicious. By skewing Western understanding of the Soviet Union, it can but negatively affect Western policy toward that country as well.

What does the phrase "the Soviet national question" mean? It refers to the political, socioeconomic, and cultural interplay among the Russian-dominated Party-state, the dominant Russian majority, and the subordinate non-Russians. That interplay consists in a perpetual tug of war between the centralizing and decentralizing tendencies built into the Union of Soviet Socialist Republics at its founding in the early 1920s. The Soviet federal system is the product of the confrontation from 1917 to 1921 between a Russian-led Communist Party based in the largely Russian cities as well as the working class and a variety of non-Russian nationalist forces drawing on the non-Russian countryside for support. The Bolsheviks eventually won, to a large extent because of their ability to win non-Russian allies by promising them the "right to self-determination up to separation." Although separation (or, in U.S. terms, secession from the Union) was declared counterrevolutionary once the "dictatorship of the proletariat" had been established and the bourgeois bases of national enmity putatively abolished, the political and ideological imperative of granting the non-Russians a degree of self-rule and cultural autonomy remained. A system of ethnically designated administrative units and republican branches of the Party was constructed, one that has survived largely unchanged to this day.

Today, approximately one-half of the 275 million inhabitants of the Soviet Union are non-Russians.[2] Like the Russians, fourteen nations inhabit so-called union republics, and more than thirty others live in autonomous republics, provinces, and regions. Each non-Russian republic has its own Party organization, Council of Ministers, Supreme Soviet, constitution, flag, hymn, and capital city. The Ukrainian and Belorussian republics even have seats in the United Nations, the International Labor Organization, UNESCO, and other international organs.[3] Although Soviet propaganda holds that the republics are sovereign entities bound together in a voluntary federation, their sovereignty is largely symbolic while their dependence on Moscow is very real. Although the reins have been loosened since Iosif Stalin's rule, political power is still lodged in the central organs of the Communist Party and government apparatus in

Moscow, and Russians continue to dominate the system politically, socially, and culturally.

Appearances to the contrary notwithstanding, the republics and their populations do, in fact, play an important role in the Soviet system in general and the process of the formulation of policy in particular. First, republican elites influence central policies by making substantive contributions to the decisionmaking process and by implementing resulting measures according to their own cultural perceptions and local requirements. Second, the very presence of the non-Russian republics demands of Moscow that it adopt ethnic policies that are specifically designed to meet their needs and address their demands. Third, the non-Russians and their sensitivities always figure in Moscow's calculations of popular reactions to its policies because virtually every technically nonethnic issue in the USSR—economic efficiency, labor supply, education, and so on—has an ethnic component that must be considered by Kremlin policymakers.

These three points illustrate the contradictory nature of the relationship between the non-Russians and central authority. On the one hand, the non-Russians willingly participate in the policy process, attempt to utilize it for their own advantage, and thereby legitimize both the status quo and their subordinate status within it. On the other hand, Moscow remains constantly fearful that non-Russian initiative will get out of hand, translate into rejection of Moscow's supervision, and spark bona fide separatist tendencies. Although non-Russian elites generally support the system and consider themselves Soviet, the Kremlin's fears are not groundless. World War I and II testify to the fact that non-Russian loyalty to Moscow is a function of its ability to maintain control over the periphery. By the same token, national communism—or the tendency of local Communists to pursue "national roads" to communism—has flourished when the Party-state has retreated to the "commanding heights" of the polity or economy, as it did in the 1920s and 1960s. To sum up, it is the proclivity of the non-Russians to define their own interests and to go their own way whenever Moscow permits them to do so by relinquishing some central control.

It is not an exaggeration to say that preventing and containing non-Russian nationalism—the belief in and pursuit by non-Russians of political independence—is the main purpose of Soviet policy toward the non-Russians. Although both nationalist beliefs and nationalist behavior are anathema to the Soviet authorities, the latter, logically, is deemed to be more unacceptable. Nationalist beliefs are the target of frequent invective, but they cannot alone undermine the state. Nationalist behavior, by contrast, can, and it has therefore always been repressed by the Soviet authorities, quickly and usually violently.

As the Soviets realize, however, nationalist behavior can be pursued out of conviction, expedience, or necessity—that is, both by bona fide believers in political independence and by nonbelievers who rationally respond to political and economic incentives and disincentives by acting *as if* independence and sovereignty were their primary goal. Indeed, the history of the international Communist movement suggests that even ostensibly internationalist goals may be best pursued—some would say, can *only* be pursued—within a nationalist framework. Coping with the subjectively nationalist behavior of genuine separatists is relatively easy for a superpower with the apparatus of a formidable secret police.[4] It is far more difficult to manage the objectively nationalist behavior of seemingly loyal Soviet elites. Here, repression alone is insufficient because the root of the problem—the political-economic conditions that induced these elites to pursue national communism in the first place—must be addressed. But these very conditions are the crux of the Kremlin's dilemma. If, as I shall argue, the circumstances that drive non-Russian elites to place the interests of their own nations above all else are the unintended consequence of central policies, then such policies have built-in limits on their ultimate success. Indeed, to use the language of Marxian dialectics, they may well result in their own negation.

The Nature of Present-day Non-Russian Republics

The most striking characteristic of the non-Russian republics today is the enormous progress they have made since the early 1920s. These previously illiterate peasant societies with little industry and tiny in-telligentsias all now possess, to varying extents, well-educated popu-lations, large working classes, extensive economic bases, and self-confident and increasingly assertive elites. Soviet propaganda may or may not be correct in attributing this progress to socialism, but one thing is certain: Developed non-Russian republics represent a qualitatively new challenge for the Soviet leadership. The 1986 Party Program implicitly accepted this view by stating that the "nationalities question *inherited from the past* has been successfully solved in the Soviet Union."[5] The political, economic, and cultural resources now possessed by the republics translate into increasing influence and weight in the Soviet system and its policy process. The national question has come into its own, not only as a policy problem but also as a central concern.

Politically, the last two-and-a-half decades have seen the rise of formidable republican Party machines. The dismantling of Stalinism, Nikita Khrushchev's subsequent encouragement of greater non-Russian representation in central and local Party-state organs, and Leonid Brezhnev's policy of "stability of cadres" have combined to create pockets of political autonomy outside Moscow. Non-Russian elites have rushed to fill this vacuum by establishing their own ethnic networks and extending local control over as much of a republic as possible. Uzbekistan's Sharaf Rashidov, Kazakhstan's Dinmukhamed Kunayev, the Ukraine's Vladimir Shcherbitsky and Petr Shelest, Georgia's Vasilii Mzhavanadze, Lithuania's Antanas Snieckus, and Kirgizia's Turdakun Usubaliyev represent the new breed of republican Party boss willing and able to dish out favors, to advance ethnic personnel, and to establish local bailiwicks not unlike old-fashioned U.S. ward politicians. Although their motives are not nationalistic, these non-Russian elites inevitably place local interests above all-Union ones and generally resist efforts to submit to Moscow's direction. For a conservative politician in Brezhnev's mold, such a locally oriented style may have been of little concern; but for a would-be radical reformer such as Gorbachev, republican empire building is inevitably a major problem.

Economically, the decades since Stalin have witnessed the emergence of two related trends. First, there has been a tendency toward economic equalization among the republics. Although vast differences still abound, especially between the industrially advanced northwest and the lagging southeast, the fact remains that the underdeveloped regions of the USSR have made enormous strides thanks to purposeful central policy. Second, serious regional imbalances have emerged, partly as a result of the trend toward equalization. Industry and infrastructure are still largely concentrated in the resource- and labor-poor European part of the Soviet Union west of the Urals. Mineral resources are increasingly found in the industrially undeveloped and sparsely populated Siberia. Surplus labor is concentrated in Central Asia, where industry is weak. Bringing industry, resources, and labor together is of great importance to the Soviet Union's continued growth and modernization. Yet, correcting these regional imbalances while maintaining a commitment to republican equalization will be difficult. Building industry in the south or east means diverting resources from the more prosperous west; modernizing the industrial base in the west, however, means investing less in the south and east. Similarly, inducing Central Asians to migrate to the north and west is problematic in light of their cultural preferences and the lack of incentive given that standards of living have significantly improved in the "sun-belt" of the Soviet Union. Some kind of balance may well be found, but it will require time and political finesse. Even General Secretary Gorbachev may not possess these in sufficient measure.

The economic problem is exacerbated by a demographic one: the enormous growth rates—three times that of the Soviet average in the twenty-year period from 1959 to 1979—of the Soviet Muslim population in Kazakhstan, Central Asia, and Azerbaijan. Even if, as is likely, the rising curve of Muslim population growth flattens out, the Soviet authorities will have to contend with two problems. First, Soviet Muslims have managed to retain a sense of community and separateness from the Russians in the face of frequent prosecution and seven decades of antireligious propaganda. Increased numbers may reinforce their sense of identity at a particularly inauspicious time, as Islamic fundamentalism undergoes a resurgence on the southern borders of the Soviet Union. Second, because of their relatively poor knowledge of Russian, the USSR's lingua franca, the ever-growing cohort of young Muslims poses a special problem for Soviet economic and military planners. A modern economy and army require language proficiency, and although there is no reason that Muslims should not eventually acquire Russian-language skills, the process is likely to be both lengthy and disruptive.

Culturally, the decades since World War II have witnessed an unprecedented expansion of national consciousness among all Soviet ethnic groups, including the Russians. It was not supposed to work out this way according to Communist ideology, which had asserted (as it still continues to do) that "friendship of peoples" and "proletarian internationalism" would grow by leaps and bounds and nations would merge to form a single "Soviet people." Indeed, the opposite has taken place. The ethnic groups of the Soviet Union are more vigorous than ever, and their concern for native languages and cultures is unquestionably on the rise. Although national consciousness does not alone pose a threat to Soviet stability, it can contribute to nationalism, which does. More fundamentally, a growing sense of ethnicity greatly complicates Moscow's management of the system. The more Soviet citizens think and view problems in ethnic terms, the more difficult it becomes for policymakers to ignore the ethnic factor in making policy choices. U.S., Canadian, and European politicians understand these constraints, and we can be sure that their Soviet counterparts do as well.

Naturally enough, education and publishing are two of the Soviet policy issues of greatest concern to the non-Russians. The Soviet ideological commitment to cultural development requires that resources be channeled in support of local languages and publications; the necessity of having a Russian lingua franca and of catering to the cultural wishes of the dominant Russian majority, however, means that Russian language, culture, and values are vigorously propagated as well. Finding a balance between the Russian and the non-Russian imperatives has proven to be virtually impossible, with the weight historically having been placed on the Russian side of the scales. As a result, where the authorities and the Russians see only the propagation and inculcation of ethnically neutral Soviet values, or Sovietization, non-Russians see a threat to their ethnic identity—they see Russification. To make matters worse, Moscow's occasional stabs at evenhandedness have often produced discontent among the Russians who resent being treated as the cultural and political equals of the non-Russians.

Education is an especially sensitive area because in the Soviet Union, as in North America and Western Europe, it is a prerequisite of social mobility. Since the early 1960s, the Soviet government has assiduously pursued educational and professional affirmative action for the non-Russians. The number of non-Russians receiving secondary and higher education has greatly increased, a non-Russian professional class has emerged, and the republican bureaucracies have become career paths for the natives. Although social mobility has doubtless contributed to stability, such a massive and rapid expansion of educational opportunities has also produced negative effects. It has resulted in a surplus of graduates of sometimes dubious ability; it has also skewed popular perception of the status associated with certain jobs and careers. It is difficult to imagine how the recent Soviet school reform, which hopes to bring the Soviet educational system more in line with the needs of a modern economy, can successfully address these problems without at least a partial reversal of affirmative action.

The educational dilemma is further complicated by the fact that the expansion of opportunities for most non-Russians has coincided with—indeed, has probably contributed to—the decline in opportunities for Soviet Jews. Traditionally better educated than most Soviet citizens, Jews came to bear the brunt of Soviet attempts to raise the educational levels of other ethnic groups. Such a policy also dovetailed with official hostility toward Israel, Zionism, and Jews. In any case, a policy of equal educational opportunities may not mix well with a policy of equal results. Some ethnic groups inevitably will do better than others.

Are these problems so great that they pose a threat to the stability of the system? No. Moreover, none of them is insoluble. For all their truculence, Sharaf Rashidov, Dinmukhamed Kunayev, and other republican bosses were in fact ousted, and a similar fate probably awaits Vladimir Shcherbitsky. Some combination of modernization and investment, coupled with Russian-language training, may resolve the problem of regional imbalance without alienating the Muslims. In principle, national consciousness can be channeled in support of the system, while genuine nationalists can always be repressed. It is important for Western observers to avoid the oversimplification they would certainly reject if it were applied to their own societies. Nevertheless, as Soviet society grows more complex and as the republican share of that complexity increases, the impact of the national question on both the system and its policy will grow correspondingly. Dealing effectively, wisely, and humanely with the increasing importance of the non-Russians may be the greatest challenge facing Soviet policymakers in the near future.

Gorbachev's Education
in the Nationality Issue

If any sphere of Soviet politics illustrates both the manner in which Mikhail Gorbachev has learned while in office and the difficulties attendant upon learning about difficult subjects, it is the national question. Gorbachev is no newcomer to this problem area, if only for personal reasons: His wife Raisa is partly Ukrainian, and Mikhail Sergeyevich himself reportedly speaks some Ukrainian.[6] Moreover, by the time he had been appointed General Secretary in March 1985, he had already accumulated a good deal of working experience with the multinational nature of the Soviet Union.

Until 1978, when Gorbachev was promoted to Moscow, his entire Party career had been centered in Stavropol, an ethnically heterogeneous north Caucasus territory that administratively encompasses an autonomous province inhabited by the Karachai and Cherkess, two small nations subjected to severe repressions by Stalin for alleged collaboration with the Germans in World War II.[7] In fact, Gorbachev made two speeches on the "friendship of peoples" as early as 1972, and despite his position as Central Committee Secretary in charge of agriculture, he was considered sufficiently expert on nationality issues to travel to Lithuania in June 1980, where he delivered an ornate oration on the "Friendship of USSR Peoples—an Invaluable Achievement," in celebration of the fortieth anniversary of Lithuania's annexation to the Soviet Union.[8]

What do these speeches tell us about the early Gorbachev? Only that he expressed the official line. His early pronouncements on the national question are notable only for their dullness, cliches, and naive optimism. They seemed to assume there was nothing more to Soviet national relations than harmony, friendship, brotherhood, and boundless love. New ideas may have been germinating in his mind in the 1970s and early 1980s, but there is nothing in these speeches to indicate that they extended to the question of the Soviet nationalities.

The tenor of Gorbachev's comments concerning nationality changed little after his appointment as General Secretary. His March 11th, 1985, acceptance speech made the obligatory reference to the "steadfast strengthening of the friendship of peoples of our great multinational state."[9] His May 8th, 1985, speech on the fortieth anniversary of victory in World War II repeated the same platitudes that Brezhnev never tired of stating: "The blossoming of nations and nationalities is organically connected to their all-round drawing together. Into the consciousness and heart of every person there has deeply entered the feeling of belonging to a single family—the Soviet people, a new and historically unprecedented social and international community."[10] If anything, the speech was regressive in that Gorbachev unnecessarily praised the "great Russian people" and Stalin for their role in the war. Gorbachev's Russocentric inclinations appeared to surface on June 25, 1985, when in an impromptu talk in Kiev he transposed the USSR with Russia.[11] Whatever the psychological importance of this misstatement, it confirmed that Gorbachev's attitude toward the non-Russians was one of complacency at best and lack of interest at worst.

But things were to change, and radically so. On May 9 and 15, 1985, anti-Russian riots erupted in Latvia's capital city, Riga. In November and December 1985 and in January 1986, meanwhile, in addition to the continuing cleanup in Sharaf Rashidov's former fiefdom, Uzbekistan, major personnel changes were implemented in several republics in preparation for the republican Party congresses planned for early 1986. New Party first secretaries were assigned to Kirgizia, Tadzhikistan, and Turkmenistan; Azerbaijan and Moldavia received new chairmen of their local Supreme Soviets. In addition, new KGB chiefs were appointed in Kirgizia and Kazakhstan, while internal affairs ministers were replaced in Uzbekistan, Tadzhikistan, and Georgia.

The changes were obviously preceded by several months' painful examination and deliberation, an experience that appears to have conflicted with Gorbachev's tranquil image of national relations. Not surprisingly, his own speech at the Twenty-seventh Party Congress in February 1986 reflected his growing doubts about the status of the national question. The six paragraphs Gorbachev devoted to the nationalities contained their share of cliches, but for the first time in his career he spoke openly of "contradictions" and other problems that threatened to undermine the "fraternal friendship of peoples." But what was the Party to do about these problems? At this point, Gorbachev recommended more of the same: uncompromising opposition to nationalism and chauvinism; sensitivity; creativity; adaptability; and other practically meaningless measures. Significantly, the most concrete of Gorbachev's suggestions—opposition to nationalism and chauvinism— was negative. His positive recommendations were so vague as to be worthless as guidelines.[12]

In the months that followed the Party Congress, some rumblings were heard among non-Russian intellectuals, but it was not until mid-December 1986 that Gorbachev's idyllic image of nationality relations was finally shattered. To make matters worse, shock after shock would follow throughout 1987. On December 17–18, mass anti-Russian riots erupted in Kazakhstan's capital, Alma-Ata, after Gennadi Kolbin, a Russian, replaced Dinmukhamed Kunayev, a Kazakh, as Party First Secretary. Thousands of students—many of them Komsomol members—participated, some carrying banners calling for autonomy and a U.N. seat for Kazakhstan. Store windows were smashed, cars burned, and policemen attacked.[13] Events such as these were said to take place only in colonialist and capitalist countries, not in the Soviet Union, which, as the Party Program insisted, had definitively and completely solved the national question.

At the other end of the country, in Riga, anti-Russian demonstrations took place in late December 1986 and early January 1987. Jewish dissidents participated in several days of protest in Moscow on February 10–13, 1987. Nationalist demonstrations again broke out in the Latvian capital on April 19. Several weeks later, in May, a newly formed Russian chauvinist group, Pamyat' (Memory), staged a series of noisy and ominously anti-Semitic public meetings. Much to the consternation of Jews and other non-Russians, the supporters of Pamyat' appeared to be legion and the authorities' handling of the group relatively lenient. Riga was the site of another disturbance on June 14.

Crimean Tatars besieged Moscow for most of July, demanding the right to return to their ancestral homeland in the Crimea. August 23— the day on which the Molotov-Ribbentrop Pact had been signed in 1939—was particularly tense as nationalist demonstrations took place in the Baltic capitals, Riga, Tallinn, and Vilnius. Then, in early October, an unofficial Ukrainian peace group took to the streets in Lvov. Finally, national unrest climaxed in February 1988, when hundreds of thousands of Armenians marched through the streets of Yerevan demanding that Nagorno-Karabakh, an Armenian-populated province in neighboring Azerbaijan, be annexed to Armenia. So many demonstrations in so short a time are unprecedented in recent Soviet history, and it is difficult to imagine that they failed to bring Gorbachev to his senses.[14]

The sobering of Gorbachev was evident at the January 1987 Central Committee Plenum. The self-laudatory and complacent tone of his earlier pronouncements was gone. Instead, it was clear that Gorbachev now realized that the roots of the Alma-Ata riots were not unique to Kazakhstan and that the Party had actually made "mistakes" in implementing its national policy. Gorbachev also accused Soviet social scientists of having painted an excessively optimistic picture of national relations, and—in what may have been an indirect form of self-criticism—he said that "it was long not accepted to speak" of mistakes. As refreshing as was Gorbachev's growing sophistication, he again had few positive recommendations. He expressed his support for equitable ethnic representation in Party and state organs, for an intensification of "internationalist education," greater candor, and so on, but all of this was familiar ground. On the other hand, Gorbachev's list of measures he opposed had grown to include "all manifestations of national narrow-mindedness and conceit, nationalism and chauvinism, parochialism, Zionism, and anti-Semitism."[15]

Still, Gorbachev was clearly learning, as became painfully clear in February 1987, when he visited Latvia and Estonia. In contrast to his upbeat 1980 speech in Lithuania, Gorbachev now sounded distinctly apologetic and ill at ease. With no trace of irony, he noted that the "Baltic peoples' road to socialism had been thorny and complex" and that there had been "omissions," "miscalculations," and "strain" in the Soviet Baltic experience. He also felt obliged to compare nationality relations in the Soviet Union with those under "imperialism" and to reject émigré "bourgeois nationalist" insinuations regarding Soviet national policy. No less striking, however, was his complete lack of openness about the shameful circumstances of Stalin's annexation of the Baltic states in 1940.[16] Gorbachev took one step forward only to take one step backward.

A similar dialectic was evident at the close of 1987. Just two months after a frank official statement on the national question appeared in the September issue of the theoretical Party journal, *Kommunist*, Gorbachev retreated to Brezhnevian platitudes in his otherwise groundbreaking November 2 speech commemorating the seventieth anniversary of the 1917 Revolution. This relapse notwithstanding, the *Kommunist* editorial, which may be assumed to represent Gorbachev's own views, remains an important milestone in Gorbachev's political growth. First, the document all but acknowledged that nationality relations were in as much difficulty as was the rest of the Soviet system; the friendship of peoples might be an ideal, but it was certainly not a reality. Second, the continued prominence of national tensions was explained in terms of Russia's backwardness at the time of the revolution—a clear-cut admission that contradictions about the national question were inherent in the system and were not merely "survivals of the past." Third, nationalist disturbances were attributed to "extremists" who misused *glasnost'* and democracy, while the "leading Soviet intelligentsia" was enjoined to be "implacable towards any manifestations" of subjectivism, passions, and political frivolity. Finally, the *Kommunist* editorial addressed non-Russian language concerns and recommended that both Russian and non-Russian languages—and not primarily the former—be cultivated in the republics and that both Russians and non-Russians be bilingual.[17] As the first substantive official statement on the national question since Gorbachev's appointment, the article was remarkable not only for engaging in public self-criticism, but also for making concessions to the linguistic demands of non-Russians as well as for strongly implying that there were clear nationality-related limits to *glasnost'*.

Regardless of whether these verbal assurances ever become policy, their importance lies in the fact that they are concessions. As Gorbachev's belated call in early 1988 for a special Central Committee plenum on nationality relations indicates, the Kremlin is reacting to and not acting upon the national question. Such meek behavior is clearly atypical for Gorbachev, who generally finds himself in the role of the radical innovator surrounded by lethargic bureaucrats and citizens. That the non-Russian elites have taken the lead in arguing for *perestroika* in national relations and have succeeded in imposing some of their preferences on the Kremlin means that it must be particularly reluctant to tinker with existing national arrangements to the point of deeming them outside the entire reform program.

What can account for this reluctance? Although it would be naive to think that Gorbachev believes all he says about the indissoluble friendship of peoples, it is nonetheless possible that the Soviet leadership acquired an idealized view of nationality relations as a result of its lack of contact with the grass roots of Soviet society in the Brezhnev era. A far more plausible explanation, however, is that Gorbachev has purposely been mouthing platitudes in order to avoid dealing with the Pandora's box of ethnicity. This is a classic example of a nondecision. Soviet leaders know of their country's frequent ethnic conflicts, of Soviet federalism's contradictory nature, and of non-Russian resentment of Russian dominance. These leaders surely understand that restructuring nationality relations is both supremely difficult and dangerously complex in that it can lead to questions regarding the Russian–non-Russian relationship that should not be raised and cannot be answered. Gorbachev's lack of interest in and seeming complacency about the nationalities are thus partly genuine and partly false. On the one hand, he is "confusing wishes for reality," as Soviet propaganda calls such self-delusionary behavior; on the other, he is intentionally avoiding an issue that can only seriously complicate the political, economic, and social reforms he wants to effect.

It is precisely for this second reason that Gorbachev continually emphasizes what should be avoided—such as nationalism and chauvinism—and the limits to *glasnost'*. Gorbachev knows that *perestroika* inevitably has profound implications for the nationality question. If it upsets the delicate imbalance between central and peripheral authority too much in the direction of the periphery, *perestroika* may also elicit nationalist tendencies and thus create an insurmountable barrier to continued reform. In view of this possibility, restructuring the national question appears to be far less pressing an issue to Gorbachev than containing it—keeping it within manageable limits and preventing it from disrupting the four pillars of *perestroika*'s support: democratization, *glasnost'*, political renewal, and economic modernization.

All four elements logically go together, and without each of them *perestroika* would be meaningless. Of course, economic modernization is Gorbachev's highest priority. But Gorbachev has come to understand that modernization is contingent on a renewal of the political system. Administrative effectiveness must be enhanced and political opposition must be quelled for the radical economic measures he envisions to take effect and to work. In turn, political restructuring means mobilizing the support of various elite and popular constituencies through greater publicity and *glasnost'* and increased popular initiative and participation (democratization). All of these are laudable goals, but even laudable goals can have unintended consequences. Unfortunately for Gorbachev, measures to cope with these consequences may be fatal to *perestroika*.

Glasnost' and *Perestroika* in a Non-Russian Context

Glasnost' and democratization inevitably go together because a more open expression of opinions is predicated on the ability to do so. The rights of citizens must be expanded and those of the police and courts curbed. This means that the powers of the secret police, the KGB, must be reduced, even if only temporarily. Gorbachev appears to have moved in this direction when he announced that a law on "USSR state security" is scheduled to appear in 1990 and when he encouraged the public exposure and censure of a KGB operative in the Ukrainian city of Voroshilovgrad.[18]

The dangers of such a policy are readily apparent. Even a weaker KGB would still be a formidable opponent, but it would mean that political adversaries would have an easier time expressing opinions and organizing oppositionist groups. It was in 1986, for example, long after the Helsinki human rights movement had been crushed, that a Latvian group was established to monitor the state's record on national and civil rights in Latvia. There followed in 1987 the *samizdat* (self-published) journals *Glasnost'* (Moscow) and the *Ukrainian Herald*, the Russian chauvinist group Pamyat', the Initiative Group for the Release of Ukrainian Prisoners of Conscience, the Committee for the Release of Political Prisoners in Armenia, the Committee for the Release of Political Prisoners in Georgia, the Ukrainian peace movement, the Armenian National United Party, the Ukrainian Association of Independent Creative Intelligentsia, the Ukrainian Culturological Club, a Soviet branch of the International Society for Human Rights, and a revived Ukrainian Helsinki

Group.[19] Where, and whether, to draw the line on such unsanctioned activity is a question that is likely to concern Gorbachev for the rest of his tenure. The longer he waits, the more the dissidents can organize. The swifter his crackdown, however, the sooner the KGB will reassert itself and the more hypocritical will Soviet democracy appear.

The dangers of *glasnost'* must be particularly evident to Gorbachev. Given that *glasnost'* represents the removal of taboos; the expansion of the permissible in literature, journalism, and scholarship; the encouragement of criticism; and the expression of real needs, desires, and values, it is inevitable that some non-Russians will use *glasnost'* to pursue their own ends. This would be acceptable if their perception of the utility of *glasnost'* matched that of the Party and if they restricted their criticism to lazy workers; corrupt bureaucrats; such social ills as drug abuse, violence, and blackmarketeering; and the like. Matters become far more sensitive when *glasnost'* is extended to nationality issues. Since early 1986, for example, non-Russians from republics as disparate as Estonia, Belorussia, the Ukraine, Turkmenistan, and Kirgizia have been publicly expressing ideas that would have landed them in prison for "bourgeois nationalist agitation and propaganda" only several years ago.

This new fearlessness was most apparent at the republican writers' congresses held in May and June 1986. Some writers openly called for the purification of foreign (that is, Russian) loan words from local languages; others lambasted the educational and publishing systems for neglecting native languages; still others demanded that true internationalism required that Russians learn to speak the language of the republic in which they live and that republican languages be enshrined in republican constitutions.[20] The following statement by Pavlo Zahrebelny, the First Secretary of the Ukrainian Writers Union, was typical of many that were expressed at the gatherings:

In what things does national dignity manifest itself first of all? From the writer's point of view, it manifests itself in the national character depicted by artistic mastery. Therefore we cannot remain indifferent to such things as the language in which business correspondence is conducted, the language in which technical, scientific, and sociopolitical literature is published or what language is used in kindergartens, in schools, in higher educational establishments, in Komsomol and Pioneer organizations, or how many theatres have already become bilingual, because such an approximate language gives rise to approximate thoughts, approximate feelings, approximate work, and, as a consequence, approximate people. Let us be frank: He whose speaking ability is poor also lives and works badly. One is convinced of this by the example of those drones and punks who have ceased to understand us, who instead of living are "sailing high."[21]

Perhaps most remarkable was the fact that twenty-eight prominent Belorussians, representatives of a nation that most Western scholars had long since dismissed as lacking a sense of ethnic identity, wrote a letter to Gorbachev in December 1986 in which they expressed concern for the "fate of the Belorussian language" and demanded a return to the policy of linguistic and cultural liberalization of the 1920s:

a. Belorussian to be introduced as a working language in Party, state, and local government in the republic. . . .
b. a compulsory leaving examination to be introduced in Belorussian language and literature (essay) in secondary schools, and in Belorussian language (dictation) in eight-year incomplete secondary schools irrespective of the language of instruction.
c. a compulsory examination for all school-leavers (except those coming from outside the BSSR and USSR) in Belorussian language and literature (essay) for entry into all institutes of higher education, and in Belorussian language (dictation) for entry into the technical colleges of the republic.[22]

Why is the language issue so important to non-Russians? At one level, the growing use of Russian is perceived as Russification. The defense of non-Russian languages thus becomes a defense of national traditions, cultures, and identities. But there is an even more important dimension to the language debate. In multinational states, such as the Soviet Union, language is inevitably politicized, which is probably the major reason that many former colonial states have retained the languages of the colonial powers as their national languages. In the Soviet Union, however, what is officially called the "language of internationality discourse" happens to be the language of the dominant nationality, the Russians, so that the use of the Russian language often becomes a virtual political statement. A non-Russian who speaks only Russian is tacitly supporting the Soviet status quo; one who insists on using his or her own language is tacitly expressing dissatisfaction with the existing political arrangement.[23] In demanding a higher status for their languages, therefore, non-Russian writers are not concerned exclusively with linguistic issues; they are engaged in an oblique form of politics and thereby testing the limits of *glasnost'* in a manner that may well alarm the critics of *perestroika* and perhaps even its advocates.

It is thus of little wonder that such radical demands concerning language are a source of distress for Gorbachev. Not only are they associated with the nationalism and chauvinism he is determined to oppose, but by implementing them, he would surely produce substantial resentment, especially among the large Russian populations living in non-Russian republics who are generally ignorant of the local languages.

But if non-Russian intellectuals are forbidden to make such demands, *glasnost'* and the Party's ostensible commitment to ethnic equality will suffer. If these demands are not met, frustration may well result.

It may be a sign of things to come that the Belorussian Party leader, Efrem Sokolov, strongly rebuffed the writers of the Belorussian letter and suggested they needed enlightenment. Indeed, he asserted, "those who would like to dramatize the situation should be aware that this does not serve the cause of restructuring."[24] In an action that was no less indicative of the new spirit in the republics, however, 134 Belorussians ignored Sokolov's admonitions and wrote another letter to Gorbachev on June 4, 1987, in which they repeated the demands of the first letter.[25]

A particularly explosive mixture is that of *glasnost'* and non-Russian history. It is one thing to go over familiar ground and criticize Iosif Stalin and his cult of personality or to reevaluate Nikita Khrushchev, Nikolay Bukharin, and perhaps even Leon Trotsky, all of whom were associated with the Soviet Party-state and its development. It is quite another to delve deeply into non-Russian history and ask awkward questions (that reinforce nationalist tendencies) about the manner in which the borderlands were subdued and annexed. (Recent Soviet willingness to examine the Katyn massacre is a positive development, but it is premised on, and can only improve, the abysmal quality of current Soviet-Polish relations.) Are the Balts to study Stalin's absorption of their countries in 1939? Are the Ukrainians to open the archives on the 1933 famine that may have claimed several million lives? Are the Central Asians to evaluate the Basmachi anti-Soviet guerrilla movement of the 1920s and 1930s, especially in light of its similarities to the Afghan *mujahidin*? *Glasnost'* has not yet gone that far, but one day Gorbachev must confront these issues and decide how much openness he actually desires.

So far, the outlook is mixed. Gorbachev's speeches in Latvia and Estonia suggest that the "blank spots" in non-Russian history will remain far larger than those in Russian history. More ominous was an otherwise openminded and reasonably argued article written by Alexander Yakovlev, a protégé of Gorbachev known for his opposition to Russian chauvinism, which contained the following passage:

> Recently, sometimes quietly, but also openly, criticism of the Revolution and of Soviet power has been voiced for their supposedly destructive policy vis-a-vis national cultures. The subtext of such arguments contains the thought that the class, socialist approach and proletarian internationalism have in practice proven to be the reason for the "impoverishment" of national cultures. This is political speculation on lack of knowledge and ignorance, as well as a prime result of the fact that the demagogy that

repeats bourgeois propaganda fables is not getting a well-argued rebuff from scholarly criticism, which is summoned to defend historical truth.[26]

If Yakovlev's opinions reflect those of Gorbachev, non-Russian *glasnost'* may soon be reduced to a pale shadow of its Russian counterpart. If that happens, disillusionment, protests, and perhaps even repression are sure to follow. When they do, *glasnost'* and with it *perestroika* will be seriously harmed.

Even if Gorbachev can produce both *glasnost'* and democratization in the non-Russian context, he is likely to discover that they will not simplify his task of restructuring the political system. Politically, Gorbachev's goals are to streamline the bureaucracy and to mold it into an effective and efficient instrument of government. Naturally, all bureaucrats, both Russian and non-Russian, may be expected to resist such a move, but the problem is likely to be more acute in the non-Russian republics, where entrenched elites, ethnic favoritism, and affirmative action represent a formidable obstacle to Gorbachev's plans of renewal.

Whereas recalcitrant locals can always be purged—although not without difficulty—and non-Russian reformers can usually be found, ethnic favoritism and affirmative action are so ingrained in the republics that these have become a part of non-Russian political expectations. A policy that emphasizes merit and not nationality in the disbursement of jobs in the Party and state bureaucracy goes against what many non-Russians now consider to be their birthright. Renovating the bureaucracy will thus involve sending an unmistakable signal to the non-Russians, one that they are unlikely to receive with equanimity. Gorbachev's appointment of Kolbin, for example, an able Russian apparatchik with a reputation for getting things done, as Kunayev's replacement in Kazakhstan was precisely such a signal. The ethnic violence that followed may have contributed to Gorbachev's far more cautious attitude toward the Ukrainian Shcherbitsky. Nationalist riots in Kiev would not only be an international embarrassment, but they would also represent a major blow to the legitimacy of the leadership. Obviously, such considerations will not keep Gorbachev from pursuing whatever personnel policy he deems necessary. But the ethnic factor will stand in the way of his search for an ideal bureaucracy and, at the same time, will impede *perestroika*.

The results of *glasnost'*, democratization, and the quest for political renewal indirectly affect the primary goal of *perestroika*—economic modernization—by undermining what Gorbachev believes are its bases. Nevertheless, it is conceivable that substantial modernization could be achieved, albeit at a slower pace, even without the benefits of openness, participation, and efficiency. Unfortunately for Gorbachev, the national question directly casts a shadow, the longest yet, even on economic modernization.

The Repercussions of Decentralization
for the Republics

Regardless of whether the Soviet economy is currently in a state of crisis, there appears to be little doubt, both among Western and Soviet economists, that it is in the doldrums. Soviet leaders appear to think that the Soviet Union is falling behind the West and is progressively becoming a second-rate power. Modernization is the solution: raising productivity and improving the quality of products by means of better technology, improved management techniques, and greater individual initiative. Gorbachev recognizes that such an economic change may be accomplished only by introducing some elements of the market and thereby decentralizing economic decisionmaking authority and devolving it to lower levels of the system. Some steps have already been taken in this direction. More private activity in the service and consumer-goods sectors is now permitted than in the past, and enterprises may now make more decisions concerning how to allocate their resources, what and how much to produce, and to whom to sell it. But if *perestroika* is to succeed, even greater steps toward decentralization are necessary, with one Soviet economist, Nikolai Shmelev, suggesting that a form of market socialism might have to be introduced.[27] How far Gorbachev intends to go is unclear, but he does appear to believe that decentralization is still in its initial stages.

Decentralization may or may not solve the economic problems of the Soviet Union, but it is certain to produce important consequences for republican participants and institutions.[28] Most basically, decentralization represents a devolution to local levels of information and of decision-making. Devolution represents a significant expansion of peripheral authority on its own terms, but it is important for three additional reasons as well. First, devolution cannot be confined to the economic sector alone—to the system of ministries and to the factories attached to them. Politics and economics are intertwined in socialist systems, and it is inevitable that economic decentralization will be accompanied by the devolution of information and decisionmaking to peripheral political organizations. Second, a genuine devolution to the periphery of information and decisionmaking is necessarily associated with increased popular participation and initiative. If the periphery is now to solve centrally defined problems, then it must involve greater numbers of people in its information-gathering and decisionmaking processes. Just as the center depends on contributions from the periphery to make decisions, so now the periphery depends on its own "periphery" for contributions. Third and perhaps most important, none of these developments is feasible if central or coercive organs (or both) continue to exert particularly close supervision of events on the periphery. Some kind of thaw is required for information processing on the periphery and peripheral decisionmaking and participation to function semieffectively. For decentralization to work, the center must reproduce at the peripheral level the conditions of decisionmaking that it enjoys—that is, the center must expand the autonomy of the periphery.

Economic decentralization, however, does far more than permit republican actors more freely to pursue their interests as they define them. Decentralization forces peripheral elites to pursue *only* their own interests. The purpose and logic of decentralization compel peripheral elites to focus their energies on the territorial unit they administer, the republic; otherwise they would be incapable of implementing the original mandate of decentralization—improved efficiency, better decisions, a smoothly functioning system. Decentralization also arms the periphery. It gives local elites the means effectively to pursue their goals. That is, it provides them with resources or with greater control of resources, such as information, finances, organization, language, ideology, jobs, and cadres. Resources, in turn, convert into rewards and sanctions that permit peripheral elites to mobilize republican support for their policies.[29]

Economic decentralization thus turns the tables on the normal structure of incentives. It rewards efficient self-centered behavior and punishes inefficient self-centered behavior, and rational, non-nationalist republican elites respond accordingly. They come to act *as if* they believed that their unit of governance should be sovereign and its interests paramount, and by acting as if they were nationalists, they become nationalists in spite of themselves. Local elites need not be nationalists, nor must they want sovereignty for their republics. Indeed, as members of the Soviet elite, the *nomenklatura*, they will probably devote themselves to the well-being of the Soviet Union as a whole. Under conditions of decentralization, however, all the incentives go in the opposite direction—that of enhancing the prosperity and modernity of one's own republic and, thus, automatically neglecting the all-union context. Economic decentralization within a centrally directed socialist federal system encourages objectively nationalist behavior, even by non-nationalists or antinationalists. Yugoslavia's constantly warring ethnic republics would appear to confirm the validity of this observation.

Objectively nationalist elite behavior affects the Soviet system in the same way as does the subjectively nationalist behavior of bona fide nationalists. Both accelerate centrifugal tendencies and aggravate the system's fundamental contradiction between Russian hegemony and non-

Russian symbolic sovereignty. Economic decentralization thus contains the seeds of its own destruction. Because decentralization logically leads to the breakup of the Soviet system, Moscow cannot permit decentralization to run its course. At some point, when it perceives that centrifugal tendencies have increased more than the system can bear, Moscow must recentralize, revoke peripheral autonomy, and reduce peripheral resources. In sum, it must retrench. The precise timing of retrenchment will depend on many circumstances—international relations, intraelite conflicts, successions, economic trends, and so on—but at some point a retrenchment must occur if the system is to survive.

This logic will hold with equal force if economic centralization is held constant and political decentralization is assumed to occur. The diminution of Party control and supervision of local political organs translates directly into increased peripheral prerogatives, political resources, and objectively nationalist behavior for the reasons I have discussed with regard to economic decentralization. Significantly, the political de-Stalinization initiated by Khrushchev and more or less maintained by his successors means that some political decentralization is now built into the Soviet system. Attempts at economic decentralization under conditions of some political decentralization are therefore all the more likely to encourage objectively nationalist behavior and produce national communism.

Both of these forms of decentralization coincided in the 1920s, with nativization and the New Economic Policy, and in the 1950s–1960s, with de-Stalinization and the Sovnarkhoz reform—periods that witnessed a flowering of national communism. Since Khrushchev's ouster, political and economic decentralization have not overlapped to as great an extent as was the case earlier. The Kosygin reforms and their progeny, wholly in fact and partly in intention, were tantamount to economic recentralization, whereas Brezhnevism represented a selective reassertion of some central control in recalcitrant republics such as the Ukraine and Georgia, together with the institutionalization of the political prerogatives of peripheral cadres. This fact, together with the political turmoil that accompanied the Brezhnev succession, enabled Rashidov, Kunayev, Usubaliyev, and other Central Asian satraps to engage in a form of national communism and convert Uzbekistan, Kazakhstan, and Kirgizia into modern versions of the ancient khanates of Khiva and Bukhara.

Mikhail Gorbachev is treading on particularly thin ice because his program combines all the necessary ingredients of objectively nationalist behavior. *Glasnost'* and democratization accelerate political decentralization, and economic modernization is equivalent to economic decentralization. The combination is a potent one, and the visible growth of aggressively national sentiments in all the republics is the first sign of the dangers ahead. Despite the fact that Gorbachev is placing his own supporters into key positions in both Moscow and the periphery, the logic of decentralization within a federal context will drive these elites to pursue increasingly objective nationalist behavior. If so, Gorbachev or his successor will come face to face with the contradictory nature of Soviet federalism, and unless he is willing to preside over the system's disintegration, recentralization of some kind will be inevitable.

To the extent that, as most economists argue, centralization inevitably leads to crises demanding economic decentralization as a solution, the Soviet Party-state would appear to be caught in a vicious cycle of its own making. Just as decentralization effectively addresses the problems of economic centralization, so, too, decentralization inevitably sets loose forces that threaten the stability of the system. Can the Soviet Union continue indefinitely in such a cycle? The answer, for better or for worse, is "yes." Because systemic survival is not now or in the immediate future an issue, temporary decentralization can alleviate certain problems, and recurrent recentralization is always a possibility. Some states manage to muddle through for centuries, and most do well for decades. In order to answer this question in the negative, we would have to assume that the crisis requiring decentralization is so severe that anything but complete decentralization will lead to collapse.

Can the vicious cycle ever be broken? Only if one of three conditions is met. The uneven federalism of the Soviet Union would have to be replaced with a more unitary state structure that dissociates administrative units from ethnic groups. Or the uneven federalism would have to be transcended, and a more genuine federation, without Russian hegemony, would have to be established. Or, finally, Soviet socialism would have to work sufficiently well—perhaps with some element of low-level marketization—that it would prevent the emergence of overcentralization. On their own, these conditions are not at present likely to emerge. The non-Russians are not prone to tolerate the abrogation of the rights they do possess; the Party and the Russians are unlikely to give up their elite prerogatives (elites, after all, generally do not self-destruct); and socialism's renewal still seems a long way off at best. Recentralization and repression appear to be inevitable, unless, as I will argue in the concluding section of this chapter, an outside force improves the likelihood that the second and third conditions will come into existence.

The Non-Russians and the West

While the side effects of *perestroika* represent a political and economic dilemma for the Soviet Union, they confront the West with a moral one. Specifically, the USSR's difficulties will put the West's putative commitment to human rights and democracy to a severe test. At some point, the West may have to choose between tolerating repression of legitimate non-Russian national aspirations and supporting the destabilization of a superpower and risking bloodshed and, perhaps, war.

The best way for the West to resolve this dilemma is to create the conditions that would enable the Soviet system to escape the vicious cycle described in this chapter. Given that the endorsement of extreme political centralization in the Soviet Union would be tantamount to violating non-Russian human and national rights, the West should opt for a combination of genuine federation and economic reform. In a word, the West should encourage *perestroika* in the non-Russian republics. There are ample incentives for all sides to support this course of action. Such a policy would permit the West to remain sincerely committed to human rights and to peace; this policy would enhance the decisionmaking prerogatives of the non-Russian elites within the Soviet context; and this policy would sweeten the pill for supporters of Russian hegemony and Party centralization by improving *perestroika*'s overall chances of success.

Is such a course realistic? Western policy toward Eastern Europe, which is no less a part of the Soviet empire than are the non-Russian republics, suggests that the answer is a qualified "yes." Whereas the post–World War II U.S. aim of rolling Soviet control back from Eastern Europe proved to be an illusion and in reality only drove the Eastern Europeans into the arms of the Soviets, the expansion of interstate and intersociety contacts—all of which were based on Western recognition of Soviet hegemony—improved the quality of life and advanced human rights in most Eastern European countries. Eastern Europe benefited, as did the West, while the USSR was generally satisfied that its imperial interests in the area were not being threatened. Greater contacts with the West were effective because they attempted to institutionalize and thus to make permanent the relative autonomy of the Eastern European countries in the context of their subordinate status within the Soviet bloc. Institutionalization proceeded along the lines of permanent political, economic, and cultural contacts between the Eastern Europeans and the West on the understanding that bridges can exist only to link separate spheres of influence.

A Western policy of bridge building toward the non-Russian republics may well be what is required today. Liberation is unrealistic, repression morally repugnant; genuine and institutionalized limited autonomy coupled with Western recognition of continued Soviet hegemony may be the best for which the non-Russians can hope. Notwithstanding the problematic nature of the Baltic states' international status,[30] a basis for expanding diplomatic relations with the other republics exists. All have ministries of foreign affairs, and the Ukraine and Belorussia are represented in a variety of international bodies and are hosts to a number of consulates. The United States has agreed to open a consulate in Kiev, and West Germany may do the same. Academic and cultural relations could also be extended. Here, too, precedents exist, such as the recent establishment of direct relations between the American Council of Learned Societies and the Soviet Ukrainian Academy of Sciences. Most important, now that Soviet enterprises may legally engage in some foreign economic relations on their own, the basis for establishing direct economic bridges, investing in and trading with the republics, the West can contribute directly to economic modernization and thus to the success of *perestroika*, which is a prospect of considerable appeal to Soviet reformers and one that may overcome their apprehensions concerning genuine federalism.

The purpose of bridge building would not be to foment nationalism and encourage the dissolution of the Soviet Party-state. Rather, the goal would be the opposite: to expand and to institutionalize the political, cultural, and economic autonomy of the Soviet republics—of their populations in general and of their nationally minded elites in particular—*within* the Soviet context. By helping the republics to acquire a form of limited, but genuinely national, autonomy—one that falls far short of Finlandization, Polonization, or Magyarization and that more closely resembles Bulgarization—while acknowledging continued Soviet rule over these territories and promoting economic reform, Western policymakers may eventually succeed in sparing Mikhail Gorbachev and themselves the unpleasant choice between repression and disintegration. For the non-Russians, of course, Bulgarization, or the possession of limited autonomy and genuine national identity under the rule of an outside hegemony, would represent an enormous step forward in terms of their cultural, linguistic, economic, and political aspirations—a result of no small magnitude.

Notes

1. For an excellent overview of the Armenian demonstrations and of their repercussions in Azerbaijan, see Elizabeth Fuller, "A Preliminary Chronology of Recent Events in Armenia and Azerbaijan," *Radio Liberty Research*, RL 101/88, March 15, 1988.

2. The largest non-Russian groups, according to the 1979 census, include the Ukrainians (42 million), Uzbeks (12.5 million), Belorussians (9.5 million), Kazakhs (6.5 million), Tatars (6.3 million), Azerbaijanis (5.5 million), Armenians (4 million), Georgians (3.5 million), Moldavians (3 million), Tadzhiks (3 million), Lithuanians (3 million), Turkmen (2 million), Kirgiz (2 million), Jews (1.8 million), Latvians (1.4 million), and Estonians (1 million). *Chislennost' i sostav naseleniia SSSR* (Moscow: Finansy i statistika, 1984), p. 71.

3. See Alexander J. Motyl, "The Foreign Relations of the Ukrainian SSR," *Harvard Ukrainian Studies*, no. 1 (March 1982), pp. 62–78.

4. See Alexander J. Motyl, *Will the Non-Russians Rebel? State, Ethnicity, and Stability in the USSR* (Ithaca, N.Y.: Cornell University Press, 1987).

5. *The Programme of the Communist Party of the Soviet Union* (Moscow: Novosti, 1986), p. 47 (emphasis supplied).

6. *Soviet Nationality Survey*, no. 9 (September 1985), p. 5.

7. On the fate of the Karachai, Cherkess, and other deported nationalities, see Aleksandr M. Nekrich, *The Punished Peoples* (New York: Norton, 1978).

8. M. S. Gorbachev, *Izbrannye rechi i stat'i* (Moscow: Izdatel'stvo politicheskoi literatury, 1987), vol. 1, pp. 50–54, 69–78, 225–236.

9. *Kommunist*, no. 5 (March 1985), p. 10.

10. M. S. Gorbachev, *Ibrannye rechi i stat'i* (Moscow: Izdatel'stvo politicheskoi literatury, 1985), p. 52.

11. *Soviet Nationality Survey*, no. 9 (September 1985), p. 5.

12. *Izvestiya*, February 26, 1986, p. 6.

13. T. K., "Nationalist Riots in Kazakhstan," *Soviet Nationality Survey*, no. 1 (January 1987), p. 3. See also Uwe Halbach, "Perestrojka und Nationalitaeten-politik. Der Schock von Alma-Ata und Moskaus gespanntes Verhaeltnis zu Mittelasien," *Berichte des Bundesinstituts für ostwissenschaftliche und internationale Studien*, no. 38 (1987).

14. "V Ryzi vidbulasia demonstratsiia," *Svoboda*, June 17, 1987, p. 1; "Russian Nationalists Test Gorbachev," *New York Times*, May 24, 1987, p. 10; "Lithuanians Rally for Stalin Victims," *New York Times*, August 24, 1987, p. 1; "Unofficial Peace Demonstration Broken Up in Lviv, Ukraine," *Ukrainian Press Agency*, no. 6 (October 8, 1987); "Wachsende nationale Spannungen in der UdSSR," *Neue Zürcher Zeitung*, March 13–14, 1988, p. 7.

15. *Kommunist*, no. 3 (February 1987), pp. 28–29.

16. *Pravda*, February 20, 1987, pp. 1–2; *Pravda*, February 22, 1987, pp. 1–2.

17. "Internatsionalistskaia sut' sotsializma," *Kommunist*, no. 13 (September 1987), pp. 3–13. Also see Mikhail S. Gorbachev, *October and Perestroika: The Revolution Continues* (Moscow: Novosti, 1987).

18. *Vedomosti verkhovnogo soveta SSSR*, no. 37 (September 10, 1986), pp. 729–736; *Pravda*, January 4, 1987, p. 3.

19. See "Latvian Helsinki Group Documents," *Ukrainian Weekly*, January 25, 1987, pp. 2, 4; Roman Solchanyk, "Former Political Prisoners Form New Human Rights Group in Ukraine," *Ukrainian Weekly*, October 18, 1987, p. 1; Bohdan Nahaylo, "'Informal' Ukrainian Culturological Club Under Attack," *Radio Liberty Research*, RL 477/87, November 23, 1987; *Glasnost'*, nos. 2–4 (July 1987), pp. 4–5; and "Herald Editors Renew Ukrainian Helsinki Group," *Ukrainian Weekly*, January 17, 1988, p. 1.

20. *Soviet Nationality Survey*, no. 9 (September 1986), pp. 1–5.

21. Ibid., pp. 6–7.

22. "A Letter to Gorbachev from 28 Belorussian Cultural Figures," *Soviet Nationality Survey*, no. 5 (May 1987), p. 8.

23. See Motyl, *Will the Non-Russians Rebel?* pp. 88–106.

24. Roman Solchanyk, "Party Leader in Belorussia Rejects Criticism About Status of Belorussian Language," *Radio Liberty Research*, RL 180/87, May 7, 1987, p. 3.

25. Roman Solchanyk, "An Open Letter to Gorbachev Sent by Byelorussian Workers, Intellectuals," *Ukrainian Weekly*, August 30, 1987, p. 2.

26. A. Iakovlev, "Dostizhenie kachestvenno novogo sostoianiia sovetskogo obshchestva i obshchestvennye nauki," *Kommunist*, no. 8 (May 1987), p. 20.

27. "Zu lange herrschte statt des Rubels der Befehl," *Der Speigel*, no. 25, June 15, 1987, pp. 135–137.

28. On the connection between economic decentralization and political liberalization, see Wlodzimierz Brus, *The Economics and Politics of Socialism* (London: Routledge & Kegan Paul, 1973).

29. On the importance of positive and negative sanctions, see Mancur Olson, *The Logic of Collective Action* (Cambridge, Mass.: Harvard University Press, 1971).

30. For the best discussion of the Baltic states' legal status, see William J. H. Hough III, "The Annexation of the Baltic States and Its Effect on the Development of Law Prohibiting Forcible Seizure of Territory," *New York Law School Journal of International and Comparative Law* 6, no. 2 (Winter 1985), pp. 303–533.

6

Politics and Nationality: The Soviet Jews

Laurie P. Salitan[1]

The most recent Soviet census, taken in 1979, counted 1,810,876 Soviet Jews, thereby ranking Jews the sixteenth largest Soviet nationality. From October 1968 to December 1987, approximately 15 percent of Soviet Jewry, or 274,726 Soviet Jews, left the Soviet Union. The number of emigrants has fluctuated annually, with the 1970s characterized by a general increase and the 1980s marked by a contrasting diminution, although 1987 saw a dramatic surge.

An international spotlight on emigration, resulting from Western concern, has been significant for its scope and durability as well as for the amount of pressure it has brought to bear on the USSR. However, Western pressure is not responsible for the course of emigration. Indeed, the policy behind emigration, rather than the international spotlight, comprises the most important aspect of the twenty-year history. Why, in a country that does not permit free emigration, were Soviet Jews able to leave? Why was a significant portion of Soviet Jewry (approximately 15 percent) permitted to emigrate? What do the fluctuations in emigration indicate? What does Mikhail Gorbachev's reform program mean for Soviet Jews and the emigration movement?

The most widespread explanation offered for the fluctuations in emigration relies on what this author calls the "barometer thesis": an interpretation that portrays emigration as a barometer of U.S.-Soviet relations, with the Soviet Jews used as pawns in, or hostages to, the superpower rivalry. Although the barometer thesis seems plausible, it is ultimately flawed and cannot account for the entire course of emigration because it fails to consider the domestic context of emigration policy. Policy decisions on emigration are rooted in a complex set of interrelationships involving demography (including population distribution), economic performance, elite and institutional politics, foreign policy, nationality policy, and the role of Jews in Soviet society.

The Rise of Jewish National Consciousness

Initially, the horrors of the Holocaust and the "black years" under Iosif Stalin stimulated a reawakening of Jewish identity among a number of Soviet Jews. Many Jews felt betrayed by their country's lenient treatment of the Soviet citizens who perpetuated the anti-Semitism of the Nazis and by the failure of the Soviet Union to recognize and commemorate the suffering of Soviet Jews in World War II.[2] The influx of more culturally aware Jews from the western territories annexed during World War II[3] was also an important factor in the growth of national consciousness. In many cases, Soviet Jews from the heartland of the USSR came into contact with the so-called *zapadniki* (westerners) as a result of the wartime evacuations. The *zapadniki* taught Judaism, Jewish history, Hebrew, and Zionist ideology to the Soviet Jews. The creation of the State of Israel in 1948 and the subsequent arrival of Golda Meir, the first minister of the Israeli legation in Moscow, were sources of great pride to many Soviet Jews; in the Jewish State of Israel they found the natural expression of their Zionist and religious aspirations.[4]

Aside from cultural and religious motivations, the limits placed on the admission of Jews to institutions of higher education also prompted many Soviet Jews to consider emigration. A *numerus clausus* (quota), instituted in the late 1940s, had the effect of diminishing future opportunities for Soviet Jews. Moreover, the policy of developing national cadres, combined with a simultaneous demand for greater representation by less professionally saturated nationalities, restricted Jews from positions of power and authority in administrative posts, the Party, the army, and the foreign service. At the same time, increased competition for jobs traditionally held by Jews[5] heightened national tensions and, in some cases, intensified anti-Semitic attitudes. Many of the Jews affected by the *numerus clausus* and cadres policy responded by developing a stronger ethnic identity, which was manifested by religious observance and/or a commitment to Zionism.

Jewish national consciousness surfaced in the thaw following the death of Stalin. The reign of terror had ended, and in its wake came a limited public expression of long-submerged sentiments. Dissatisfaction with the quality of Jewish life in the Soviet Union and with anti-Jewish or anti-Zionist policies (or both) in the USSR became important concerns for the group of Jews who had quietly maintained a commitment to Zionism. Yet it was not until significant international events in the 1960s, principally the 1967 Arab-Israeli War, the officially sponsored anti-Semitism in

Poland, and the 1968 Soviet invasion of Czechoslovakia, that Soviet Jewish cultural and religious leaders began to lose hope in the possibility of domestic reform. In 1968, the convergence of these external events and the rise of dissident activity within the USSR led to the development of an emigration movement. In reality, the term *movement* is used loosely for it includes divergent groups of Soviet Jews who share little more than the common goal of emigration.

Unlike the dissident groups, the Jewish emigration movement did not strive for internal reform. The Jewish activists had lost hope for the possibility of living as Jews (in the broadest sense of the word) in the Soviet Union; instead, they had one goal: emigration. The catalyst that sparked the emigration movement was the 1967 Arab-Israeli War, which triggered an outpouring of anti-Zionist attacks in the Soviet media that have continued unabated to the present. Although the objectives of Soviet Jews differed from those of the human rights activists, the former employed the tactics of the latter primarily by using Soviet and international law as the basis of their campaign for emigration. The Gomulka regime in Poland had made Jews a scapegoat for the government's problems and forced several thousand Jews to leave the country. Despite what amounted to an expulsion of the Jews from Poland, Soviet Jews were encouraged nonetheless by the fact that emigration was "allowed" at all. In 1968, Soviet Jews became hopeful that Polish Jewish emigration would set a precedent that the Soviet Union would follow.[6]

Characteristics of the Emigrants
and Their Decision to Leave

The first period of mass emigration (1968–1973) was characterized by an emigrant pool drawn largely from Georgia, the Baltic republics, Transcarpathia, the western Ukraine (primarily Bukovina), and Moldavia. Bukharan and Mountain Jews constituted smaller percentages. The overrepresentation of *zapadniki* and Georgian Jews reflected the lower rate of Jewish assimilation in those areas. Although the majority of Soviet Jews reside in the Soviet heartland (the territory longest under Soviet rule[7]), the bulk of the 1968–1973 emigration was from the annexed areas, Georgia, and Central Asia, which are regions in which less than 20 percent of Soviet Jews lived. The reasons for this imbalance have as much to do with the Soviet Jews themselves as with the Soviet authorities.

Jews of the periphery (the southern republics and the annexed territories), who had retained a greater attachment to Jewish culture and/ or religion, were less "Sovietized" than the more assimilated Jews from the Soviet heartland. The periphery Jews also had strongly rooted Zionist aspirations. Indeed, among the Jews of the periphery, Zionism was the strongest motivating factor for emigration to Israel. Family reunification and religious considerations were also important determinants for this group, particularly among the elderly. In the case of the Baltic Jews, their well-established ties with Western Jews and previous exposure to emigration, primarily as a result of the Soviet-Polish Repatriation Agreement (effective from 1957 to 1959), which repatriated about 200,000 Poles (30,000 of whom were also Jews), were additional factors contributing to the decision to leave the Soviet Union.[8]

Preference for the United States and other Western countries rather than Israel as a final destination highlights the declining importance of Zionism to emigrants after 1973. Many of the post-1973 emigrants identified themselves more strongly as Russians than as Jews. Mostly educated urban professionals, their high level of assimilation reflected the predominance of heartlanders among them. As the group of emigrants began more closely to correspond to the geographic distribution of Soviet Jews, the chief considerations prompting the decision to leave the country changed. Factors that were not principally important to the earlier emigrants became more significant to the later group. Letters sent from recent emigrants to friends and family remaining in the Soviet Union detailed negative experiences in Israel resulting from absorption difficulties, high inflation, competition for professional jobs similar to those held in the USSR, and the compromises necessitated by life in a country surrounded by hostile neighbors. This news had greatest impact upon those who lacked a strong Zionist commitment and therefore did not feel particularly drawn to Israel. By 1979, when the number of emigrants peaked at more than 50,000, the majority were choosing to settle in the United States.

When emigrants from this period were surveyed, they cited discrimination on the basis of nationality, cultural or political motivations, economic reasons, and family reunification as chief factors motivating their decision to emigrate.[9] The survey findings revealed that the most assimilated Soviet Jews left the USSR for cultural and political reasons, whereas those from the annexed areas, who more openly identified themselves as Jews, attributed their emigration to ethnic (including Zionist) and economic factors. The lesser-educated, rural Jews were motivated primarily by economic considerations.[10] These results reflected the views of the majority of emigrants after 1976, namely, those who chose not to go to Israel.

Emigration Policy in the 1970s

The factors shaping emigration policy can be identified as primary and secondary. Primary factors are those that are directly responsible for and/or have a clear impact on policy decisions. Secondary factors are those that accrue as positive or negative results of the policy and as such may be important by-products; however, they do not themselves drive policy. The primary determinants of emigration policy in the 1970s and beyond related to domestic factors rather than to international relations. Although détente with the West, specifically U.S.-Soviet relations, was the overarching backdrop for the period, it was not a primary factor in determining emigration policy.

The need for Western technology and grain, the desire for a Strategic Arms Limitation Talks agreement (SALT I), and the fear of a Sino-U.S. rapprochement were key reasons the USSR pursued détente with the United States. Soviet negotiators surely realized that increased emigration helped to maintain a more relaxed international atmosphere and could be used as a concession to advance the goals of détente. This would seem evident from the fact that Soviet officials were and continue to be routinely made aware of the weight the emigration issue carries domestically in the United States. However, it is doubtful that emigration was orchestrated as part of a grand Soviet scheme to curry favor with the United States. The perspective of time shows that emigration could not have endured if its fate had been linked to that of U.S.-Soviet relations, a key point that underscores a crucial flaw in the barometer thesis.

Emigration served a number of Soviet objectives, as did détente itself. If viewed in isolation, the linkage the barometer thesis establishes between détente and emigration seems plausible, for emigration levels rose in the early 1970s as U.S.-Soviet relations grew warmer. Yet emigration began several years before détente became a significant factor in the U.S.-Soviet relationship. The Soviet Jews themselves created the emigration movement. Although support of Western friends and sympathetic governments focused an international spotlight on Soviet Jews, the initial reason the Soviet Jews began a public campaign for their right to leave the Soviet Union was their sense that the time was ripe *internally*.

The Soviet decision to permit emigration was a response to the Jewish demand for it. For a small price, it afforded domestic social, economic, and political benefits. These were the primary reasons for the Soviet decision. The Soviet authorities calculated that they could curtail the movement by permitting the relatively small group of unassimilable Jews to leave before their activities became an example to others. In particular, this may have been true in the case of the Georgian Jews, whose emigration would eliminate a potentially destabilizing element in an area of the Soviet Union where national identity has traditionally been strong. Additionally, many of the Jews who had left the country prior to 1973 represented the least productive and therefore the least economically valuable segment of Soviet Jewry. Allowing the elderly and infirm to leave meant that funds would no longer have to be used to pay their pensions.

Jewish emigration policy in this initial period also represented a new Soviet approach to the management of politically sensitive issues.[11] Détente brought with it a broader exposure of Soviet citizens to Western society and values and an increased presence of Western correspondents in the USSR. The Soviet Jews made effective use of the foreign media corps, which regularly monitored their situation. Although Soviet policy-makers may not have anticipated the magnitude of Western concern for human rights issues, they quickly made clear their intolerance of foreign intervention into areas they considered entirely domestic. However, once the decision was made to permit emigration, the policy could be used effectively to further a wide range of goals. Increased emigration in the early 1970s enabled Soviet officials, when confronted on their poor human rights record, to demonstrate improvement. In this way, the USSR would appear as if it were moderating its stance, without making any significant changes in its approach to domestic pressure for greater liberalization. Indeed, as the number of emigrants increased, so, too, did the level of harassment and repression directed at the broad spectrum of dissidents.

That détente was only a secondary factor in emigration policy is clear from the basic position toward Jewish cultural and religious activities, which remained harsh and in fact grew more severe as exposure to the West increased. No amount of pressure, applied in the spirit of détente or tied to concessions in other areas, succeeded in moderating the treatment of Jewish activists and other dissidents. Emigration, a policy the Soviet decisionmakers had already decided to pursue, brought the added bonus of appeasing Western critics. What remains unclear is whether policymakers anticipated that the decision to permit Jews to leave would expand rather than shrink the size of the movement. As greater numbers of Jews were granted permission to leave, still more filed applications to do so. Because the Soviet authorities had to confront a continually expanding movement, factors motivating decisions on emigration in the early stages, when the proportions of the movement were not yet clear, differed from those affecting decisions in later years.

As the 1970s progressed, both the domestic and the international parameters affecting emigration changed. The second period of mass emigration, 1974–1979, was characterized by fluctuating emigration levels and the diminishing importance of Zionism as the chief factor motivating emigration. The full impact of what is known as the "drop-out" phe-nomenon—the decision to go to countries other than Israel—was felt during this period as increasing numbers of Soviet Jews chose the United

States and to a lesser degree, Australia, Canada, New Zealand, and Western Europe as their final destination.

The domestic factors motivating emigration policy remained the primary ones, although arguments to the contrary abound. Proponents of the barometer thesis argue that the Jackson-Vanik amendment passed by the U.S. Congress in 1974,[13] which linked U.S.-Soviet trade to free emigration, was responsible for the drop in emigration during 1974–1976. However, the evidence casts doubt that there was a direct cause-effect relationship between the amendment and emigration levels. Despite the 1974–1976 drop and the fact that the amendment has remained in effect since 1974, emigration levels began to increase in 1977 and rose to all-time highs by the end of the decade.

The mid-decade reduction in emigration was a function of the Soviet Union's reassessment of the emigration policy in the wake of the expanding parameters of the movement. This reduction was also conditioned by the would-be emigrants' reevaluation of Israel as their desired destination. Many Soviet Jews delayed filing emigration applications while waiting to hear news about the United States (which faced a deep recession in the mid-1970s) as well as other potential destinations. At the same time, Soviet officials tightened the policy, thus discouraging would-be emigrants from applying. However, by 1977, emigration levels began to rise again as a result of the emigration policy being relaxed and growing numbers of Soviet Jews choosing to go to the United States.

Emigration increased dramatically at the end of the decade. The number of emigrants was 16,736 in 1977, 28,864 in 1978, and 51,320 in 1979. Nonetheless, as the decade wore on, U.S.-Soviet relations deteriorated. Despite the signing of the Final Act of the Conference on Security and Cooperation in Europe (CSCE) in 1975, tensions flared. The stalled SALT negotiations and the Sino-U.S. entente further tarnished relations. If emigration were a barometer of U.S.-Soviet relations, these negative factors should have combined to stall or impede emigration, yet they did not. Proponents of the barometer thesis point instead to legislation in the summer of 1979 superceding the Stevenson amendment,[14] to rumors that the waiver to the Jackson-Vanik amendment would be invoked in 1979,[15] and to the U.S. Senate debate on ratification of the SALT II treaty as factors motivating the tremendous increase in emigration at the end of the decade. However, such analysis has three major flaws. First, it is internally inconsistent for it does not account for large-scale emigration during years of tense relations (1976–1979). Second, in the context of poor relations, the thesis does not satisfactorily explain why the Soviet Union would pay an unduly large price with little guarantee of a positive return. Third, the one-to-one correlations the barometer thesis establishes between annual emigration levels and significant events in U.S.-Soviet relations are methodologically unsound because they do not leave room for time lags in policy implementation.

The pattern of Soviet German emigration during these same years adds further evidence that weakens the barometer thesis. Despite improvements in West German–Soviet relations during the late 1970s, Soviet German emigration was curtailed after 1976.[16] Thus, on the one hand, while U.S.-Soviet relations deteriorated, Jewish emigration increased, and on the other, while West German–Soviet relations grew warmer, German emigration was reduced. These trends indicate that the international climate was not determining the flow of emigration.

The increase in emigration during the latter half of the 1970s suggests that détente was the major secondary motivation for mass emigration but was not the essential determinant. Instead, emigration policy in the second half of the 1970s was conditioned by issues relating to the process of elite integration,[17] the resolution of nationality tensions via a policy of anti-Zionism, and the necessity of the leadership to confront the demands of a significant segment of the population, which could not, as was the case during Stalin's rule, merely be imprisoned as a solution. The fluctuations in emigration rates and the inverse levels of Jewish and German emigration indicate that although there may have been a consensus regarding the agenda of broad goals to be pursued by the Soviet Union, the policy for attaining those objectives was not consistent.

Emigration from 1980 to 1986

Soviet Jewish emigration during the first half of the 1980s was drastically reduced from the level of the previous decade. Emigration fell from the 1979 total of 51,320 to annual levels of 21,471 (1980), 9,447 (1981), 2,688 (1982), 1,314 (1983), 896 (1984), 1,140 (1985), and 914 (1986). This decrease was accompanied by a correspondingly significant increase in the number of refuseniks (Jews who applied for and were denied permission to emigrate). Additionally, the late 1970s practice of suppressing Jewish religious and cultural activities and harassing Jewish activists, which included the use of imprisonment for religious and ideological beliefs, was expanded.

As in the previous decade, the primary determinants of emigration in the 1980s continued to be internal. Domestically, the impact of many far-reaching internal changes, some of which had been developing since the 1950s, began to be felt in the late 1970s. A combination of slow economic growth, a declining birthrate for most of the Soviet population, and demographic changes had a profound impact on Soviet Jewish emigration in the 1980s. Census data show a drop in the rate of population growth since the 1950s. Whereas the natural population increase was

17.8 per thousand in 1960, the figure had fallen to 8.0 per thousand in 1980[18] and was projected to decline even further to perhaps less than 2.5 per thousand in the year 2000.[19] The full impact of low birthrates (lower in the 1960s than in any period of Soviet post–World War II history) is being felt in the second half of the 1980s, as the children of the late 1960s attain working age. A labor shortage could have devastating effects on future economic growth as well as on the maintenance of a balance between productive and dependent sectors of the population.[20]

In addition to decreasing population growth, the Soviet Union has been faced with a major realignment of its population centers. An increasing population growth rate in the predominantly Muslim Central Asian and Transcaucasian republics and a decreasing birthrate and higher mortality rate in the more industrialized Baltic and Slavic republics will translate into profound changes for the Soviet Union. Projections for the year 2000 show an increase from 8 percent in 1970 to 13–16 percent in the Central Asian republics' share of the total population and a decrease from 54 percent in 1970 to 47–49 percent in the Russian republic's share of the total population, to cite but one example.[21] As the largely Slavic-dominated governing elite begins to lose its demographic advantage to non-Slavic nationalities, the Soviet leaders face important decisions regarding how to secure their own power base, manage the increased assertiveness of non-Russian nationalities, allocate jobs and resources, stimulate the economy, and rectify the disparity between centers of population and regions of industrialization.[22]

The cumulative effect of these developments has been a drastic limitation on emigration. Jewish emigration fell to 914 in 1986, thereby indicating that emigration had been virtually ended. The dramatic increase in 1987 (when 8,155 Soviet Jews left the USSR) is significant but does not represent a policy reversal. Indeed, a liberal policy at this point would be counterproductive to the goals of *perestroika* (restructuring). Whereas emigration in the 1970s bolstered the anti-Zionist policy, offered a mechanism for resolving nationality tensions, served the goals of elite integration, and helped to rid the country of unwanted citizens whose demands for emigration could incite disaffection among others, emigration was not the policy choice for addressing these issues in the 1980s. Indeed, emigration would neither serve immediate needs nor further broad-ranging policy objectives as defined by the Soviet Union in the 1980s.

The scale of actual and potential Soviet Jewish emigration could not be ignored in the 1980s, a time of declining economic and population growth. Most Soviet Jews are highly assimilated and are closely akin to the Slavic nationalities, which makes their presence in the USSR increasingly important. The loss of Jews from the Caucasian and Central Asian republics (where the growth of the native population is outpacing population growth in other regions), plus the departure of a large percentage of the Jewish population from the western annexed territories (where nationalism is already strong), were considered by the leadership to be impediments to the Soviet goals of economic restructuring and democratization. It would seem that the traditional reliance on a physical presence of significant numbers of Slavs[23] as cultural and ethnic safeguards against the potential national self-assertion of other groups had again become operative. In a period when the Soviet Union must stimulate its labor force, contend with increased national assertiveness, and entice workers to industrial areas, emigration does not present a positive alternative for Soviet policymakers.

Moreover, the realization by Soviet decisionmakers that family reunification is a never-ending process—indeed by 1980 it was apparent that controlled emigration had led to the departure of approximately 12.7 percent of Soviet Jewry—contributed to the curtailment of emigration in the 1980s. Granting permission to individuals to join relatives abroad further divides families and increases the number of people who can petition to leave for the purpose of family reunification. Along these lines, there probably came a point when the Soviet leadership deemed it important to assert and actively demonstrate control over the emigration movement, lest would-be emigrants and others think they could manipulate the system. Emigration from the Soviet Union is highly regulated and severely restricted, and emigration to nonsocialist countries is ideologically problematic, for it is viewed as an indictment of the Soviet system.

Despite the array of domestic problems and considerations that confronted the Soviet Union in the 1980s, proponents of the barometer thesis routinely cite international events to explain the curtailment of emigration. Although both the sanctions imposed by the United States in response to the December 1979 Soviet intervention in Afghanistan and the withdrawal of the SALT II treaty from Senate consideration may have played a secondary role in Soviet emigration policy throughout 1980 and beyond, it would be difficult to substantiate an argument that those actions were responsible for initiating the rapid decline. Indeed, the monthly number of visas decreased as early as November 1979, which casts doubt on claims that the reduction was a direct outcome of U.S. sanctions. Similarly, it is doubtful that an antiemigration policy was engendered by the January 1980 congressional approval of the Sino-U.S. bilateral trade agreement, which granted the People's Republic of China most-favored-nation status. Although such a policy was not inconsistent with the progressive deterioration of U.S.-Soviet relations in the 1980s, the primary mechanism driving emigration policy was the maturing of several domestic issues of the 1970s to full-blown crises in the 1980s.

Gorbachev's Objectives
and Soviet Emigration Policy in 1987

The year 1987 was characterized by a turnabout in the number of Jewish emigrants but not in the basic emigration policy. Soviet officials began making statements regarding the decision to handle emigration cases in a more timely fashion and to review refusenik cases with an eye to resolving contested visa decisions and permitting the refuseniks to leave.[24] (At the beginning of 1987, there were an estimated 11,000 refuseniks.) Emigration in 1987 did not stem from the thaw in U.S.-Soviet relations, nor was its purpose to enhance relations prior to the December 1987 Reagan-Gorbachev summit meeting. Emigration on the magnitude of 1987 did not occur before the 1985 summit meeting in Geneva or the 1986 summit meeting in Reykjavik. In order to understand the 1987 increase, it must be viewed in the context of Gorbachev's overall policy objectives.

The USSR Council of Ministers' resolution (effective January 1, 1987) amended the regulations on emigration and immigration. The resolution clarifies the rules concerning eligibility for emigration by restricting emigration to reunion with first-degree family members (spouses, parents, or siblings). It also outlines the grounds on which exit may be refused.[26] The resolution serves as the legal foundation for decisions on emigration, and because it is restrictive regarding eligibility, it has the potential to be used to impede emigration. An updated codification of the precise terms of emigration is consistent with Gorbachev's emphasis on the rule of law.

Traditionally, one of the results of filing an emigration application has been the loss of employment. The inability to find reemployment in one's profession has characterized the situation of the refuseniks. The emigration of refuseniks means that Gorbachev will be able to rid himself of a large group of disgruntled, mobilized emigration activists whose skills are already lost to the Soviet Union. Emigration of the refuseniks also enables Gorbachev to reduce the number of divided families, a problem the USSR committed itself to resolve by signing the Final Act of the Conference on Security and Cooperation in Europe. Fulfillment of the obligations of the Final Act enhances Gorbachev's standing among liberals at home and appeases critics abroad. Most importantly, resolution of the refusenik problem allows Gorbachev to put the situation behind him, rid himself of its legacy, and move on to the pressing issues on his agenda.

Free emigration is not a likely option for the future because it would be difficult for Soviet policymakers to support ideologically and also because it is counterproductive to Gorbachev's long-term goals. There are several reasons why a liberal emigration policy is not in the best interests of *perestroika*. First, in the context of greater democratization, the restriction of emigration to several select groups is increasingly indefensible and could easily lead to demands by other nationalities for the freedom to emigrate. Second, Gorbachev has been clear about the importance of the intelligentsia's support for his reforms. Jews constitute a significant segment of the Soviet intelligentsia, and Gorbachev will need to coopt the Jews by improving their lot and by providing those considering emigration with incentives to remain in the USSR.

Although it is evident that maintaining large numbers of refuseniks is a liability, it remains to be seen whether the domestic situation will change sufficiently to discourage pressure for future emigration. In addition to coopting the Jews along with the rest of the intelligentsia, Gorbachev's emphasis on skill, efficiency, and productivity could mean that Jews, whose performance in these areas is considered strong, may benefit from *perestroika*.[27] If so, they will benefit at the expense of other groups, which could again trigger demands for affirmative action. In turn, this pressure could, in its worst manifestation, lead to increased anti-Semitism.

A survey of recent changes in the USSR indicates that Gorbachev is attempting to alter the modus vivendi, or social contract, affecting the Jews. All of the Jewish prisoners of conscience have been released, and a number have been permitted to emigrate. However, there are still several former prisoners who remain in the USSR. Greater access to professional and educational opportunities are high on the list of grievances frequently mentioned by would-be emigrants. It is too early to tell whether Jews have been afforded increased opportunities in these areas, but some limited improvements have been made in the cultural and religious spheres. These changes include the November 1986 airing on Soviet central television of a forty-five minute show on the Chamber Jewish Musical Theater of Birobidzhan; the permission given to a small group of Soviet Jews to study for the rabbinate in the United States, provided they return to the USSR to assume posts at Soviet synagogues; the establishment in November 1987 of a kosher refectory at the Moscow synagogue; a major exhibit of Marc Chagall's work, which opened at the A. S. Pushkin State Museum of Art in September 1987; and far greater access than ever before of Jewish book publishers and spectators to the Jewish bookstalls at the Moscow Book Fair in September 1987. Moreover, a number of these events were reported in the Soviet press.

Nonetheless, other developments are not as favorable. Democratization has brought with it greater freedom of expression for a wide variety of groups. One of these is Pamyat' (Memory), an organization ostensibly created for the preservation of Moscow's historical and cultural monuments that has emerged as an extreme Russian nationalist, anti-Semitic group. Pamyat', which has revitalized the notion of a Zionist-Freemason conspiracy to take over the world, a theme first popularized in the 1905 *Protocols of the Elders of Zion*, has received a good deal of Soviet media coverage. Although most official discussion points critically to the excesses of Pamyat', it is interesting to note that some of the well-published Soviet anti-Zionist propagandists of the 1970s and early 1980s, absent from the literary scene in recent years, have resurfaced in Pamyat'.[28]

Additionally, some reports in the Soviet press have been openly critical (as in the past) of Jews who wish to emigrate. A piece published in *Pravda* by Fedor Burlatsky, a journalist with *Literaturnaya gazeta*, discussed the new political culture developing in the Soviet Union and the multiplicity of views that are emerging.

> And now something has been discovered that could have been predicted. We have views that do not coincide fully, although all of us believe in socialism, Soviet rule and the Party's leadership of the country. . . . I remember a person who, during a meeting, demanded unlimited "freedom to demonstrate." This is typical ochlocracy (ochlocracy, according to Aristotle is mob rule). . . . Who in our country is for an unlimited "right to demonstrate"? Local nationalists, extremists from Pamyat' and certain other groups of similar orientation, *people pursuing selfish interests, so-called "refuseniks" who want to emigrate, etc.*[29]

Charges that the Western intelligence community and "Zionist circles" are undermining *perestroika* and *glasnost'* (openness) have also developed. An *Izvestiya* editorial stated that

> the plan is varied and adapted to different situations. At present, Zionist circles and Western intelligence services are trying to prevent their "human rights activitists" from leaving the USSR; they would rather have them remain in our country and attempt to use the development of *glasnost'* and democratization against our society.[30]

What is disconcerting about statements such as these is that they were made by official organs of the Party and the government. It seems that some of the messages intended for domestic consumption are harsher and, on occasion, even contrary to those designated for the foreign audience. At this early date, it is difficult to discern the scope of these discrepancies and harder still to assess their significance. However, they do indicate that the antiemigration policy remains unchanged.

Finally, if Gorbachev is to undertake the full de-Stalinization of Soviet society, he will need not only to carry out the social, political, and economic changes he is proposing but also to address Stalin's specific abuses. He began this process in his November 2, 1987, speech on the occasion of the seventieth anniversary celebration of the October Revolution and continued it with the official rehabilitation of Nikolai I. Bukharin, Lev B. Kamenev, Grigory Y. Zinoviev, and others in 1988. Presumably, Gorbachev will go further when he has enough political strength to do so. With respect to Stalin's treatment of the Jews, issues such as the Doctors' Plot, deportation, executions, and Jewish cultural annihilation will have to be addressed. So too, will the fate of the Jews during the Holocaust, which is still not specifically treated in Soviet textbooks.

In sum, it would seem that Gorbachev has taken some steps toward improving conditions for Soviet Jews, but it is not clear how far he will go or whether those steps will be significant enough to preempt future demands for emigration. As with all aspects of his reform plan to date, Gorbachev has experienced some difficulties and is moving more slowly than he would have liked. The treatment of the Jewish question is an important indicator of Gorbachev's ability to rewrite the social contract and establish new norms. Treatment of the Jewish question also provides additional evidence to support the view that domestic rather than international factors motivate Soviet emigration policy.

Notes

1. The author is pleased to thank Marc A. Kushner for his assistance in the preparation of this chapter, which is based on an article forthcoming in *Political Science Quarterly*.

2. See Benjamin Pinkus, "National Identity and Emigration Patterns Among Soviet Jewry," *Soviet Jewish Affairs* 15 (November 1985), p. 12.

3. The Baltic republics, Eastern Poland, and Bessarabia-Bukovina were annexed in 1939–1940.

4. See Yehoshua A. Gilboa, "The 1948 Zionist Wave in Moscow," *Soviet Jewish Affairs*, no. 2 (November 1971), pp. 35–39.

5. Jews represent about 15 percent of all Soviet physicians and constitute similar proportions among economists, musicians, and other professionals. Theodore H. Friedgut, "Soviet Jewry: The Silent Majority," *Soviet Jewish Affairs* 10 (May 1980), p. 8.

6. Joshua Rubenstein, *Soviet Dissidents: Their Struggle for Human Rights* (Boston: Beacon Press, 1980), p. 158

7. The largest percentages of the Jewish population live in the RSFSR (38.7 percent), the Ukrainian SSR (35.0 percent), and in the Belorussian SSR (6.6 percent). These figures are based on population distribution statistics in *Vestnik statistiki*, no. 2 (1980), pp. 27–28.

8. Victor Zaslavsky and Robert J. Brym, *Soviet-Jewish Emigration and Soviet Nationality Policy* (London: Macmillan, 1983), pp. 32–35; Yochanan Altman and Gerald Mars, "The Emigration of Soviet Georgian Jews to Israel," *Jewish Journal of Sociology* 26 (June 1984), pp. 35–45.

9. See "Leaving the Soviet Union: The Emigrant's Experience," in United States, Congress, House, Committee on International Relations, *Implementation of the Final Act of the Conference on Security and Cooperation in Europe: Findings and Recommendations Two Years After Helskinki*, report by the Commission on Security and Cooperation in Europe, 95th Cong., 1st sess., September 23, 1977, p. 183; Zaslavsky and Brym, ibid., pp. 49–51; and James R. Millar and Peter Donhowe, "The Classless Society Has a Wide Gap Between Rich and Poor," *Washington Post: National Weekly Edition*, February 17, 1986, p. 17.

10. Zaslavsky and Brymn, ibid., pp. 61–62. Similar results were reported by Gitelman in a survey conducted in 1976 among 244 recent Soviet immigrants in Detroit. Gitelman reported that the heartlanders indicated they left the USSR for reasons of political alienation and anti-Semitism, whereas the *zapadniki* were motivated by family and economic considerations. See Zvi Gitelman, "Soviet Jewish Emigrants: Why Are They Choosing America?" *Soviet Jewish Affairs* 7 (Spring 1977), pp. 41–43.

11. At the same time, the policy toward the emigration of Germans and Armenians was liberalized.

12. Invitations were sent to 79,711 Soviet Jews during 1968–1971, to 67,895 in 1972, and to 58,216 in 1973. Z. Alexander, "Immigration to Israel from the USSR," *Israel Yearbook on Human Rights* 7, special supplement (Tel Aviv: Tel Aviv University, 1977), p. 326. These figures refer to first-request invitations and do not include those requested in order to replace expired invitations. The emigration process must be initiated by an invitation (*vyzov*) from a relative in Israel, inviting the Soviet relative to join him or her. Invitations are valid for a limited period of time; only a portion of those who receive invitations apply to emigrate.

13. See United States, Congress, *Trade Act of 1974*, Pub. L. 93-618, Title IV, § 402, reprinted in *United States Code Congressional and Administrative News*, vol. 2 (1974).

14. The Stevenson amendment was one of the 1974 Export-Import Bank amendments. It limited the dollar value of credits the Export-Import Bank could grant to the Soviet Union to $300 million during a four-year period and required congressional approval for any decision to exceed the $300 million ceiling. See United States, Congress, *Export-Import Bank Amendments of 1974*, Pub. L. 93-646, § 8, reprinted in *United States Code Congressional and Administrative News*, vol. 2 (1974).

15. The amendment authorizes the president to waive the restrictions if (1) the waiver will substantially promote the objective of free emigration and (2)

the country under consideration provides assurances that its emigration practices will more closely reflect the objectives of the amendment. A waiver is to remain in effect only for a specified period and may be extended annually if approved by a concurrent resolution of both houses of Congress.

16. German emigration reached 9,701 in 1976. Annual levels dropped to 9,274 (1977), 8,455 (1978), 7,226 (1979), 6,954 (1980), 3,773 (1981), 2,071 (1982), 1,447 (1983), 913 (1984), 460 (1985). The number of German emigrants rose to 914 in 1986 and to an astounding high of 14,488 during 1987.

17. Elite integration was designed to neutralize independence and disaffection among the national elites by promoting allegiance to the system through expanded professional and educational opportunities. An anticipated by-product of this practice was greater local support for economic revitalization.

18. *Narodnoe khozyaistvo SSSR v 1984 godu: statisticheskii ezhegodnik* (Moscow: Finansy i statistika, 1985), pp. 34–35.

19. Godfrey S. Baldwin, "Population Projections by Age and Sex: For the Republics and Major Economic Regions of the U.S.S.R., 1970 to 2000," *International Population Reports*, Series P-91, no. 26 (Washington, D.C.: U.S. Department of Commerce, Bureau of the Census, Foreign Demographics Analysis Division, 1979), p. 14. Baldwin uses a projection series (high, medium, low) for natural increase rates in the year 2000. His projections are 8.4, 5.5, and 2.4 per thousand, respectively. (According to *Narodnoe khozyaistvo SSSR v 1985 godu: statisticheskii ezhegodnik* [Moscow: Finansy i statistika, 1986], p. 33, the natural population increase in 1985 rose slightly to 8.8 per thousand. It remains to be seen whether the long-term [Western] forecasts for continued decreases will prove accurate.)

20. See report to the Twenty-seventh Congress of the CPSU by Nikolai Ryzhkov, as reported by TASS, in *FBIS Daily Report: Soviet Union—National Affairs* 3 (March 3, 1986), pp. O 23–O 26.

21. Baldwin, "Population Projections by Age and Sex," p. 11.

22. For detailed discussions see Ann Helgeson, "Demographic Policy," in *Soviet Policy for the 1980s*, ed. Archie Brown and Michael Kaser (London: Macmillan for St. Antony's College, Oxford, 1982), pp. 139–145; Gail Warshofsky Lapidus, "Social Trends," in *After Brezhnev: Sources of Soviet Conduct in the 1980s*, ed. Robert F. Byrnes (Bloomington: Indiana University Press in association with the Center for Strategic and International Studies, Georgetown University, Washington, D.C., 1983), pp. 200–232.

23. Jews are often taken for Russians (or other Slavs) because they tend to be highly assimilated.

24. See *Pravda*, January 19, 1987; *New York Times*, March 30, 1987, p. A13; *New Times* (Moscow), no. 28, July 20, 1987, pp. 24–26.

25. This figure was provided by the National Conference on Soviet Jewry.

26. See Resolution of the USSR Council of Ministers, "On Making Amendments to the Regulations on Entry into the Union of Soviet Socialist Republics and on Exit from the Union of Soviet Socialist Republics," *Sobranie postanovlenii pravitelstva SSSR* [section one], no. 31 (1986), item 163, pp. 563–566.

27. During an interview with Tom Brokaw, Gorbachev spoke about the need to protect against a brain drain. See David K. Shipler, "Gorbachev Mix on TV Is Tough But Cooperative," *New York Times*, December 1, 1987, pp. A1, A12.

28. See Howard Spier, "Russian Chauvinists and the Thesis of a Jewish World Conspiracy: Three Case Studies," Institute of Jewish Affairs, *Research Report,* no. 6 (August 1987).

29. *Pravda,* July 18, 1987, p. 3 (emphasis added).

30. *Izvestiya,* September 19, 1987, p. 5.

(Author's note: Since this chapter was completed, developments in the Soviet Union indicate that a new trend in immigration policy may be under way.)

7

The Changing
Soviet Political System:
The Nineteenth Party Conference
and After

Seweryn Bialer

"A single week in the life of a revolution," according to Robespierre, "is often richer in historical events than a year of normal times." The brief history of Mikhail Gorbachev's reform has been rich and has already produced a number of milestones. The Nineteenth Party Conference that met in Moscow from June 28, 1988, to July 1, 1988, and the Plenum of the Central Committee that followed it a month later are two such milestones. To understand their importance it is necessary to see how they fit into the extraordinary process of reform that Gorbachev has begun.

*   *   *

Gorbachev was selected by his peers in the leadership for the post of the Party's General Secretary in March 1985. He came to power against major opposition and without a personal political machine to support him. Yet he had a clear mandate from the political elite to reform the Soviet Union, to arrest its stagnation and decay, and to reverse its decline. This mandate did not, however, specify what to do or how to do it. Moreover, at the time of his appointment Gorbachev did not yet grasp the depth of the Soviet crisis, nor had he identified the remedies to overcome it. It took the General Secretary approximately a year and a half of improvisation and analysis to develop even the outlines of his program. The years 1985 and 1986 therefore constitute the prelude to *perestroika* (restructuring).

Perestroika can be divided into three phases. The first lasted from the late fall of 1986 to the summer of 1987. Gorbachev's aim during this phase was to establish and energetically pursue the policies of democratization and *glasnost'* (openness) as instruments of mass mobilization against bureaucratic resistance and inertia. He sought to establish a conceptual framework that would become an entire plan of structural economic reform. Finally, he pursued the parallel goal of consolidating his power at the level of the top leadership.

Perestroika's second phase lasted from the fall of 1987 to April 1988 and represented a pause in the implementation of *perestroika*. This phase was characterized by a confluence of unanticipated events that complicated Gorbachev's political situation, by a growing bureaucratic resistance to *perestroika,* and by an open attack by his opponents on key elements of *glasnost'*.

The third phase began in April 1988 and, if the General Secretary has his way, will conclude with the election of a new Soviet of People's Deputies in 1989. The third phase began with Gorbachev's counteroffensive against the opponents of *perestroika*. The main goal of this phase is a thorough transformation of the Soviet political system that will make *perestroika* irreversible and place Gorbachev in a commanding position of power.

The First Phase

The first phase of Gorbachev's efforts to transform the Soviet Union sought to establish a plan of radical political, cultural, and economic reforms and begin their implementation. Gorbachev also pursued the goal of consolidating his power in the institutions of Soviet leadership— the Politburo, the Secretariat of the Central Committee, and the Presidium of the Council of Ministers. He had achieved both to a large extent by the summer of 1987. By building on the ideas and policies of his first years in office, Gorbachev was able, from January to June 1987, to launch an unprecedented offensive that started and ended with plenary meetings of the powerful Central Committee. They were devoted to the two pillars of his program—the political-cultural and the economic.

In January 1987, the Central Committee adopted resolutions and promulgated policies that sought to democratize the USSR at the grassroots level. The committee also initiated vigorous efforts to promote a less restrained flow of information; greater openness of discussion in all fields of endeavor; freer press, radio, and television; and greater freedom of expression in theaters, films, and culture in general. In June 1987, it adopted an outline of a radical economic reform, one that sought to move the Soviet Union away from its traditional centralized, overradministered, and economically ineffective form of socialism. The purpose of this reform was to create a system in which market forces and individual enterprises would play a major role and in which the traditional stress on quantitative growth would be replaced by an emphasis on productivity of labor and capital, technological progress, material incentives, profit, and quality.

During this period, Gorbachev effectively consolidated his power. By the summer of 1987, through a combination of forced retirements, expulsions, and cooptations, he was able to command a clear majority within the Soviet leadership. He could thus count on support for his policies from leaders who not only shared his commitment to radical reforms but were personally loyal to him as well.

Gorbachev also seized control of the military. The landing near Red Square of the nineteen-year-old West German pilot Matthias Rust, in a small aircraft he had flown in undetected—demonstrating, wry Muscovites said, that the Soviet Union was an "open society"—became the pretext for a shake-up of the high command. General Dmitry Yazov, Gorbachev's man, was appointed minister of defense, and this appointment bypassed more than twenty senior marshals and generals. Some two hundred lower-ranking generals were retired or fired. At no other time since the era of Nikita Khrushchev a generation earlier had the political clout, the visibility, and the prestige of the armed forces been as low.

After the flurry of activities during the first six months of 1987, the General Secretary and his close associates took a brief hiatus. Gorbachev went to the Crimea for more than six weeks to finish his book *Perestroika*, which was designed for both Western and domestic audiences, and to prepare himself for the new task of supervising the implementation of the radical reforms already adopted. Official Moscow settled down for a temporary lull.

By now, the aims of the second phase of the Gorbachev revolution were becoming clear to the Moscow establishment, the General Secretary's friends and foes, and Western observers. These aims were twofold: The first was to reform the Soviet political system. *Glasnost'* and democratization, as well as purges of personnel, had already affected the existing traditional Soviet political system. But the purges, the pressure from below, and the pressures from the media were insufficient to restore vigor to the political system and to break bureaucratic resistance to *perestroika*. *Structural* change in the stagnant political system was urgently needed.

Gorbachev had planned all along to accomplish this at an all-union Party conference. No Party assembly of lesser magnitude and political weight was equal to such a task. At the January 1987 Plenum of the Central Committee, Gorbachev raised the idea of convening such a conference, which is second in importance to a regular Party congress, for the first time since 1941. The attempt failed; Gorbachev was unable to persuade the Central Committee to convene such a conference. After major preparations, he had greater luck at the June 1987 Central Committee meeting, and a conference was scheduled for June 1988 after Gorbachev informally agreed that he would not follow Iosif Stalin's 1941 precedent of using the conference to make major personnel changes.

The other aim of the second phase of reform was to create within two years all the organizational, political, cultural, and psychological conditions necessary for the Soviet Union's entry into modernity. The Central Committee Plenum of June 1987 adopted an economic restructuring more sweeping than anything in the post-Stalinist past and promising even more daring innovations to come. Gorbachev defined his proposals as a plan of "fundamental reconstruction of the management of the economy" that would go far beyond those he introduced in his first two years as General Secretary. The purpose of these reforms was to reduce central planning and give new independence to managers of enterprises and firms; to install a system of quality control and pricing; to encourage competition; and to increase the importance of money, credit, and profit. These goals stood in dramatic contradistinction to the inherited Stalinist system of centralized planning and bureaucratic interference.

Yet as they were adopted at the June 1987 Plenum, the economic reforms were only preliminary because at the crucial junctures of Soviet economic activity, such as price formation, quality control, and competition, market forces will not be decisive. A multitude of committees, commissions, boards, and offices will continue to perform the roles that are fulfilled in economically more successful societies by the market and competition. Bureaucrats may act more rationally, but their actions will not erase the system's underlying irrationalities: the artificiality of costs, prices, and profits, which are divorced from the quantity and quality of labor and capital expenditures, from the laws of supply and demand, and from unhampered competition. But these preliminary reforms were nonetheless needed to create a climate for the more dramatic changes that were to come in the second phase of *perestroika*.

The Second Phase

The second phase of *perestroika* was to start with the celebration of the seventieth anniversary of the Bolshevik Revolution and was to be inaugurated on November 2, 1987, by the General Secretary's speech to a combined meeting of the Party's Central Committee, the Supreme Soviets of the USSR and the Russian Republic, as well as a large group of foreign guests. But things began to go wrong in late summer. The combined effects of increasing bureaucratic resistance, the Yeltsin affair, unrest in the non-Russian republics, and an open conservative attack on *glasnost'* visibly slowed Gorbachev at a critical juncture. *Perestroika* lost its momentum. The General Secretary was forced to the defensive.

It became clear in the summer of 1987 that *perestroika* was facing open resistance from the administrative bureaucracies. No one, particularly not Gorbachev, thought the reform of a failing system would be easy, but by the fall of 1987, even Gorbachev publicly claimed to be surprised by the intensity of resistance. This resistance grew at a time when Gorbachev's position of power within the top leadership had been consolidated beyond question. Yet from a political point of view, the relationship between Gorbachev's power and the resistance to his *perestroika* processes was only logical.

During his first year and a half in office, Gorbachev spoke of the need for change in a generalized way. He had neither a detailed program nor sufficient power to act decisively. The process of Gorbachev's self-education and the increase in his authority led in 1987 to policies that took aim at the vested interests of clearly defined groups. As long as Gorbachev spoke of change in *general*, he enjoyed wide support. Everyone saw the need for change in the old, stagnant, and corrupt system. But as the reforms became specific and their radical nature sank in, the bureaucracies mounted a fierce resistance in defense of their privileges and indeed their very livelihood. In words, the bureaucracies agreed publicly with the fundamentals of Gorbachev's *perestroika*, but in deeds, the bureaucracies opposed its implementation. Thus, the growth of Gorbachev's authority was accompanied by growing resistance at the middle levels of power.

The Yeltsin Affair

At the October 1987 Plenum of the Central Committee, Gorbachev was confronted by a new challenge from a surprising source—the Moscow Party leader Boris Yeltsin, a passionate advocate of reform. As the Party prepared to celebrate the Seventieth Anniversary of the Bolshevik Revolution, Yeltsin gave a stunning indictment of the Party, and thus of Gorbachev, for moving too slowly and promising too much (see Chapter 3). Yeltsin also disclosed differences of views within the ruling Politburo. It was Gorbachev's first open crisis of political leadership, and he only partially contained the damage.

From the point of view of *perestroika*, the domestic repercussions of the Yeltsin affair were entirely negative. They encouraged the conservatives to greater resistance against change, particularly against criticism from below and honest investigative reporting from without. Before the Yeltsin affair, the only enemies of *perestroika* that Gorbachev had identified were the forces of inertia, bureaucratization, and defense of vested interests. Now a new enemy was identified: the forces of "political adventurism" and those who "want to jump through stages"—that is to say, those who, like Yeltsin, wanted a stronger push for reform and who were ready to purge utterly the inherited apparatus. As one strongly pro-Gorbachev Party leader expressed it, "The main enemies still remain the conservative opponents of *perestroika*, but the superliberal supporters of *perestroika* have to be contained because, by their exaggerations, they provide the ammunition for the conservatives."

The Yeltsin affair sent a strong cautionary signal to those within the power structure who were wholeheartedly committed to Gorbachev's course. It discouraged those in the intelligentsia who were still cautiously waiting on the sidelines, uncertain whether it was safe to lend active support to the General Secretary's programs and policies. Gorbachev admitted as much on January 11, 1988, at a meeting with leading Soviet newspaper and magazine editors. Although he did not refer to Yeltsin by name, Gorbachev publicly acknowledged for the first time that the events surrounding Yeltsin's dismissal had caused wide anxiety and doubt about the leadership's commitment to change: "We shall not conceal the fact that the party's rebuff was viewed by a certain part of the intelligentsia, especially young people, as a blow to *perestroika*."

Nationalistic Ferment

While Gorbachev was recovering from the consequences of the Yeltsin affair and trying to reignite the flame of *perestroika*, he was dealt another serious blow. It took the form of bloody rioting, with many deaths, in Transcaucasia. Armenians took the new liberalization as license to demand annexation to Armenia of the Armenian-majority enclave of Nagorno-Karabakh in Azerbaijan, which unleashed traditional mutual animosities with the Azerbaijanis. This has been the most dramatic, but by no means the only, side effect of Gorbachev's liberalization among Soviet ethnic groups.

Deepening nationalistic ferment—a long-delayed reaction to Stalinist suppression—has begun to rock the multinational Soviet state. Beginning with Stalin, non-Russians within the Soviet Union have endured economic, political, and cultural subordination to the Russian elite. Russian officials have supervised the bureaucracies and blocked the promotion of non-Russians to the upper-echelon political positions in Moscow. Gorbachev confronts hundreds of petitions for justice from non-Russians. Native Tatars demand restoration to the homeland they left at Stalin's order. Kazakhstan continues to seethe more than a year after the Kazakh Party chief was fired (on December 16, 1986) in favor of a Russian. Unrest is a constant in the Baltic states.

The issue of relations among the nations of the Soviet Union, particularly between the non-Russians and the Russians, is clearly an important, if not primary, matter to be addressed in the process of *perestroika*. Gorbachev had hoped to resolve the nationalities issues in an orderly manner. The Azerbaijan-Armenia conflict, which continued for many months and required troops to restore the peace, has demonstrated that this may not be possible.

Whereas it is difficult for Gorbachev to overcome the apathy and indifference to his program, it is much easier for that program to release forces detrimental to his cause. Gorbachev and his loyalists within the leadership have begun a process that cannot be entirely controlled or directed. Actions that positively affect the progress of *perestroika* will inevitably be accompanied by unintended and unwelcome consequences. If in the long run Gorbachev is genuinely committed to *perestroika*, which seems unquestionable, a retreat from the principle of *glasnost'* in dealing with those unintended consequences will harm *perestroika* without preventing those consequences.

It is to be hoped that the Soviet leadership will treat the violent events in Transcaucasia and their consequences with openness, without curtailing *glasnost'*. Such a course will help to put those events in the proper perspective and will underscore the necessity to deal seriously with the legacy of accumulated grievances.

Conservative Opposition and Bureaucratic Resistance

In the meantime, however, the nationalistic unrest in the Soviet south has strengthened all those who urged caution in planning and implementing *perestroika* and who could say, "We told you so." Encouraged by Gorbachev's increasing difficulties, the conservative opposition has become emboldened and increasingly active. Active conservative opposition to *perestroika* must be distinguished from simple bureaucratic resistance. These two currents of anti-Gorbachev activity mutually reinforce each other, but they are not identical. They have far different social bases and take distinctly different forms. The bureaucratic resistance has its base in the administrative-managerial apparatus of the Party and state. Its most pronounced form of activity is a combination of passive resistance and camouflaged sabotage of the reforms. The bureaucratic resistance has no ideology of its own. The disgruntled bureaucrats, while clandestinely defending their privileges, mouth the slogans of *perestroika* in public and do not defend their positions in open forums. (The bureaucratic-administrative apparatus, according to Gorbachev, consists of 18 million officials.)

A young technocrat, Sergei Andreyev, described how managers sabotage government decisions. In an article in *Nedelya* (April 25, 1988), he called this sabotage "the braking mechanism" and outlined three ways to use it effectively. The first is to break up the "big" resolution into small ones that are in sum different from the big one. The second is to find loopholes in the "big" resolution and thus to water it down. The third is worth quoting verbatim:

> The third method is not only simple but brilliant, if there is such a thing as brilliant corruption. 'In conformity' with directives from above, managers issue orders to their subordinates, but *in exaggerated and over-zealous form,* and therefore unsupported by economic calculations—in effect, they send below a peremptory command: Do it, and that is all there is to it. . . . As a result, disproportions develop in the national economy that cannot be adjusted—and the government is forced to take a step backward to correct them by making changes in its own decisions.

The social base of the conservative opposition is particularly heterogeneous and only partly coincides with the base of bureaucratic resistance. It is composed of such groups as a large segment of the Party's ideological, educational, and propaganda apparatus; the Party activists who are engaged in agitation, propaganda, and Party schooling; a powerful minority of writers, journalists, and those who work in the media, particularly outside Moscow in the Russian Republic; a part of the academic profession in the social sciences; and a large group that may be called the "semi-intelligentsia," the hundreds of thousands of teachers of Marxism-Leninism in the universities, institutes of higher education, and high schools.

Members of these groups have embraced conservative opposition to *perestroika* for many different reasons. The most important ones, however, are not difficult to fathom. The education of these conservatives has consisted of the assimilation of the most narrowly conceived Marxist-Leninist dogmas. Their only qualification for occupying positions of status and authority, indeed their only skill, is their command of the "eternal truths" for every occasion. The Russian writers and journalists within this group are predominantly, although not exclusively, from the provinces, and they are masters of "socialist realism." They have been able to earn significant salaries and to achieve positions of status despite their sheer simplemindedness and actual lack of talent. They have controlled the unions of "creative workers" and are now faced with the danger of losing everything. Their views and deepest beliefs are a mixture of Russian nationalism, Slavophile anti-Western orientation, simplified Marxist-Leninist dogmas, and commitment to the glory of past Soviet and Russian achievements. Some of these writers are clearly anti-Semitic obscurantists.

The conservative opposition is openly critical of Gorbachev's *perestroika* and particularly of democratization and *glasnost'*. They see these movements as alien to the USSR and to the Soviet tradition that they cherish. They regard *glasnost'* and democratization as the Trojan horse that will destroy the Soviet system as they know it in its neo-Stalinist form. The conservative opposition has relatively easy access to the media and even partial control over many provincial and some Moscow journals and newspapers, among them the Central Committee organ, *Sovetskaya Rossiya*, which is published in 7 million copies; the organ of the Russian Writers' Union, *Literaturnaya Rossiya*; and the Communist Youth League organ, *Molodaya gvardiya*.

The conservative struggle against *perestroika* is quite open, enjoying the support of powerful patrons. One of them is Viktor Afanas'ev, the editor in chief of the main Party daily newspaper, *Pravda*, and a member of the Central Committee. The conservatives' main defense against *perestroika*, however, rests in the hands of Yegor Ligachev, the second-ranking member of the Party Secretariat and one of the most powerful members of the Politburo.

Gorbachev and other members of the Soviet leadership deny the existence of any opposition, either to the General Secretary or to *perestroika*, at the highest levels of government. Yet, it is generally, and justifiably, accepted in Moscow and the West that Gorbachev's key opponent in the Politburo and the Secretariat is Ligachev. Soviet and Western sources have asserted that Ligachev is not an enemy of *perestroika* but wants only to proceed more cautiously with economic reforms, abandon the strong critique of the past, and limit but not abolish *glasnost'* and democratization. Nevertheless, to say that Ligachev is not an enemy of *perestroika*, but only of some of its features, is utter nonsense.

Ligachev seeks a vastly different *perestroika* than that to which Gorbachev and his associates are committed. Ligachev is a proponent of the types of reform that were attempted so many times in the past rather than of the radical, comprehensive, and speedy reforms envisioned by *perestroika*. Ligachev's formula appears similar to that of Deng Xiaoping in China, according to whom, "In the political, ideological, and cultural realms, the enemy is liberalism; in the economic realm, the enemy is conservatism." Yet, even in the economic field, Ligachev's vision of *perestroika* is far different from that of Gorbachev. Ligachev is against bureaucratic resistance to the most basic steps of the economic reform that has started in the Soviet Union. But from what is known, he is far more restrained than the General Secretary in his support of the introduction of market forces as the basis of economic activity. He is certainly unhappy with the spontaneous development of the so-called cooperatives (private enterprise) in production, marketing, and services. He appears to support heavy taxation of those enterprises (such taxation existed until it was limited by recent legislation). Ligachev is not alone in the higher Party circles in his attempt to dull the cutting edge of *perestroika*. Often named as his associates in the Politburo are Vitaly Vorotnikov, the prime minister of the Russian Republic, and Mikhail Solomentsev, the head of the Party Control Committee.

There is yet another, crucially important difference between bureaucratic resistance and conservative opposition to *perestroika*. The bureaucrats who defend their privilege and position in an underhanded manner are unable to count on either sympathy or help from the mass Communist Party or from the workers. Gorbachev's attack on the bureaucracy and his goal of reducing its size and limiting its administrative powers are the most popular parts of his program within the Party and among the people.

The situation is entirely different with the cause of the conservative opposition. As in other industrial countries, so in the Soviet Union the working class is by and large anti-intellectual, deeply patriotic, and traditional in its values. In part at least, whether they are members of the Communist Party or not, workers provide a ready-made constituency for the values and sentiments that are being expressed by the conservative opposition. The workers, for example, hate the bureaucrats and call them *bumazhnye dushi* (paper souls) but like the predictability of the old order. Workers are egalitarian not so much in their dislike of the perquisites and privileges of the *nachalstvo* (bosses) as in their support of equality at the lowest common denominator within their own class—not unlike the solidarity of the peasant *mir* (collective) against the *khutor* (the individual farm) at the time of the Stolypin reform during the decade before the October Revolution. Workers hate the instant affluence of the *deltsy* (entrepreneurs) in the cooperative enterprises and regard profits made by individual efforts as "dirty money," although this does not prevent them from making money through collective stealing from state enterprises or through work *na levo* (under the table), done either after work or during official working hours. Workers have a deep-seated and instinctive dislike of intellectuals and the media and are jealous and critical of the newfound freedom of such groups. The older workers are against the Western mass culture adopted by the younger generations. They glorify the Soviet past and the role of their class in it. In the final analysis, they are the conservative opposition's greatest source of power, and their vocal opposition to *glasnost'* and democratization is the greatest danger to Gorbachev.

March 1988—Dual Power

The offensive of the conservative opposition culminated on March 13, 1988, with an article in *Sovetskaya Rossiya* that burst like a bombshell on the Moscow political scene and spread like wildfire quickly around the country. The article, written in the form of a letter to the newspaper, covered an entire page and was purportedly written by Nina Andreyeva, a chemistry teacher at the Leningrad Technological Institute. The article, entitled "I Cannot Compromise Principles," attacked Gorbachev's program and attempted to rehabilitate Stalin and refute Gorbachev's critique of the past; the article even employed arguments intended to appeal to the anti-Semitic feelings among the Russian people.

The nonetheless well-written article contained a highly emotional attack on the "left liberals" who were destroying everything valuable in the Russian and Soviet past. (In one relatively benign paragraph on p. 3, the author criticized the "traditionalists" of the organization Memory who "do not understand the importance of the October Revolution for our fatherland.") The article accepted the Stalinist past without excuse or justification. It could easily have been published, unchanged, in Stalin's time. The dictator would have been delighted to learn that he was very "humble" and "ascetic in his lifestyle." Stalin's cultural commissar, Andrei Zhdanov, would have been pleased that his favorite "enemies of the people"—the "Cosmopolites" (meaning Jews and Zionists)—had returned after thirty-five years' absence to the pages of the Soviet press. Andreyeva's article was not simply a return to a Brezhnevian judgment of the past, with its slightly embarrassed "on the one hand" and "on the other hand" approach; this was a full-fledged apology for Stalin and all he stood for.

Some details of how this article was produced are known. Andreyeva was selected to be its author for a number of reasons: She was a chemistry teacher who was intelligent enough to write a complex article but simple enough to reflect the voice of "the people"; her father and mother were workers in the Putilov factory in Leningrad, where the revolution was born; and a member of her family was "repressed" under Stalin and posthumously rehabilitated in 1953. In short, hers was a perfect biography.

The letter-article, of course, was not written by Nina Andreyeva, or even by her husband, who as a teacher of Marxism-Leninism at an institute of higher education at Leningrad had even better qualifications for the task. The article was in fact written by a team of propagandists and coordinated by the editor of *Sovetskaya Rossiya*. More importantly, it was inspired by Ligachev, who gave it to the newspaper for publication. It is notable that during the month before the publication of the article, the atmosphere in Moscow was heavy with the intelligentsia's foreboding about an impending all-out conservative counteroffensive against *glasnost'*. In the February issue of *Novy mir*, for example, publicist Andrei Nuikin had predicted it.

It seems worth quoting at length from an extraordinary essay by the Russian literary critic Yu. Karyakin, published in June 1988, who wrote as follows of the Andreyeva letter:

> A year ago one of the models for my Incognito [a reference to an earlier essay], apparently also a chemist, by the way, withdrew his denunciation from publication with the words, "It is not now the time to strike." I can imagine how pleased he must be with his colleague's letter: the time, it seems, has arrived. . . . I can imagine how much you all found it to your liking. —Here they are, your new "Fundamentals," your new "Short Course," your first ideological "Manifesto," soaked through with "zhdanovite fluid." I can also imagine how you mobilized all your intellectual, moral, and organizational abilities in order to turn this "Manifesto" into the signal for an immediate counterattack, but . . . it backfired. (*Inovo ne Dano* [There Is No Other Way], edited by Yu. N. Afanas'ev [Moscow: Progress, 1988])

Gorbachev's Critique of the Soviet Past. Ligachev chose to concentrate the attack on Gorbachev's program on an issue where the General Secretary is most vulnerable—his passionate denunciation of Stalin (and Leonid Brezhnev) and, more broadly, of Soviet tradition. Under Gorbachev, the critique of the Stalin era from its inception in the 1920s had already gone far beyond Khrushchev's most radical attacks on the person of the leader. It is still gaining momentum, as is the attack on the "period of stagnation" under Brezhnev. It is unprecedented in its scope and its depth. In providing archival data to support its thesis, it often goes beyond Western analyses and is very similar to the writing of dissident historian Roy Medvedev; sometimes it even attains the intensity of an Aleksandr Solzhenitsyn exposé.

There are many reasons that the critique of the entire Soviet past is so intense. It seems that for the General Secretary and his loyal associates, it fulfills an emotional need to speak out on things they have learned to hate and have maintained silence about for many years. It provides them with a historical sense of and intellectual perspective on what they want to accomplish in the Soviet Union. It is also natural for them to want to discover what went wrong in the past. As one pro-*perestroika* author expressed it, "The most important thing that we are doing is, for the first time, to learn the truth about ourselves and our country."

In the Soviet Union under Brezhnev, research institutes were created to study virtually every country in the world and every aspect of international relations. Thousands of experts, with free access to original sources, were involved in research that was to serve Soviet global-power aspirations. There were no comparable institutes established to study the Soviet past or present. Such academic research institutes that did exist partly for this purpose, such as the Institute of Economics, the Institute of State and Law, the Institute of the History of the USSR, had no access to either historical archives or to contemporary data. Their conclusions were dictated by the Party line of the moment, and their "production" was, as a rule, not unlike the articles in *Pravda*. Winston Churchill spoke of the Soviet Union as an enigma wrapped in a mystery; but the Soviet Union was also a mystery for its own citizens, its own scholars, and, as bizarre as it may appear, for its own leaders as well, all of whom were deprived of accurate statistics and information.

Knowledge about the Soviet past and, especially, the Soviet present has depended heavily on views and information from the West. For economists, for instance, who did not have detailed *Gosplan* figures or did not believe its statistics, the publication of the "Green Books" from the United States (the biannual compendium from the U.S. Congress that analyzes the state of the Soviet economy) was awaited with great eagerness. The numerous Soviet books written to debunk "the falsifiers of Soviet history" provided the teachers and students of Soviet history with the views and arguments of Western historians through lengthy quotations, from the Western sources, that were supposedly being intellectually "annihilated."

Gorbachev's revision of the Soviet past is also, perhaps even primarily, advanced for other more directly instrumental reasons. First, this critique is a necessary ingredient of *perestroika;* it provides the policy with legitimation and ideological justification. Gorbachev is asking the Party and the people to dramatically change their way of life. They will agree to it only if they believe that the key components of their tradition were wrong and that the alternative offered by Gorbachev is better.

Like every Soviet leader before him, Gorbachev has used Leninism as the ideological basis of his policies. But he must show that the "real" V. I. Lenin was the one whose thoughts and ideas would support *perestroika* and then, from the vantage point of historical experience, would reject the alternatives of Stalin and Brezhnev. So radical a break with sixty years of tradition cannot be justified unless this tradition was either criminal (in Stalin's case) or drastically wrong (in Brezhnev's case).

At the same time, the ideological base of Gorbachev's legitimacy is far different from that of Nikita Khrushchev, the other anti-Stalinist Soviet leader. In the words of Khrushchev's son-in-law, Aleksei Adzhubei, in my interview in April 1988, "Khrushchev tried to dethrone *Stalin*. Gorbachev is fighting *Stalinism*, the system that Stalin created and that in its basic outlines survived in Russia through the eras of Khrushchev's and Brezhnev's leadership." This view was substantiated by Gorbachev in his speech, "The Ideological Basis of *Perestroika*," delivered at the February 1988 Plenum of the Central Committee.

Moreover, Gorbachev's anti-Stalinism is a prerequisite to his credibility in the eyes of the intelligentsia. Gorbachev's power base is not a traditional one. It is not built on an alliance with any of the basic Soviet bureaucracies. It depends to a great extent on the support of the mainstays of Party and public opinion—writers, journalists, filmmakers, television personnel, scientists, and academics. Gorbachev is their natural leader, and, therefore, even if he is often vexed by what he considers their ideological excesses, he must be in step with their burning desire to come to terms with the Soviet past in the interest of the future.

Finally, Gorbachev's critique of the past, precisely because it is sensitive, is an attempt to shock the Party and the people out of their conformity with it. The critique is designed to create an atmosphere of free thinking in which a person can question the traditional authority that is still so much in the control of Gorbachev's opponents and enemies and that is still so plagued by the inertia of the past. This critique is an attempt to mobilize people to whom he still has very little to offer through a spirit of emancipation, freedom, and individual dignity.

Yet, the attack in the March 13 article on Gorbachev's historical revisionism was aimed at a particularly vulnerable point. Although Gorbachev's denunciation of the Soviet past is a necessity, the Soviet people, especially the older ones, are traditionalists. Some resented the attacks; others were confused or made uneasy by the harsh critique of the greater part of their past. Within the Party, and among its powerful bureaucracy, the feeling was widespread that Gorbachev had gone too far.

Gorbachev's Historical Revisionism. That Gorbachev was conscious of his vulnerability in this respect is clearly shown by the very tactics that he used in revising history. First, in his speeches on this subject, such as that of November 2, 1987, to celebrate the Seventieth Anniversary of the October Revolution and in February 1988 at the "ideological" Plenum of the Central Committee, he took centrist positions. He denounced the past but only generally and in terms much less harsh and more ambiguous than those used by liberal Party intellectuals. The most important function of his speeches was to stimulate more detailed and harsher revisionism, especially in the early stages of *perestroika*. After late 1987, an equally important function of his speeches could be detected in what he did *not* say. By not passing judgment on many issues of history, he was in fact saying that there was no binding Party line on those issues and that they were open for free discussion. When he did go into detail, his views were intended to prescribe, not always successfully, the limits of revisionism. This was the case with his denunciation of Leon Trotsky and his defense of the Nazi-Soviet pact of 1939.

Second, Gorbachev's denunciations of the past have increased in intensity and depth following a period of sharp media discussion of an issue, such as Stalinist collectivization or the centralization of the party apparatus. It is as if Gorbachev has waited for the people, particularly Party members, to become accustomed to reading of or hearing about certain historical subjects before he has joined the critique. The battle of historical revisionism has been conducted primarily by "shock troops" drawn from among the creative intelligentsia within the Party. Gorbachev tried to preserve freedom of maneuver on individual historical issues. He knew how sensitive the process of historical revisionism could be and tried not to complicate his job by becoming too openly and deeply involved in the heated battles. There was, of course, little doubt about where his sympathies lay.

Ligachev's Maneuvers. The March 13 article was both inspired and exploited by Ligachev. He made a well-publicized congratulatory call to the editor. For three weeks after its appearance, Ligachev and his associates used their considerable influence to praise the article, to make it required reading at the educational meetings of Party organizations throughout the country as well as within the Soviet armed forces, and to encourage the appearance in the press of similar articles and supportive letters from readers. At meetings with newspaper editors and agricultural managers, Ligachev and his supporters praised the article as reflecting the true Party line. Viktor Afanas'ev openly declared that he regretted that this article had not been published in his newspaper (*Pravda*). The intensity and self-confidence of Ligachev's attack engendered panic among the creative intelligentsia. It presented an image of Gorbachev in full retreat from his program. It encouraged the conservative middle and lower strata of the bureaucracy and gave rise to their attack on investigative journalism. It created despondency and frustration among Gorbachev's supporters. For a full three weeks, it generated the impression of "dual power" at the top.

Karyakin described his trip to Leningrad, the alleged source of the Andreyeva letter, in the following manner:

Quite recently (March 24–26), while in Leningrad, I heard and read plenty that glorified [Andreyeva]. I witnessed a very real recurrence of the Zhdanov period. I inhaled and was intoxicated by the "zhdanovite fluid." This glorification swung about as if on command. But, why—how? And it was even very organized. We've seen it all before: "The moral burden has blown over. The pillars have been cut down; the fences will fall by themselves. . . . " I heard, "Finally!" "Finally, the slanderers have been given a rebuff." "Finally, everything's been put in its place." . . . I heard, "Here is the ideological tuning-fork of the Nineteenth Party Conference!" I heard, "This is the sort that we should send there as delegates!" . . . and is it surprising that the April 5 article in *Pravda* did not raise any enthusiasm among the organizers of the "moral relaxation"?

It is sobering. There is still no guarantee of the irreversibility of renewal. Instead, they have graphically and gladly demonstrated for us a small rehearsal of the smothering of *perestroika*, a micromodel of revenge. We will be grateful for the lesson: the only guarantees are in ourselves. (Inovo ne Dano, p. 420)

Ligachev's attack was encouraged by a range of difficulties that the General Secretary had encountered during the previous five months, and its timing had an additional purpose. Throughout the Soviet Union, delegates to the Nineteenth Party Conference were being elected by local Party organizations. Ligachev sought to create an atmosphere within the Party that would discourage the reformers, strengthen the hand of the conservatives, and thus promote the election of anti-*perestroika* delegates to the conference. By so doing and by continuing his campaign, Ligachev could have nullified Gorbachev's hopes that the conference would provide a decisive push for the implementation of his program. Gorbachev's political momentum was losing ground.

Phase Three

At the beginning of April, Gorbachev responded with a determined and largely successful counteroffensive. He began by convening a special Politburo meeting that lasted (with recesses, of course) more than two days. He and his closest associates attacked the *Sovetskaya Rossiya* article in the harshest terms. They forced Ligachev and two members of the Politburo who were in sympathy with his views to explain their role in the appearance and the dissemination of the article. Gorbachev's associates rebuffed, point by point, the views that the article promoted and characterized them as being directed against the Party line and against the General Secretary personally. They voted to publish in *Pravda* a full-page article to strongly repudiate the views promoted by Ligachev. This article appeared on April 5. It described the *Sovetskaya Rossiya* article as a "manifesto of all anti-*perestroika* forces" and an "open challenge to the party line." It was unsigned and therefore left no doubt that it represented the views of the Party leadership. The article in *Pravda* addressed the seriousness of the challenge contained in the "letter" of March 13 in the following way:

> It seems to us that the readers [of the Soviet press] have been exposed for the first time to this 'letter to the editor' not with a search, not an attempt to think through, and not even simply an expression of confusion, of a mix-up when faced with the complex and difficult questions that life poses for us, but a rejection of the very idea of renewal, a sharp, brutal expression of a specific point of view, in essence conservative and dogmatic. In substance two basic propositions run like a red thread through the entire letter: why do we need *perestroika* and have we not already moved too far in questions of democratization and *glasnost*?

The *Pravda* article saw the "letter" as a defense of Stalin and Stalinism and as a call to turn back because "socialism is allegedly in danger and has to be saved." The *Pravda* article concluded, "The school of [*perestroika*] is not a simple one. To free oneself from the old in thoughts and actions has shown itself to be more difficult than we expected. But the most important thing that unifies us today is the recognition that there can be no way back. It is clear that a turning back would be fatal" (p. 1).

Gorbachev called a meeting of all Party functionaries working in the Central Committee in Moscow, explained to them what the general line of the Party was, and warned them that they were dutybound to give it their wholehearted support or to quit. He reportedly met alone with all the First Secretaries of the Russian provinces and the non-Russian republics to make clear to them as well what the Party line was and to express his dissatisfaction with their lack of strong, public, and negative reaction to the March 13 article. The April 5 *Pravda* article was widely disseminated and became an essential document for Party schooling.

At the end of April, the editor in chief of *Sovetskaya Rossiya* admitted in print that he had made a major political error in publishing the anti-*perestroika* "letter." Beginning on April 5, a virtual avalanche of articles, speeches, and TV and radio programs began to appear. Almost all went further than ever in criticizing the Soviet past and attacking bureaucratic inertia and the opponents of *perestroika*. Tens of thousands of letters were sent to the newspapers. A torturer from Stalin's police wrote about his feelings of shame and guilt and signed the letter with his initials only so that his family would not learn the truth about his past. A Jewish physician who in the last months of Stalin's life was arrested with other prominent Jewish doctors and accused of poisoning Soviet leaders in the service of "international Zionism" published his memoirs in a large-circulation monthly. A top scientist denounced the conservatism of the Soviet scientific establishment. Arthur Koestler's antitotalitarian classic, *Darkness at Noon*, as well as Boris Pasternak's *Doctor Zhivago*, were published in a Soviet literary monthly. Another antitotalitarian classic, George Orwell's *1984*, was translated for publication. Many of those who had been committed to *perestroika* and those who continued to wait on the sidelines, when faced with the actual danger of reverting to the past with the publications of the March 13 article, decided to fight.

In April 1988, I spent two weeks in the Soviet Union. For the first time, I had the impression that large parts of the Soviet working and middle classes, whether in agreement or in opposition, had started to believe in the seriousness of Gorbachev's program. They had begun to understand that the process of *perestroika* will not simply fade away, as have so many reforms during their lifetime. For the first time I also had the impression that the struggle for *perestroika* and against the totalitarian past had become highly personal; had acquired the intensity of a struggle for a cause and not simply for a new policy; and had become straightforward, spurning the use of Aesopian language and camouflage.

A Belorussian cultural figure, Ales' Adamovich, wrote:

> The editor-in-chief of a journal that strongly supports *perestroika* was asked: And if *perestroika* does not succeed, how will you live? It is said that he answered: "In that case, why should I live at all?" My answer would have been less personal: "In that case, how long will life last at all, life in general? After this attempt to make the two parts of the planet find each other, to accept each other, does not succeed." I asked the same question of a well-known party activist. His answer was to the point: "To go back to the past, they will have to kill us all." (*Inovo ne Dano*, p. 273)

Yet despite the apparent success of his counteroffensive, what must have been vexing and disappointing to Gorbachev was the behavior during the three weeks from March 13 until April 5 of the mass Party membership and that part of the political and cultural elite that normally supported his program. Most of his supporters displayed confusion, lack of resolution, and fear. No counteroffensive from below was mounted against the attack by the anti-*perestroika* forces. The authoritative statement in *Pravda* was needed to reactivate and revitalize the broad strata that supported Gorbachev's program. Most of the people behaved in accordance with the Soviet tradition of avoiding risks, waiting for instructions from the top, and biding their time to see who would emerge victorious from the leadership struggle. These were the tactics of the best people, those committed to Gorbachev's reforms.

To be sure, the way in which the issue was resolved was far from an example of democratization in action. *Sovetskaya Rossiya* and its supporters were denied their right to express their anti-Gorbachev views and had to recant and "confess" the error of their ways. (The difference between supporting *perestroika* in general and doing so in a democratic way is similar to the difference in the economy between adjusting prices toward greater rationality and creating a market mechanism for setting prices.)

Many speeches were made against the March 13 letter, but to my knowledge only two articles against the letter appeared *before* April 5. One in the *Moscow News* and the other in the *Tambovskaya pravda*. (Tambov is a Russian town approximately 250 miles from Moscow.) The mood of the Party activists supportive of Gorbachev in those three weeks was captured in an article that appeared in *Izvestiya* under the title, "The Turnaround That Did Not Take Place." Its author, a Moscow Party activist, said openly that he did not like the March 13 letter and was frightened by it, but because it was published in an organ of the Central Committee, he assumed that it represented a new Party line. This impression was strengthened by the fact that for three weeks there appeared no critique of the article. He acted as he would have in the past, before *perestroika*, and remained silent, fearing to criticize the Party line. Yet now he was determined to think and act independently if a similar situation arose in the future. His conclusion: You will not catch me again; one has to think for oneself without waiting for instructions from above.

The Repercussions of Gorbachev's Counteroffensive

As a result of the events in March and April, Ligachev's power declined, at least temporarily. He lost face and showed his supporters and co-believers that the degree to which he could help them was limited. Repercussions for his political position also followed swiftly. The informal, but traditionally sanctioned position of Second Secretary of the Central Committee, which he held, was simply abolished. The importance of the Secretariat of the Central Committee was downgraded. Its members started to chair the weekly meetings of the Secretariat on a rotating basis. Ligachev's responsibilities were curtailed. A decisive part of his work in supervising personnel (the *nomenklatura*) was taken over by Georgii Razumovsky, a candidate member of the Politburo and Central Committee secretary, and the role of chief ideologue passed to Politburo member and Central Committee secretary Alexander Yakovlev—both close friends of the General Secretary. Ligachev and his friends had to shift to a defensive stance. Even his speech to the Nineteenth Party Conference, although demagogic and vitriolic toward *glasnost'*, was defensive in nature, a rear-guard attack against the growing pressures in support of *perestroika*. There was, however, no talk of his removal from the Politburo or Secretariat.

Nevertheless, Ligachev's influence among the powerful provincial Party apparatus remained strong. Gorbachev, a most cautious politician (sometimes too cautious, in the view of his supporters), knew that to remove Ligachev from the Politburo without changes in the composition of the Central Committee and of the provincial Party leadership could jeopardize Party unity, which Gorbachev valued, if not the General Secretary's own security in office. Ligachev's fate is closely tied to the reconstruction of the Soviet political system. The extent of its success will determine how soon he is retired or put into a symbolic post with little power.

From April to June, with the Gorbachev offensive in full swing, the election of the delegates to the Nineteenth Party Conference moved ahead in a different atmosphere but, as events showed, with the provincial and district Party bosses fighting against the selection of the candidates most identified with *perestroika*. On the wave of Gorbachev's offensive, the Soviet press reported fraudulent practices in the selection of delegates. *Izvestiya*, for example, on June 8 reported mass protests against such "behind closed doors" elections in Yaroslavl. Gorbachev made a speech urging Party members to choose delegates not according to rank but rather on the basis of their support for *perestroika*.

The party secretary of the Union of Soviet Cinematographers, Aleksandr Gelman, expressed the hopes and the potential importance of the conference in a simple but dramatic way. He opened an article in *Sovetskaya kultura* on April 9 thus:

> Three years from the moment of the introduction of *perestroika*, what is its main positive result? In my opinion it is the fact that, although three years have passed, *perestroika* still exists. What is its main negative result? In my opinion it is the fact that, although *perestroika* has existed for three years, it has not yet become irreversible. . . . The main task of the Nineteenth Party Conference is to develop and adopt decisions, the implementation of which will guarantee the unquestionable irreversibility of the democratization of our country. (p. 5)

Preparations for the Conference

The theses of the conference, published in *Pravda* on May 27, 1988, in the name of the Central Committee, made clear that Gorbachev's hopes for making *perestroika* irreversible were tied to a radical change in the Soviet political system. The Central Committee's theses were supported, supplemented, and made more detailed by the resolutions adopted at the Party meetings that elected delegates to the conference. The delegates were instructed to present the conference with these proposals for change in the internal order and activities of the Party. By a provisional count of only the published proposals, it would appear that more than three hundred such mandates, often overlapping in their concerns, were directed to the Central Committee for consideration by the conference. They proposed greater openness in party life: for example, live and complete transmission of the conference, publication of the proceedings of plenary meetings of the Central Committee, systematic and frequent reports by all Party officials—including the secretaries of the Central Committee—about their work and attitudes toward *perestroika* so that Party members can form an opinion of the individuals within the Party leadership and what differences of opinion exist among them.

The most frequently repeated resolutions involved the establishment of limited tenure in office for elected Party officials—including the top leadership and the General Secretary himself. These resolutions most often called for a four- to five-year term that in some cases could be extended for an additional term. A compulsory retirement age of sixty-five or seventy years for Party and state officials was also proposed. Other resolutions called for similar changes in the work of local soviets and the state administration. These resolutions also proposed elections with a choice among several candidates, a strict separation between the work of the Party apparatus and that of the state administration, the granting of greater responsibilities and rights to trade unions, and a speedy change in the legal system and in Soviet law.

The conference promised to be a major benchmark in the progress of *perestroika* as well as an arena of confrontation among the liberals, the moderates, and the conservatives. As an all-union assembly of the powerful, the vocal, and the active, its resolutions would have a significant effect on Gorbachev's ability to influence the Central Committee to take a radical road; the conference would provide Gorbachev with a democratically achieved mandate to push the recalcitrant.

All-union Party conferences have a long and respectable history in the Soviet Communist Party. They were convened regularly under both Lenin and Stalin until 1932. Conferences gave Party leaders and activists a forum in the years between regular congresses so that they could deliberate and enact binding resolutions on timely and fundamental issues. From 1917 to 1930, eight Party congresses and eight Party conferences took place. After Stalin became an unrestrained dictator, only two congresses took place, the eighteenth in 1939 and the nineteenth in 1952. The last Party conference, the eighteenth, occurred in 1941, on the eve of the war. (The Seventeenth Party Conference convened in 1932.) In fact, under Khrushchev an all-union Party conference took place in all but name, although it was called the Twenty-First Extraordinary Party Congress.

One important distinction between a congress and a conference is that the latter traditionally does not elect a new Central Committee. This tradition was partly broken by Stalin in 1941 when the Eighteenth Party Conference expelled a few members and coopted many new ones to the Central Committee (leaders from the territories annexed after the Eighteenth Party Congress of March 1939—Eastern Poland [or Western Belorussia and Western Ukraine], Estonia, Lithuania, Latvia, and Romanian Bessarabia [Moldavia] but mostly new top generals).

Whether he did not consider it seemly to follow Stalin's example rather than the older Party tradition, or whether he did not have the strength to manage it, Gorbachev did not include in the conference agenda the election of a new Central Committee or expulsions or cooptations of individual members. Gorbachev's dilemma in this matter is worth noting. At first glance, it would seem that Gorbachev's position was not all bad. He was able at the Twenty-Seventh Congress in 1986 to replace 41 percent of the voting members of the Central Committee (125 out of 307). Since he came to power, he had replaced ten of the fourteen First Secretaries of the non-Russian republics. Only 19.7 percent of the provincial First Secretaries were holdovers from Brezhnev's time, 21 percent were holdovers from the times of Yuri Andropov and Konstantin Chernenko, and Gorbachev himself replaced 59.2 percent. In the Presidium of the Council of Ministers, of the thirteen members only two remained from the time before Gorbachev, and 80 percent of the entire Council of Ministers (92 ministers) were appointed by him. Yet many of the new appointments were made at the relatively nonradical stage of *perestroika*, and not all appointments were Gorbachev's, as distinct for instance, from Ligachev's, preferences.

The top personnel problem was, however, exacerbated by an additional factor. Since the time of the Twenty-Seventh Congress in 1986, about 20 percent of the Central Committee members had lost the executive positions to which their Central Committee membership could be ascribed (for example, provincial First Secretary). Yet, in the spirit of democratization, they retained their titles as Central Committee members, but these "dead souls" probably did not participate in the meetings of the Central Committee.

Of far greater importance was the fact that many of Gorbachev's highly placed supporters had not acquired the rights of Central Committee members, despite the fact that their executive posts entitled them to this privilege. The redress of this anomalous situation will have to wait for the Twenty-Eighth Congress, which according to the existing Party statutes is to convene in early 1991, unless, of course, Gorbachev finds a way to change the statute. Despite this anomaly, it seemed certain before the Nineteenth Party Conference that Gorbachev could nonetheless expect a resounding success.

The Nineteenth Party Conference

The Nineteenth Party Conference opened on June 28, 1988, and lasted three days. There were 5,000 delegates, each representing 3,780 Party members. Fifty-nine percent of the delegates came from the Russian Republic; of those, Moscow and Leningrad alone accounted for almost 10 percent of all delegates. About 33 percent of the delegates were workers; about 16 percent were farmers and farm workers; about 8 percent belonged to the "creative intelligensia"; and about 17 percent came from the Party apparatus. The others were drawn from the state and government organs. Twenty-five percent of the delegates were women. Of the delegates to the conference, 29.1 percent were forty years old or younger; 36 percent were between forty and fifty years old; 27.2 percent were between fifty-one and sixty years old; and 7.7 percent were older than sixty. Forty-seven delegates entered the Party between 1919 and 1940; 143 entered the Party during the Nazi-Soviet war (1941–1945); 1,948 entered the Party between 1946 and 1965; and 2,862 entered the Party between 1965 and 1988. The conference opened and closed with a speech by Gorbachev. There were no other lengthy speeches. All other speakers had to limit their time to ten to fifteen minutes.

Before and during the conference, rumors in Moscow held that some 80 percent of the delegates were conservative, but there was no evidence to support these estimates. The rumor could have represented an official attempt to mobilize the supporters of *perestroika* for the conference. No accurate judgment can be made concerning the composition of the delegates based on their political orientation. Judging the political distribution among the speeches at the conference (which may not, however, be a representative sample) on the basis of the reaction of the conference to these speeches and by the general atmosphere, I would suggest that the conference was dominated by centrists. This means that a clear majority of delegates were strongly against what the conservatives called the unseemly excesses of *glasnost'*, highly supportive of economic reform, strongly against bureaucratic resistance, not against the conservative opposition, and oddly neutral concerning changes in the political system. Here the difference between those who represented the Party apparat and those who represented the government and economic administration was noticeable, the latter showing greater genuine satisfaction with the direction of systemic political changes.

Both liberals and conservatives had their say at the conference. The liberals (for example, Leonid Abalkin, the head of the Institute of Economics; and Vitaly Korotych, the editor in chief of *Ogonyok*) were more aggressive and unabashed in their speeches, but received less applause than their opponents. The conservative speeches (including those by V. V. Karpov, the First Secretary of the Union of Soviet Writers, and Yuri Bondarev, the secretary of the Union of Writers of the RSFSR), while in substance clearly against *glasnost'*, were in tone a far cry from the Andreyeva article. The conservatives tried hard to be anti-Stalinist and ingenuously characterized "the excesses of *glasnost*" as representing the legacy of the past—the *Stalinist past*.

Given his behavior at the conference, Gorbachev had few good words to say for the liberals and supported the conservative allegation that there was a danger of leftist excess in the process of *glasnost'*. He made an effort to convince the delegates that he should not be identified with those "excesses." He confirmed that he felt his liberal supporters often went too far, thus providing ammunition for his main enemy on the Right.

The two leaders that visibly lost out at the conference were the chief antagonists of the October 1987 Plenum: Boris Yeltsin and Yegor Ligachev. Yeltsin made a convincing pro-*perestroika* speech to the conference that was well received and published in full. However, he then went on to attack Ligachev and, most damaging of all, to plead for his own political rehabilitation. By doing so Yeltsin created an inescapable impression, within and without the Kremlin's Great Hall, that he had tried to use the conference to settle *lichniye schoty*—his "personal accounts."

Ligachev's speech, by attacking Yeltsin in strong and graphic terms, gave the impression of someone trying to get even with a man who was already down (in the unmistakable tradition of the Soviet past). The speech also contained a vitriolic attack on the press and on the liberals, as well as an attempt to at least partly rehabilitate the Brezhnevian past: "When people ask me where was I then, my answer is: I was in Tomsk and I was building Socialism" (*Pravda*, July 2, 1988, p. 11).

The Drama of the Conference

The Nineteenth Conference confirmed its advance billing as a major steppingstone in Gorbachev's program of radical reforms. The conference produced a serious and exciting political theater of the highest order. It contained both substance and drama. It was not surprising that almost all Western reporting from the conference exuded excitement and wonder.

This event caught the imagination of virtually all Western journalists as had no other domestic event during Gorbachev's tenure in power.

The drama had many dimensions. There was the drama of its comparison with other important Party meetings in the Soviet past, including the Twenty-Seventh Party Congress in the spring of 1986. The conference illuminated the difference between what the Soviet Union was a few years earlier and what it had become by mid-1988 and gave a glimpse of what it could be in the future. This gathering of the Party faithful, a political theater in the best meaning of the word, was performed according to a far different script than had similar events in the past. This well-orchestrated script still left significant room for the spontaneous expression of the participants' emotions and thoughts. No one who witnessed this conference could help but be impressed by its genuineness and authenticity.

The drama of the conference was also evident in the significant changes of the Soviet political system proposed by its leaders and delegates. The resolutions attempted to institutionalize Gorbachev's plan of grassroots democratization and *glasnost'*. They were directed at the introduction, for the first time in Soviet history, of a system of checks and balances into the traditionally authoritarian system. The implementation of these checks and balances will mark the most profound change of the Soviet political system since the advent of Stalinism. In only three days of deliberation, the conference considered the experience of three years of *perestroika*, its achievements and pitfalls. As if in a flash, the conference brightly illuminated what is new and what is old in Gorbachev's Soviet Union.

The drama of the conference was continued and enlarged in its interaction with the people on the streets of Moscow and other Soviet cities. The deliberations of the conference found a surprisingly positive resonance among rank-and-file Party members and average Soviet citizens that was sorely lacking in the previous endeavors of the General Secretary. The political theater of the conference was communicated not only to its 5,000 delegates but to tens of millions of people at home and abroad.

The conference confirmed that Gorbachev was secure in his office and in control of the top Party establishment. With energy, with total self-assurance, with great political skill, and without significant challenge, he dominated the entire proceedings of the conference. Moreover, the position of the Chairperson (President) of a new national legislature (a reformed Supreme Soviet), which the conference agreed to institute, will without doubt go to Gorbachev. His position as Chairperson as well as General Secretary will add to this stature, influence, and power and will surely lead to the retirement of the seventy-nine-year-old Andrei Gromyko.

An arresting feature of the conference was its concentration on the political rather than the economic aspects of Gorbachev's program, although the question of improving food supplies was discussed, and a resolution on this matter was adopted. On its face, this would seem unusual and, indeed, startling. The key goal, and the very rationale of the *perestroika*, was, after all, economic: to overcome the economic stagnation of the last two decades; to accelerate economic development and modernization; and to stabilize and eventually narrow the widening gap between Soviet and Western levels of technological advancement. Moreover, in Gorbachev's three-and-a-half years in office, no visible progress had been made in the realization of these goals.

Delegate after delegate, especially those of the working class, emphatically confirmed this from the podium. Yet, Gorbachev, in his many ad hoc interventions, appealed to the delegates to concentrate on political questions. Clearly, the Party leadership had deliberately decided to focus on political issues. This was, in fact, made clear by Gorbachev at the outset of his speech when he said, "Today we are facing many complicated problems. Which of these problems is the key one? The Central Committee of the Party considers that it is the reform of our political system" (*Pravda,* June 29, 1988, pp. 2–7).

Concentration on political issues when economic problems were pressing reflected the political logic of Gorbachev's situation as well as the imperatives and the fate of his *perestroika.* It confirmed Yugoslav leader Marshal Tito's profound insight into the nature of Communist systems: "Economic reforms are impossible in Communist systems; what is possible are political reforms that have economic consequences."

The Soviet economy is owned by the state and run by the Party and state bureaucracy. To be run differently than in the past, and with different results, the Soviet economy requires the existence of three *political* conditions. First, major cuts and changes must be made in the administrative personnel (unfortunately, the people who broke the economic machinery are the least willing or prepared to repair it). Second, the very process of macro- and micro-decisionmaking must change. It has been proven again and again that the Party bureaucracy cannot run the economy and that constant Party interventions in the economic policymaking process, rather than facilitating economic growth, produce disorder and gross inefficiencies. Third, to get the party apparatus out of the everyday business of running the economy (and to provide much greater freedom for the economic managers), the Soviet political system must be restructured in a way that will provide safeguards and checks and balances for implementing national economic policies. It was precisely on these political conditions of more effective economic reform that the leaders of the Kremlin focused the attention of the conference.

The Achievements of the Conference

Although the proposed changes in the political system are potentially very significant, they are still on paper. Without doubt, the most important and immediate consequence of the conference was its dramatic, and from Gorbachev's point of view, fully positive impact on Soviet public opinion. Gorbachev's great enemy was the resistance of the Party and state buraucracy to this program. An even greater obstacle to the program of *perestroika* was the apathy of the working class, the cynicism of the Party's rank-and-file members, and the unwillingness of a large part of the intelligentsia to risk involvement in *perestroika*. Gorbachev's modernizing revolution, like many in the Soviet and Russian past, is primarily a revolution from above. The weakness of the General Secretary's traditionally Soviet power base (the Party bureaucracy) makes his victory possible only, however, if it is simultaneously supported by a revolution from below that will place the recalcitrant bureaucrats and the conservative opposition between the anvil and the hammer of pressure from above and below.

In April 1988, a change in the popular mood toward *perestroika* seemed evident in Moscow. This mood was still a far cry from an active commitment to support the reforms or from a belief that Gorbachev will succeed in implementing his program. The mood was still a skeptical, "What is in it for us?" Since then, however, people have started to believe that Gorbachev's proposed reforms are serious and different from the would-be reforms of the past, that the *perestroika* will not simply fade away, and that Gorbachev will not change his mind and capitulate to bureaucratic opposition.

What the Nineteenth Party Conference seemed to have achieved by breaking with the old standards and taboos—by televising a genuine discussion and controversy even among the leaders, by telling at least a large part of the truth about the difficult economic situation—went much further. For the first time in Moscow, as well as in other metropolitan centers and even distant cities, a genuine mass interest in *perestroika* seemed to be emerging, and mass support seemed to be forming. Gorbachev, the first modern leader that the USSR has ever had, was finally reaching his citizens through modern means of communication. His energy, his enthusiasm, and his faith were at last becoming contagious.

When Gorbachev took power, the country was in the midst of an acute systemic crisis. A plundered economy, a parasitical Party, and a scavenger society had put the Soviet Union on the edge of an abyss. Unfortunately, the systemic crisis persists. Yet, Gorbachev's program of *perestroika* has created the hope and the potential for reversing the trend of Soviet development that has been characterized by a breakdown of authority, alienation (even of the Party rank and file), and economic stagnation.

The Changes in the Soviet Political System

The Nineteenth Party Conference generally followed the agenda set forth in advance. There were, however, certain surprises. The most important concerned how the system of the soviets would be transformed into a real legislative branch of the government and how the fusion of the positions of the top Party and state leaders on all administrative levels would be accomplished. Two possible reasons for the surprise: Gorbachev wanted to heighten the drama of the conference by introducing proposals that were totally unexpected or/and he wanted to discuss these proposals only within the Politburo shortly before the conference to avoid discussing them at the Central Committee meeting because he did not know what its reaction would be. Thus, he presented the Central Committee with a conference resolution in the form of a fait accompli.

The Nineteenth Party Conference and the Central Committee Plenum that followed it provided a blueprint of the new Soviet political system that Gorbachev sought to create. They also raised these questions: What were the key aspects of the new political system that Gorbachev was able to have adopted by the conference? What elements of the new system were still unclear? What were the chances that the proposed system would ever be implemented? How realistic was the expectation that the new political system, even if organizationally implemented, would change the behavior of the Soviet Party and state bureaucracies? To answer these questions, it is necessary to analyze the key elements of the radical political reform that emerged from the Nineteenth Party Conference and the July 1988 Plenum of the Central Committee. Such an analysis must consider six aspects of the Soviet Party-state: the process of democratization; the mass Communist Party; the Communist Party apparatus; the system of soviets; the function of the First Secretaries; and the "legal" state.

The Process of Democratization

At the core of the procedural aspects of Gorbachev's program of political change was the proposed process of democratization. The Soviet Union under Stalin, Khrushchev, and Brezhnev probably held more elections on all levels of the Party and state than any democratic society did, but these elections had no democratic substance. Gorbachev promised to give meaning to these elections as well as to the legislative process.

To do so, only a few new laws and regulations were, in fact, necessary. More importantly, existing Party statutes, election laws, and procedural codes would have to cease being mere symbols and become authentic channels for the expression of the will of the Party's rank and file and of the general electorate. To achieve this, Gorbachev's program proposed principles that in many instances were absent in the past but in most cases simply reinterpreted existing laws and stressed their centrality in the life of the Party and the state. The most important of Gorbachev's principles were as follows:

- The Party and the state electorates should have the right to propose a multiple-candidate slate for each office. (Although this is a right of the electorate, *it is not a duty*—elections *can* take place with only one candidate.) The right to propose additional candidates will in practice rest on the lowest levels, with the primary Party organizations or the electoral meeting of voters at the village or urban district level. On the higher level, it will rest in the Party with the delegates to a city, province, republic, or all-union conference. In the state elections—elections to the soviets   the members of the lower level soviet will choose the candidates for the next higher level soviet (county soviet for province, province soviets for republics, republic soviets for the Supreme Soviet in Moscow). Whether mass organizations, trade unions, and professional unions, for example, will also enjoy the right to appoint candidates for the elections to the soviets is not clear; nor is it clear what percentage of the delegates in a Party or soviet meeting is necessary to place an additional candidate on the electoral slate.
- The tenure of high officials on all levels should be unconditionally limited to two five-year terms. This is clearly the case with *elected* officials in the Party and state (Politburo members, Central Committee members, and Chairpersons of soviets). It is not entirely clear, however, whether *appointed* officials (such as ministers of the central and republican government, heads of departments in the Party apparatus)—who constitute the majority of high Party-state officials—will be subjected to the same limits.
- The balloting on all elections in Party and state institutions should be secret and controlled by a specially selected electoral commission or committee.
- Resolutions and laws should be adopted only after a truly free discussion.
- The Party or general electorate should have the right to recall officials that it appointed if they do not perform satisfactorily. The movement for recall can be initiated by any voter or Party member.

Any student of democracy will note that this plan for democratization depends upon two conditions: first, that there will be enough energetic and committed individuals within the Party and state electorate to take the initiative, to withstand political risk, and to mobilize support in their social units or areas; second, that a large segment of the Soviet electorate and of the Party *aktiv* (activists) can be educated to understand their new rights and trained to use them. In a country with a sixty-year history of enslavement, of resignation, and of actual denial of citizenship, to learn democracy in practice will, at best, be extremely difficult and gradual. Whereas the citizenry has little experience in asserting itself in conditions of democracy, those in positions of power on all levels are skilled in manipulation, blackmail, the side-stepping of electoral minefields, and the use of the letter of the law to destroy its spirit. Without major structural adjustments and changes, the democratization for which Gorbachev hopes will die on the vine. It is to these structural changes decreed by the Nineteenth Conference and the Plenum of the Central Committee that I now turn.

The Mass Communist Party

Gorbachev's goal with respect to the mass Party was to transform it into an authentic political movement, an association of members who shared basic political views and who influenced others to accept these views. The Bolshevik Party that Lenin created was such a movement in the first postrevolutionary period. As is typical of parties in power, the Bolshevik Party's membership grew from about 200,000 in October 1917 to almost 1 million when Stalin took power and is now at more than 19 million. By the late 1920s, and particularly after the Great Purge of 1936–1938, the mass Party became a manipulated appendage to the Party apparatus. The mass Party was transformed from a political movement into an increasingly corrupt and parasitic centralized military order.

Khrushchev attempted to revitalize the Party as a movement through ideology. Because he had not made fundamental changes in the internal rules and structure of the Party, and the system within which it acted, Khrushchev failed. Gorbachev wanted to change the Party through his process of democratization. (This will require a change in behavior more than a change in rules.)

Nothing that Gorbachev proposed at the Nineteenth Party Conference that would transform the inner life of the Party and increase its positive impact on the socio-political environment, even if it were implemented, suggested that he would succeed where Khrushchev failed. The fact that the phrase "democratic centralism" was not mentioned in Gorbachev's speech might have been an indication of his intentions to abolish this formula, which constitutes one of the key distinctions between the Soviet Communist Party and political parties in the West. In my view, it indicated instead that "democratic centralism" would, in fact, be preserved.

Democratic centralism implies three propositions:

1. Every issue of Party life should be discussed freely at Party meetings on all levels.
2. Once an issue is voted on, the views of the majority should be adopted as the Party line that is binding on all members, even those who opposed the majority. The minority must adopt the majority position, reject its own beliefs, and work whole-heartedly to implement the decision.
3. The distribution of authority in the Party is unitary and follows a vertical structure. The upper-echelon organs of the Party, committees, and bureaus have a right to issue instructions to, or even overturn the decisions of, those of the lower levels.

Democratic Centralism as a tenet was invented by Lenin and adopted as a resolution of the Tenth Party Congress in 1921. Under Stalin, the "democratic" elements were entirely eradicated, and the "centralist" aspects were applied to their absolute limits. This remained true throughout the entire post-Stalin period. Gorbachev planned important changes in this political formula, and, to a certain extent, he has already implemented several. The "democratic" modifier is being rescued from total atrophy and strengthened. Gorbachev intends to shift the "democratic" and the "centralist" elements closer to the form that they had under Lenin. But the essence of the concept, which is undemocratic, remains unchanged. Lenin called the Soviet Communist Party a "party of a new type" to distinguish it from what he saw as the "decadent" Social Democratic parties in the West. No one can predict what will happen in the distant future, but for the foreseeable future, the Soviet Communist Party will remain a party "of a new type."

Many factors suggest that even if the necessary intentions exist, without abolishing the principle of democratic centralism it will be extremely difficult to shift the mix of its two ingredients even to the proportions of Lenin's time. Today's Party members are different from the strong-willed revolutionaries and true believers of Lenin's time. The administration of the inner life of the Party is in the hands of a major bureaucracy, set in its authoritarian ways, that was only in its infancy at Lenin's time. The reform of the Party apparatus proposed by Gorbachev may serve to increase the bureaucracy's preoccupation with the internal mass Party life relative to its other activities.

In both the long and the short term, the outlook for democracy within the Party is very limited, indeed. Without institutionalized political competition the centralist principle will dominate. This competition can best be achieved by freedom for other autonomous, aggregative political organizations (freedom that is not limited to a single profession or is not geographically restricted). Such competition can be achieved with only one Party in the Soviet Union, although the principle of democratic centralism and the resolution of the Tenth Party Congress of 1921 banning the creation of factions would have to be abolished. Neither appears likely. The Soviet Party is the ruling party of a gigantic, multinational state. Its leadership and part of its political elite want to strengthen it, not to abdicate power.

In offering the foregoing analysis, I do not wish to minimize Gorbachev's democratizing intentions or the extraordinary process of *perestroika* that has already changed the meaning and practice of "innerParty democracy." While the difficult shift from totalitarianism to an authoritarian reality continues, Gorbachev still emphasizes the need for the unity of the party. Without doubt, the tasks at hand require such unity for the sake of *perestroika*. But strong unity and democracy cannot coexist at the same time. The price of democracy is a certain degree of disunity.

The experience of the inner life of mass organizations under different systems has confirmed the overall validity of the German sociologist Robert Michels's "iron law of oligarchy." According to Michels, organizations that may have originally been democratic develop needs that are served by the "organization men" who take over the administration of the organization and run it according to authoritarian principles. This is apparent in the majority of U.S. trade unions. In democratic countries, however, the authoritarianism *within* organizations is combined with free competition *among* them. In the USSR, with its conservative tradition, its lack of democratic culture, the existence of a powerful Party bureaucracy, and the Party's monopoly on political power, the strength of democracy in inner Party life is, and will remain, limited. Only those who have not lived under the traditional Soviet system can dismiss as unimportant the chasm that separates Gorbachev's democratizing policies from the policies of all his predecessors. But only those who equate their wishes with reality and reject the lessons of the past can fail to see the confining limits of this democratization.

The Communist Party Apparatus

The Party apparatus is the most powerful bureaucracy in the Soviet Union. It is composed of some 200–250,000 functionaries for whom work in the Party is a full-time job. They are paid by the Party, administer its activities, supervise all other bureaucracies, and speak *for* the Party. They perform their functions at all levels of the Soviet party-state: village, county, district, city, province, republic, and central. The Party apparatus is comparatively small in size but extremely powerful. Built by Stalin, it enhanced its position of power under Khrushchev and Brezhnev. Gorbachev, who throughout his life was a Party apparatchik, assumed its leadership at the most conservative point of its history.

Work within the mass party (the majority of which is composed of blue- and white-collar workers and farmers) was not, until now at least, the main preoccupation of the party apparatus. This mass Party activity occupied only a relatively small portion of Party effort. It was most visible when the Party apparatus was performing the function of a mass political mobilizer and political educator. Yet the essence of this activity was directed at the leading personnel of *all other bureaucracies:* the state administrators, government officials, economic and technical management, the armed forces officer corps, the *kolkhoz* (collective farm) and state farm chairpersons, and the like. The mass Party's main function with regard to these "client" bureaucracies was to pass judgment on their political loyalty and professional competence. Personnel policy, known as *nomenklatura,* the right to appoint or dismiss the occupants of any significant managerial positions, was the prerogative of a particular unit or member of the Party apparatus. Just as important, the apparat was to coordinate the interaction among all other bureaucracies and in fact supervise their activity.

The Party apparatus is a supervisory structure whose organization is parallel to all other existing state and government entities. The division of labor among all state and government bureaucracies is thus duplicated by the division of labor within the Party apparatus. For each unit of the state-government structure there is a supervising unit, or an individual, of the Party apparatus. For example, the Ministry of Education in Moscow will have a parallel unit in the Party apparatus—the Department of Education attached to the Secretariat of the Party's Central Committee in Moscow. Similarly, the Ministry of Education in a republic will have a department of education of the republican Party Central Committee and so on.

The political power of the Party apparatus is immense. In practice, the Party apparatus intervenes constantly on all levels in the everyday running of the economy. Agriculture in particular has been the domain of this bureaucracy. While supervising, intervening, ordering around managers, and exercising its prerogatives to the utmost, the party apparatus has in fact assumed only minimal responsibility for the work of these other bureaucracies. The other bureaucracies (such as the economic ones) have paid the full price of failure.

The central feature of the resolutions adopted by the Nineteenth Party Conference concerned the changes in the functions and activities of the Party apparatus:

- The Party apparatus is to be, to quote the exact language of the resolution, "significantly cut in size." According to my calculations, if the other steps concerning the Party apparatus are implemented the cut may be as great as 50 percent. If the cut is proportionate to the current geographic distribution of the Party apparatus, it will have the greatest impact at the county and district apparatus levels, which are most directly concerned with economic matters.
- The economic sectors and departments of the apparatus are to be abolished. The noneconomic departments that supervise or duplicate the governmental organizations (culture or education, for example) will probably also be curtailed. If logic were to prevail, the position of the secretaries on the county, district, city, or provincial levels who supervise these departments and sectors would also be abolished. It is still unclear whether on the level of the central Party apparatus in Moscow these departments will be abolished. In the place of the numerous economic departments and sectors, each responsible for a particular economic branch, one such department or sector will most likely be preserved to deal with overall economic matters, particularly the implementation of the economic reforms. Although detailed instruction from the Central Committee ordering these cuts has not yet been issued, the Party apparatus will certainly fight to restrict the cuts.
- The individuals eliminated from the payroll of the Party apparatus will retire with the promise of good pensions or be transplanted into government administration or managerial jobs primarily in economic enterprises and factories, supply organizations, commerce, state farms, and the like.
- The work of the Party apparatus will be concentrated in two departments or sectors, each supervised by a secretary—the ideological-propaganda department and the organizational-personnel department. The first will supervise Party schooling and promote the ideological line in primary Party organizations and in the country at large. The second will deal with the internal Party organization and with the *nomenklatura*—that is, the personnel policy within the Party apparatus and in the administrative and economic state bureaucracies. Both departments will be involved in the mobilization of Party members and working people in fulfilling the tasks ordered by the central leadership in elections, campaigns, and harvests.

Can Gorbachev Change the Party Apparatus? The present-day Party apparatus enjoys significant rights and is burdened by only limited responsibilities. It supervises and orders around the state administrative and economic bureaucracies but is not responsible for the final results of their activities. Khrushchev attempted to change this by dividing the Party apparatus into industrial and agricultural sections, tying them directly with economic management, and making them responsible for economic performance. Gorbachev is trying to do just the opposite—to remove the Party apparatus from economic activity and thus drastically curtail its power.

Can Gorbachev succeed in changing the power and the role of the Party apparatus? The odds against him are high. A number of major factors, aside from the opposition of the still powerful apparatus, argue against any but limited success in this endeavor; the disastrous Soviet economic condition, where reserves are lacking and even the minimal level of production to satisfy basic needs is difficult, makes mobilization of resources for crucial operations (such as harvesting, cutting waste, conserving natural resources, making the commerce network work adequately) absolutely necessary and unavoidable. Such mobilization in the Soviet Union takes the form of campaigns that depend on massive human resources as a substitute for good management. The state administration and economic bureaucracies are utterly helpless in organizing such mobilizational campaigns. The Party apparatus is the only organization that is adept at it. Such campaigns involve a tremendous waste of human and material resources. Nevertheless, as long as the Soviet economy is characterized by major shortages and a lack of reserves, these mobilizations and campaigns will continue. It is unreasonable to expect that the Party apparatus will perform this vital role without gaining power over the state administrative and economic bureaucracies.

Another issue is the *nomenklatura* rights of the Party apparatus. The theses of the Central Committee for the Conference addressed the question as follows:

> The party's cadres policy needs serious renewal in the conditions of democratization. The formal *nomenklatura* approach toward the selection and placement of cadres has outlived its usefulness. The basic method of party committees' work must be to organize the training and retraining of cadres, to educate them, and to recommend Communists and nonparty people alike for leadership posts. The final decision on cadre questions must be determined by elections results. (*Sovetskaya kultura*, May 28, 1988, p. 2)

This is a statement of great importance that, incidentally, was not repeated in either the resolutions of the conference or of the Central

Committee Plenum that followed it. Authentic elections will restrict the power of the *nomenklatura*, even though most *nomenklatura* positions are not "electable" by popular or mass Party vote; rather, they are appointments (for example, ministers). Moreover, the preconference thesis just cited is correct in its last sentence: *"The final decision* on cadre questions must be determined by election results." This leaves unanswered, however, the issue of the "prefinal decision"—that is, the selection of candidates for the "electable" office.

In my view, the Party apparatus, having been significantly reduced in size, will continue to exercise enormous power over the state administration and the economic bureaucracies. Gorbachev's main intention is not to abolish the *nomenklatura* but to remove the party functionaries from, in his words, "everyday and petty intervention into economic management." The significant words here are "everyday" and "petty." By eliminating the economic departments and cutting the size of the apparat, Gorbachev hopes that the apparatus will concentrate on the discussion, supervision, and solution of the major economic problems. In the foreseeable future this will mean the adoption, implementation, and adjustment of the radical economic reform to local conditions. The General Secretary may partially succeed in this regard, but there is yet another reason the Party apparatus probably will not keep its distance from the economic bureaucracies' "everyday" and "petty" preoccupations.

Until the marketizing economic reform is by and large accomplished— and this will at best take many years—the Party apparatus will for all practical purposes remain the only countrywide institution that can provide the on-site coordination of Soviet economic activity. The "everyday" and "petty" preoccupations of the state economic administration and managers can be decisive for the level of performance of the basic economic units—the more than three hundred thousand factories, mines, construction firms, commercial trusts, and collective and state farms. The functioning of each of these units depends on the supply of new materials, energy, half-finished products, spare parts for machinery, labor supply, transport, and credit and financial appropriation from other units. Instructions from the *Gosplan* or contracts with other economic units are of no help whatsoever if there are breakdowns in these deliveries. Moreover, the "normal" administrative method of surmounting these bottlenecks only increases the difficulties because each of the other units on which an enterprise depends may be, and invariably is, supervised by yet another ministry or a separate geographic administration. Almost all Soviet enterprises have created a special job that does not exist in any table of organization: that of *tolkach,* the "pusher" whose task it is to arrange *by any means* to get needed supplies in an environment of chronic shortages. The Party apparatus is the most important *tolkach* of them all for the economic units within its geographic jurisdiction. The Party secretaries in a city or county do not have to offer their "petty tutelage" to the economic administrators or managers. These people will ask for help in difficult situations.

According to Gorbachev, the Party apparat must concentrate on its political rather than its administrative role, although by "political" he cannot simply mean propaganda, organization of elections, or mobilization. He means that the *apparat* should be preoccupied with the broader picture, which in the Soviet Union of today means the implementation of the radical economic reform and personnel policy. This in itself gives the *apparat* great power. Moreover, the existing plans of production and distribution cannot wait for their fulfillment until reform changes the conditions under which an enterprise can operate. One of the monumental difficulties of the reform is that it must be accomplished simultaneously with the enterprises fulfilling their plans and in conditions where no reserves, no slack in the economy, can carry the country through until the positive effects of the reform have taken hold. Indeed, the Nineteenth Party Conference stipulated as a major goal rapid improvement in the areas of food and consumer goods.

It is possible that when and if the new economic order has been established, the power of the party apparatus, both through its control of the *nomenklatura* and its *tolkach* functions, will truly decline. The success of a director of an enterprise will be measured in rubles of actual profit and depend very little on the *kharakteristika* (recommendation) of the Party secretary. The necessary ties with other economic units will be coordinated primarily through the market rather than through a *tolkach*. But it will be many years before such a situation exists.

The System of Soviets

The reform of the system of soviets may be the most significant of changes adopted by the Nineteenth Party Conference. The term *soviet* as applied to the Soviet Union's political structure has two connotations: The first refers to an institution that is supposed to perform the function of a legislature; the second connotes the unity of the legislative and executive power because the legislature purportedly appoints the executive and the leading members of the executive branch are elected to the legislature.

The soviets (the Russian word means councils) first came into being during the 1905 revolution as an organization of the workers. After the Bolsheviks seized power in 1917, the Soviets were chosen by Lenin as an alternative to a parliamentary government in a one-party state. Thus, the soviets are political bodies of representatives elected by the people in direct, proportional, and secret balloting on all administrative levels. The Soviet Union has 49,176 such soviets, in which more than 2.3 million deputies serve. Service in the soviet at any level is not a full-time job. Each deputy combines service (with the exception of the chairperson and his or her first deputy) with regular employment in other positions. The composition of the soviet according to occupation consists of 44.4 percent workers, 24.8 percent farmers, and the remaining 30.8 percent intelligentsia and members of the administrative apparatus. The Supreme Soviet in Moscow has 1,500 deputies who are chosen by the voters in electoral districts throughout the Soviet Union. Elections to the national Supreme Soviet and republican supreme soviet are held every five years. At the provincial level and below, elections are held every 2½ years. The plenary meetings of the soviets take place twice a year and last no more than five days each. The soviets also have standing committees, elected by the deputies from among themselves, that convene more often. These include an agricultural committee, a financial committee, and, in the Supreme Soviet, a foreign affairs committee.

The term *soviet* also connotes the executive branch of the government, whose leading members, again on all levels, are appointed by the people's deputies who constitute the soviet as a legislative body. These people are also members of the legislative bodies elected by a popular vote. The executive bodies at the level below a union republic are called the Executive Committee of the Soviet of People's Deputies (Ispolkom); at the republican and all-union level they are called the Council of Ministers (the Cabinet). The Ispolkoms and Councils of Ministers employ, control, or supervise the activity of close to 20 million administrative and clerical personnel. The All-Union Council of Ministers in Moscow is composed of almost a hundred ministries, permanent committees, and commissions.

Until now, the soviets as legislative bodies were a total farce. The deputies were "elected" by voters who had no choice of candidates. In fact, the deputies were preselected by the Party apparat or bureau of each administrative geographic unit. In brief meetings they rubber-stamped the decrees and resolutions issued in their name by the Ispolkoms or Council of Ministers. They had no voice whatever in who among them would be appointed to the Ispolkom and Council of Ministers because this had already been decided by the Party apparatus or Party Bureaus.

The Nineteenth Party Conference decided to make significant changes in the system of the soviets in both functions. Gorbachev wanted to separate the legislative from the executive functions of the system of the soviets on all levels and to increase greatly the power of the legislative soviets over the executive bodies. To this end, a resolution of the Nineteenth Party Conference decreed a number of changes, many details of which remain unclear:

- The voters will have an opportunity to select from among a number of candidates for election of the deputies of the soviet; the Party organizations (or committees) as well as other mass associations and working collectives can nominate different candidates for the ballot. It is not yet clear how many candidates can be placed on the ballot, by what rules and procedures this will be decided, and by whom it will be decided. But it does appear that the voting districts will be divided into two types. In the first only one candidate will be placed on the ballot (*odno-mandatnye*); in the others there will be a choice of candidates (*mnogo-mandatnye*). The first will likely be for the candidates of the Party leaders, the second for the less prestigious candidates.
- As for the national (and probably the republican) legislatures, the elections to the soviets will be conducted in two steps. In the first, the electorate will choose people's deputies; in the second, the people's deputies will elect from among themselves the members of the soviet. About one-third of the people's deputies will be selected by mass associations and organizations (for example, the trade unions, the Academy of Sciences, the Writers' Union, the League of Women or of Youth). For the national legislature in Moscow this would mean that about 1,500 people's deputies will be elected through a popular ballot in an equal number of voting districts that will cover the entire country, and 750 delegates will be selected by the mass and professional organizations or associations. At their first meeting after the election, the 2,250 people's deputies will elect from among themselves 400 members that will constitute the Supreme Soviet of the USSR.
- The entire body of the people's deputies on each level will meet more often than do the present soviets, but they will combine their legislative duties with full-time work at their other jobs. The members of the Supreme (or republican) Soviet will devote most, and perhaps even all, of their time to their work as legislators. (The intention seems to be for the soviets to meet regularly and for long periods, as Western parliaments do, with their work divided among many standing committees.)
- Leading members of the executive branch, such as members of the Ispolkom or Council of Ministers, will not be eligible for election as people's deputies; the leading personnel of the executive branch and the membership of the legislative soviet will be strictly separated.

(It remains unclear whether this restriction will also include members of the Party apparatus.)

- The soviets will appoint the leading personnel of the executive branch of the government by ballot. (We do not yet know, on the all-union level for example, whether this process will be carried out by the entire body of the people's deputies or by the 400-member Supreme Soviet.

- The legislative soviets will supervise the activity of the state executive branch, adopt laws, and discuss the domestic and foreign policies of the government. Resolutions of the Party organs up to the Central Committee *must* be discussed in the legislating soviets and can be altered before they become law or established policy. The current fusion of the Party and the soviet executive personnel will be undone to the point that joint resolutions of Party committees and respective soviets (or their executive arm) will be forbidden.

- The central government will provide an economic and financial base for the activity of the local soviets by dramatically enlarging their jurisdiction over local economic resources and enterprises, as well as a degree of economic independence from the central or republican government.

These changes are potentially important ones and will require major constitutional amendments. Without knowing the precise details, which have yet to be worked out, we cannot judge how effective they will be in achieving Gorbachev's primary goals of bringing government closer to the people, checking the activities and performance of the executive branch, and democratizing the Soviet political system. But even without knowledge of such details, some critical observations are possible. Conceptually, the entire scheme itself appears promising. But for that matter, the existing Soviet constitution reads as a model of democracy. The structural changes must inspire the changed *behavior* of leaders, bureaucracies, and voters in order to become a reality. In this respect, a verdict must be withheld until the new reality promised by those changes is available for close scrutiny.

The new scheme raises two problems that are particularly vexing. First, the spirit if not the letter of these new changes will surely be circumvented if the actual fusion of the Party apparatus and the Ispolkom leading cadres on the local level is not broken. Gorbachev seeks to separate the executive from the legislative branch through the immense strengthening of the legislative sector. But the Party apparatus, even if drastically reduced in its economic functions, will continue to maintain close ties with the government executive. Moving part of the personnel of the defunct Party apparat to the *Ispolkom* may even reinforce the existing fusion and interchangeability of Party and governmental executive personnel. A unity between the Party apparatus and the *Ispolkom* will make the independence of the legislative soviet difficult to maintain.

The second troubling problem concerns the leading role of the Party in the soviets. Under the best of circumstances, assuming the Party apparatus does not change, the Party will still exercise its influence and press its point of view on the soviets through the Communist Party members of the soviets and through the "Bolshevik faction" in the soviets (as it was described in Lenin's day), who will almost certainly have a majority or near majority. Leading members of the soviets will also be members of the local Party Committee, and some will even sit on the Bureau of the Party Committee. They will take their cues from the Party Bureau and push its line through the soviets, whose Communist members are bound by Party discipline (under conditions of democratic centralism) to support its positions. If Gorbachev's entire plan goes well, the Communist members of the soviets will either have to convince the non-Party members that their position is right or will have to provide a line of communication to the Party Committee and the Party Bureau that will persuade them to change their line (and persuade the higher Party organ to change its position). This situation will be an enormous step toward democratization, but it indicates once more the dilemma of true democratization when political competition is absent in a one-party regime. This dilemma is all the more pressing in light of Gorbachev's plans for the function of the First Party Secretaries in his new scheme.

The Function of First Secretaries

The single most controversial, although not the most important, aspect of Gorbachev's proposed change concerns the First Party Secretaries at all levels, including the General Secretary. The First Party Secretaries, or as Professor Jerry Hough of Duke University has called them, "the Soviet Prefects," are the symbols of Communist Party rule in the Soviet Union. In practical terms, they are the backbone of the Party apparatus and of the centralizing principles of the Soviet political order. The First Party Secretaries are Party generalists who are, in principle, responsible for the overall performance of the geographic-administrative territory in which they serve. They do not participate in the division of labor within the Party apparatus or among the other bureaucracies, but they are the Party functionaries in whose hands almost all the reins of power are joined.

In the Party organization, there are 15 republican First Secretaries, 157 provincial First Secretaries, 2,113 city First Secretaries, 630 district First Secretaries and 2,113 county First Secretaries. There are also more than 400,000 First Secretaries of primary Party organizations. Of those, however, no more than 1,000 are full-time Party apparatchiks, and about 90 percent of the Party First Secretaries of primary organizations combine this function with their everyday jobs.

The Party First Secretaries chair the Party Committees, Bureaus, and decisionmaking bodies and lead the Party's executive branch—the Secretariat and its entire apparatus. Although a reform that aimed for checks and balances to lessen the power of the first party secretaries might have been logical, Gorbachev instead proposed and pushed through a change that initially appeared to add to the First Secretaries' power—the permanent chair of the legislative soviet was added to their functions.

Gorbachev's proposal met with widespread consternation and astonishment among many conference delegates and his supporters throughout the country. More than 250 delegates were courageous enough to vote against it and to discuss its merits openly. Their main argument, and fear, was that this change could lead to a concentration of power that would be dangerous in light of the past. How are we then to understand this proposal?

Faced with bureaucratic resistance and conservative opposition (particularly within Party apparatus), Gorbachev has sought to enhance his stature by combining his top Party position with the chair of a changed and potentially powerful legislature—a move that would also serve to make him head of state. Khrushchev's formula of combining the two top executive positions (Party First Secretary and Prime Minister) failed. Brezhnev's formula of combining the top Party position with that of chair of the Supreme Soviet (the head of state) was meaningless in light of the purely symbolic nature of the Supreme Soviet. Gorbachev's formula makes sense if the Supreme Soviet is to play a truly major role in the governmental structure. Through his proposal, Gorbachev has told his supporters that he will lead and supervise the new and untraditional legislature and through his authority will help to keep the legislature democratic and powerful.

But can Gorbachev accomplish a fusion of the top Party and legislative positions only for himself without doing the same thing for the Party bosses in republics, provinces, and localities—where so many of the First Secretaries do not care about democracy? Under the new circumstances this was likely to be either dangerous or unpopular. The trial balloons that Gorbachev launched before the conference, which proposed to establish a presidential post with the occupant to be elected directly in a national vote, did not fare well. It seems to me, however, that this change will take place if Gorbachev is successful. In any event, if he assumes the position of the chair of the Supreme Soviet during the upcoming elections, he will for all practical purposes be a president who was not elected by a nationwide presidential vote. An even simpler explanation for Gorbachev's proposal is that in the era of democratization and diffusion of authority a major enhancement of the role of the Party secretaries is a back-door way of guaranteeing the hegemony of the Party in the new political system.

Gorbachev's own public explanation of his proposal was straightforward: The fusion of the top Party and legislative positions expresses, without hypocrisy, the existing hegemony of the Party First Secretary within his or her geographic-administrative area. This will not change much or in the near future. Placing the authority of the Party First Secretary in the service of the development of a new and truly legislative soviet will increase the odds in favor of its success. A top Soviet propagandist, Fedor Burlatsky, wrote during the preconference discussion:

> I believe that the separation of the posts of party leader and state leader proposed by some participants in the current debate is wrong. In reality, it would lead to a struggle for personal power and total subordination of the state to the party. On the other hand, the unification of these two posts would lend a legitimate, legal nature to the practice which has existed for more than 70 years now and conforms with the political awareness of our people, who personify supreme power. (*Literaturnaya gazeta*, June 15, 1988, p. 2)

In *Moscow News* (August 7, 1988), G. Popov, a defender of the conference decision wrote that "in practical terms the fusion of the two offices will not bring any increase of power of the first secretaries beyond what they already have." Although this may be so, the new legislative soviets are intended as a counterweight to the Party apparatus and therefore are not intended to *preserve* the power of the First Secretary but are committed instead to its *decline.*

The fusion of these positions is likely to diminish the chance of a confrontation on the local level between the Party Committee/Bureau and the soviet. The question remains, however, whether such confrontations or the threat of them is not in the interest of democratization. In my opinion it is; therefore, the fusion of the positions, although quite practical in that it will smooth relations between the two centers of power and thus save Gorbachev a lot of trouble, will not serve the cause of democratization.

There is still another argument for the fusion. In a situation in which the size of the Party apparatus has been cut significantly and its prerogatives restricted, the First Secretary as chair of the soviet will increasingly exercise the Party's prerogatives through the soviets. He or she will work increasingly through the personnel of the Ispolkom and not through the Party apparatus. But this is unlikely to happen during the life of the present generation of Party secretaries, who come from the Party apparatus and whose ties with it are not only instrumental but emotional as well.

It is possible also that Gorbachev's proposal was no more than a tactical move. He offered an olive branch, a compromise, to the powerful Party First Secretaries for their acquiescence in his political reforms and for their neutrality. If this is true, then in the future when Gorbachev is stronger, this fusion of roles will probably be overturned and presented as a sign that the Soviets have matured and no longer require the tutelage of the First Secretaries.

Legal State

The resolutions of the Nineteenth Party Conference posed important questions about law, legality, and the Soviet judicial system. Yet these subjects were virtually absent from discussion at the conference, although they are crucial if the Soviet political system is to undergo a meaningful transformation. It was at once fascinating and discouraging to witness a conference devoted to a blueprint for a new political system in a country that to a large extent remains a police state in which the initials KGB are never mentioned. These initials, for most Soviet citizens, represent the reality of Soviet life no less than the word "Party."

Nevertheless, most of the conference's deliberation was directly or indirectly devoted to issues of central importance to the rule of law in the Soviet Union. Honest and meaningful elections, a real legislature, *glasnost'*—all are necessary to limit the arbitrariness of the Soviet police state and are necessary as well for the institution of the rule of law. The conference also outlined the evolution in this direction when it said in one resolution that "prime attention should be paid to the legal defense of the citizens' rights, and strengthening the guarantees of the political, economic, and social rights and freedoms of the Soviet people" (*Pravda*, July 5, 1988, p. 3).

New rules of law, reorganization of the political system, separation of the investigative organs of the state from the police and procuracy, and the independence of the public defender from the courts are being considered in professional and public discussion. But the facts of everyday life in the Soviet Union and the almost total absence of conference discussion of these issues reinforce the sense that it will take Gargantuan, sustained efforts to make the Soviet Union a country governed under a system of fair laws.

The very concept of a "state of law" only recently entered the Soviet vocabulary even in the juridical literature. The term *legitimacy* has no equivalent in the Russian language; the term that is used, *zakonnost* (lawfulness), has different connotations. The Soviet Union is a country that formally (under Stalin) and informally (after his death) subscribed to the principle that the "defendent is guilty until and unless he proves his innocence." How much time it will take to move from the principle of "what is not explicitly permitted is forbidden" to the principle of "what is not forbidden is permitted" is not only a question of the comparative force of the KGB and harsh laws, on the one hand, but also of permissive, investigative, and judiciary procedures, on the other. There exists a total lack of a legal tradition of "citizenship" among both the ruled and the rulers.

As an editorial from the government's main organ, *Izvestiya* (July 16, 1988, p. 1) said, "We want to be frank: constitutional law, the theory of the State, the history of democratic institutions that originated with the ancient Greeks, the experience of the governmental structures of other countries and nations, even if this experience is 'not the one that we need'—all this is hidden for most of us behind seven seals." Initial steps have been taken to instilling a legal culture in the nation, its rulers, and citizens alike, but this is a long and arduous process.

After the Conference

As Professor Kenneth Jowitt of the University of California at Berkeley aptly remarked, what Gorbachev wants to achieve in reforming the Soviet system is a combination of some of the principles of Martin Luther and James Madison. Gorbachev seeks to destroy or radically weaken the ruling church and return the faith directly to the people. He wants to establish a system of checks and balances of power and influence that will preclude the repetition of the murderous and stagnant past. There is no doubt that he believes in this goal and in his chances for realizing it; but he is also improvising a great deal and sees only vaguely the elements of the structure that he wants to build. Gorbachev is, however, certain of the direction in which he must move. The Nineteenth Party Conference showed what has already changed in Soviet political life and the main directions in which Gorbachev is struggling to move his country.

Aside from the substantive deliberations of the conference and its relative openness, and aside from the boost it gave to *glasnost'* and the atmosphere it created in the country, two elements of Gorbachev's position appear encouraging. First, both he and the conference resolutions, as well as those of the Plenum of the Central Committee, confirmed that the steps already taken or proposed are only the initial ones in the long task of making the Soviet Union a "normal" country by the common

standards of civilization, regardless of the name by which the country
is known—be it socialist, Soviet, or any other. Second, an ambitious
timetable has been adopted for putting the specific proposed changes
into effect. The reorganization of the Party apparatus is to be accomplished
by the end of 1988. The Party's reporting and election meetings are to
take place, in the case of the primary Party organizations, in September–
October 1988; the county, district and city organizations, in October–
November; and the provincial organizations, in November–December.
The republican reporting-electoral conferences may take place in 1989.
If the Party statutes are not changed, the All-Union Party Congress will
take place only in early 1991. It is likely that the Assembly of the
People's Deputies of the USSR will be elected in April 1989 and should
in turn elect the new, different Supreme Soviet, which will begin its
work immediately. The Supreme Soviet will then order the elections of
people's deputies on all levels, which should be completed in December
1989. Many other conference proposals should be transformed into Party
or state law in 1989 or 1990. Gorbachev is clearly a man in a hurry,
as well he should be. The regained impetus of *perestroika* must be
maintained if he is to have any chance of succeeding.

I do not expect Gorbachev to be ousted in the foreseeable future
(which in a revolutionary period can mean no more than two to three
years). Nor do I expect that he or his close associatees will change their
minds, their ideals, or the direction in which they are pushing the USSR.
Quite the contrary, I expect that the most radical steps of *perestroika*
have yet to occur.

My optimism, however, is tempered when it comes to the third
condition of the short-term development of *perestroika*. My doubts concern
the economic situation before the radical steps of marketizing economic
reform are implemented and before they have a chance to produce any
significant economic improvements. As has been repeated often by
Western and Soviet analysts, without visible improvements in the economic condition of the workers and lower managerial personnel in the
great industrial centers and of the peasantry and farm workers and
managers, the economic reform has very little chance of taking off, as
scheduled, in 1991. Moreover, if such improvement does not occur soon,
a dangerous asymmetry will develop in the Soviet Union: The progress
of *glasnost'* and democratization and the greater freedom and activization
of the working class will go hand in hand with a lack of economic
improvement for the working people. This is surely a prescription for
industrial and consumer unrest.

That in the fourth year of *perestroika* nothing improved for the average
consumer testified to the shortcomings of analysis and undue short-
range optimism of both Western and Soviet analysts. Many Western

economists, but more importantly Gorbachev, his associates, and their economic advisers had expected that the infusion of younger, more energetic personnel into the economy, combined with common-sense policies that would correct the irrationalities and stupidities of the Brezhnev era, would lead to fast economic improvements that would carry the consumer through the difficult transitional period.

In light of the performance of the economy under Gorbachev, and Soviet discussions of economic statistics, these evaluations appear to have been in error. As one Soviet economist recently argued in *Sotsialisticheskaya industriya* (January 5, 1988), because past growth has been so much below expectations, it is entirely unrealistic to expect a dramatic increase in real rates of growth. There is no massive capacity waiting to be used efficiently; there is only a fictitious capacity that exists on paper. Thus, the only way that a significant boost in consumption—so necessary for the success of *perestroika*—can be achieved is through a dramatic cut in the share of national income going to investment, particularly in the engineering industries. Coupled with the rights and incentives granted in the new enterprise law, this policy would encourage a significant increase in the rate of growth of consumption without further damage to the overall industrial performance.

The most urgent economic problems are merged with urgent political problems that were only partly dealt with at the Nineteenth Party Conference. Many Western analysts of the Soviet Union see Gorbachev's key task to be the decentralization of power and authority in the economy, polity, and society. This is clearly what the radical reforms of *perestroika* require. It seems to me, however, that it is just as important for Gorbachev to centralize power successfully in his office, in the leadership of the Party-state, and in central political institutions. I would argue, further, that in the present situation the centralization of political power is a necessary condition for decentralization and that the decentralization of power is a condition for its more effective centralization.

In the last decade of Brezhnev's rule, and during the interregnum that followed his death, a far-reaching breakdown took place in the Soviet political system. The flow of authority from the top down was successfully circumvented and made ineffective. Information flowing from the bottom up was falsified on a gigantic scale. The ties between the lower and higher centers of power, between the peripheries and the center, were interrupted. The Soviet bureaucracies acquired a "corporatist," egocentric political orientation that in practice denied authority to the leaders and any degree of autonomy to the "clients" (whether the mass Party or the consumers).

To decentralize political power, the Soviet leadership must first control it. Gorbachev must have a Central Committee to his liking and a Party apparatus that will accept and pursue his policy of greater autonomy for local soviets. Decentralization of economic power requires a much greater centralization of accurate information as a prerequisite for wise politico-economic decisions, effective control over *Gosplan* and the ministries in order to prevent their attempts to render powerless the economic reforms, and control over distribution. These will in turn require further major revisions in personnel and structural changes, of which the conference resolutions provide an example. At the beginning of Gorbachev's rule his economic slogan was *"uskorenie"* (acceleration), to which one Moscow wag replied, "One cannot accelerate something that does not move." With regard to Gorbachev's goal of decentralization of political and economic power, we can similarly say, "One cannot decentralize something one does not possess."

A true centralization of economic power is realistic within a highly decentralized environment only if the instruments of centralized control are at once sophisticated and indirect. In a gigantic, multinational, and industrialized country, the centralization of all forms of power can occur only if a government is selective about the number and relative importance of the items it wishes to control. By trying to centralize the control of everything, a government ends up controlling nothing. Only by allowing a freer flow of market forces, greater autonomy to local government, and the adaptation of national policies to the heterogenous areas and republics can the centralization of power in Moscow in the central leadership groups be truly effective.

Gorbachev's political coalition is a heterogeneous one. This was clearly demonstrated at the conference. In fact, there were a number of parallel conferences going on. The speakers from the creative intelligentsia urged the adoption of the most radical of Gorbachev's proposals and were primarily preoccupied with defending the achievements of *glasnost'* and enlarging the spirit of free discussion. The worker delegates were uniformly preoccupied with economic difficulties and immediate improvements in the standard of living. The provincial Party officials were pressing for less radical economic reform and were unified in their fury against investigative reporting, against what they called the "negativism" of the media. The delegates from the non-Russian republics emphasized the urgent need for greater autonomy from Moscow.

At the moment, Gorbachev is a political juggler who must keep many balls in the air through tactical skill, flexibility, and maneuvering, but he cannot juggle forever. What Gorbachev needs most is time. But he lacks time in the economic sphere, where quick improvements are *politically* imperative; and he may also lack time with regard to the unintended consequences of his reforms. The genie that the General Secretary let escape from the bottle does not always perform according to his liking. In this respect, two particular dangers are especially important: the national question within the Soviet Union and the situation in Eastern Europe. The conflict between the Azerbaijanis and Armenians provides only a foretaste of the most explosive issue that Gorbachev has to handle. He must respond to this challenge in two ways simultaneously: He must at least partly satisfy the autonomous aspirations of the non-Russians while keeping the multinational Soviet state intact; he must also centralize power in Moscow on key issues and decentralize it on others. This will require time, skill, and luck.

The nationality question received only perfunctory treatment at the conference. The conference resolution confirmed, however, that Moscow and the leaders of the non-Russian republics must prepare proposals on this issue by the end of 1988 and that a plenum of the Central Committee in early 1989 will be devoted entirely to this nationality problem.

The juggling act in Eastern Europe is as dangerous as the domestic one and even more unstable. How much time does Gorbachev have before some country in Eastern Europe, encouraged by *perestroika* in the USSR, explodes or stakes its claim to independence? The aspiration to transform the Soviet system requires the acceptance of such dangers, which may be fatal to *perestroika* and to the evolving *détente* with the West. Gorbachev's argument must be that without a fundamental *perestroika*, the dangers would be even greater.

The Nineteenth Party Conference was in every respect Gorbachev's show. Although he was forced by the conservatives to accept some compromises, his radical vision of *perestroika* dominated the scene. The General Secretary began his speech by saying that "the fundamental question with which this conference is to deal, is how to deepen and make irreversible the revolutionary reconstruction [*perestroika*] . . . that has developed in our country." There can be no doubt that the conference intensified and enhanced the process of *perestroika*. But there is also no doubt that despite the conference and its achievements, despite what Gorbachev has done so far, despite the fact that people in the Soviet Union are at last beginning in large numbers to believe in it, *perestroika* remains a process that is still very much reversible.

Selected Bibliography:
Recent Works
on the Soviet Union

Books

Aganbegyan, Abel. *The Economic Challenge of Perestroika*. Bloomington: Indiana University Press, 1988.

Agursky, Mikhail. *The Third Rome: National Bolshevism in the USSR*. Boulder, Colo.: Westview Press, 1987.

Akiner, Shirin. *Islamic Peoples of the Soviet Union*. London: KPI, 1986.

Alexeeva, Ludmilla. *Soviet Dissent. Contemporary Movements for National, Religious, and Human Rights*. Middletown: Wesleyan University Press, 1985.

Avis, George, ed. *The Making of the Soviet Citizen*. London: Croom Helm, 1987.

Bassow, Whitman. *The Moscow Correspondents. Reporting on Russia from the Revolution to Glasnost*. New York: William Morrow, 1988.

Beissinger, Mark, and L. Hajda, eds. *The Nationalities Factor in Soviet Society and Politics: Current Trends and Future Prospects*. Boulder, Colo.: Westview Press, 1988.

Bialer, Seweryn. *The Soviet Paradox*. New York: Alfred A. Knopf, 1986.

Bialer, Seweryn, and Michael Mandelbaum, eds. *Gorbachev's Russia and American Foreign Policy*. Boulder, Colo.: Westview Press, 1988.

Colton, Timothy J. *The Dilemma of Reform in the Soviet Union*, 2nd ed. New York: Council on Foreign Relations, 1986.

Conquest, Robert, ed. *The Last Empire: Nationality and the Soviet Future*. Stanford, Calif.: Hoover Institution, 1986.

D'Agostino, Anthony. *Soviet Succession Struggles: Kremlinology and the Russian Question from Lenin to Gorbachev*. Winchester: Allen and Unwin, 1987.

Dallin, Alexander, and Bertrand Patenaude, eds. *Knowledge, Power, and Truth: Scholarship and Humanities in the Gorbachev Era*. Stanford, Calif.: Center for Russian and East European Studies, 1988.

Dallin, Alexander, and Condoleeza Rice, eds. *The Gorbachev Era*. Stanford, Calif.: Stanford Alumni Association, 1986.

Desai, Padma. *The Soviet Economy, Problems and Prospects*. Oxford: Basil Blackwell, 1987.

Dibb, Paul. *The Soviet Union: The Incomplete Superpower*. Chicago: University of Illinois, 1986.

Dizzard, William P., and S. Blake Swensrud. *Gorbachev's Information Revolution: Controlling Glasnost in a New Electronic Era.* Boulder, Colo.: Westview Press, 1987.

Doder, Dusko. *Shadows and Whispers: Power Politics Inside the Kremlin from Brezhnev to Gorbachev.* New York: Random House, 1987.

Dyker, David, ed. *The Soviet Union Under Gorbachev: Prospects for Reform.* London: Croom Helm, 1987.

Frankland, Mark. *The Sixth Continent: Russia and the Making of Mikhail Gorbachev.* London: Hamish Hamilton, 1987.

Goldman, Marshall. *Gorbachev's Challenge. Economic Reform in the Age of High Technology.* New York: W. W. Norton, 1987.

Gorbachev, Mikhail. *Perestroika: New Thinking for Our Country and the World.* New York: Harper & Row, 1987.

Goudoever, Albert van. *The Limits of Destalinization in the Soviet Union.* London: Croom Helm, 1986.

Hammer, Darrell. *Russian Nationalism and Soviet Politics.* Boulder, Colo.: Westview Press, 1988.

Hazen, Baruch. *From Brezhnev to Gorbachev: Infighting in the Kremlin.* Boulder, Colo.: Westview Press, 1987.

Herlemann, Horst G., ed. *The Quality of Life in the Soviet Union.* Boulder, Colo.: Westview Press, 1987.

Juviler, Peter, and Hiroshi Kimura, eds. *Gorbachev's Reforms: U.S. and Japanese Assessments.* New York: Aldine de Gruyter, 1988.

Laird, Roy D. *The Politburo; Democratic Trends, Gorbachev, and the Future.* Boulder, Colo.: Westview Press, 1986.

Lane, David. *Soviet Society and Economy.* London: Basil Blackwell, 1985.

Lane, David, ed. *Labor and Employment in the USSR.* New York: New York University Press, 1986.

McAuley, Martin, ed. *The Soviet Union Under Gorbachev.* London: Macmillan, 1987.

Medvedev, Zhores A. *Gorbachev.* New York: W. W. Norton, 1986.

Millar, James R., ed. *Politics, Work, and Daily Life in the USSR: A Survey of Former Soviet Citizens.* New York: Cambridge University Press, 1987.

Miller, R. F., J. H. Miller, and T. H. Rigby, eds. *Gorbachev at the Helm: A New Era in Soviet Politics.* London: Croom Helm, 1987.

Motyl, Alexander. *Will the Non-Russians Rebel? State, Ethnicity, and Stability.* Ithaca, N.Y.: Cornell University Press, 1987.

Narkiewicz, Olga. *Soviet Leaders: From the Cult of Personality to Collective Rule.* Brighton, England: Wheatsheaf, 1986.

Naylor, Thomas. *The Gorbachev Strategy: Opening the Closed Society.* Lexington, Mass.: Lexington Books, 1987.

Nove, Alec. *The Soviet Economic System,* 3rd ed. Boston: Allen and Unwin, 1986.

Olcott, Martha B., and L. Hajda, eds. *The Soviet Multinational State.* New York: M. E. Sharpe, 1987.

Pravda, Alex. *How Ruling Communist Parties Are Governed.* London: Macmillan, 1987.

Rowen, Henry S., and Charles Wolf, Jr., eds. *The Future of the Soviet Empire.* New York: St. Martin's Press, 1988.

Sacks, M. P., and J. G. Pankhurst, eds. *Understanding Soviet Society.* Winchester: Allen and Unwin, 1988.

Shlapentokh, V. E. *The Politics of Sociology in the Soviet Union.* Boulder, Colo.: Westview Press, 1988.

Schmidt-Hauer, Christian. *Gorbachev: The Path to Power.* London: I. B. Taurus, 1986.

Smith, Gordon. *Soviet Politics: Continuity and Contradiction.* New York: St. Martin's Press, 1987.

Treadgold, Donald W., and Lawrence W. Lerner, eds. *Gorbachev and the Soviet Future.* Boulder, Colo.: Westview Press, 1987.

Tucker, Robert C. *Political Culture and Leadership in Soviet Russia from Lenin to Gorbachev.* New York: W. W. Norton, 1988.

Articles

Amann, Ronald. "Searching for an Appropriate Concept of Soviet Politics: The Politics of Hesitant Modernization?" *British Journal of Political Science* 16:4 (October 1986), pp. 475–494.

Bialer, Seweryn. "Gorbachev's Move." *Foreign Policy,* no. 68 (Fall 1987), pp. 59–87.

Bialer, Seweryn, and Joan Afferica. "The Genesis of Gorbachev's World." *Foreign Affairs* 64:3 (1986), pp. 605–644.

Brown, Archie. "Change in the Soviet Union." *Foreign Affairs* 64:5 (Summer 1986), pp. 1048–1065.

_____. "Gorbachev: New Man in the Kremlin." *Problems of Communism* 34:3 (May-June 1985), pp. 1–23.

_____. "Soviet Political Developments and Prospects." *World Policy Journal* 4:1 (Winter 1986-1987), pp. 55–87.

Colton, Timothy J. "Moscow Politics and the El'tsin Affair." *The Harriman Institute Forum* 1:6 (June 1988), pp. 1–8.

Dunlop, John B. "Soviet Cultural Politics." *Problems of Communism* 36:6 (November-December 1987), pp. 34–56.

Ericson, Richard E. "The New Enterprise Law." *The Harriman Institute Forum* 1:2 (February 1988), pp. 1–8.

Evans, Alfred B., Jr. "The Decline of Developed Socialism? Some Trends in Recent Soviet Ideology." *Soviet Studies* 38:1 (January 1986), pp. 1–23.

Gill, Graeme. "The Future of the General Secretary." *Political Studies* 34:2 (June 1987).

Goldman, Marshall. "Gorbachev and Economic Reform." *Foreign Affairs* 64:1 (Fall 1985), pp. 56–73.

Gross, Natalie. "Glasnost': Roots and Practice." *Problems of Communism* 36:6 (November-December 1987), pp. 69–80.

Gustafson, Thane, and Dawn Mann. "Gorbachev's First Year: Building Power and Authority." *Problems of Communism* 35:6 (May-June 1986), pp. 1–19.

————— . "Gorbachev's Next Gamble." *Problems of Communism* 36:4 (July-August 1987), pp. 1–20.

Hough, Jerry F. "Gorbachev's Strategy." *Foreign Affairs* 64:1 (Fall 1985), pp. 33–55.

————— . "Gorbachev Consolidating Power." *Problems of Communism* 36:4 (July-August 1987), pp. 21–43.

Lapidus, Gail. "Gorbachev and the Reform of the Soviet System," *Daedalus* (Spring 1987), pp. 1–30.

Lukacs, John. "The Soviet State at 65." *Foreign Affairs* 65:1 (Fall 1986), pp. 21–37.

Moses, Joel C. "Consensus and Conflict in Soviet Labor Policy—The Reformist Alternative." *Soviet Union/Union Sovietique* 13:3 (1986), pp. 301–348.

Odom, William. "How Far Can Soviet Reform Go?" *Problems of Communism* 36:6 (November-December 1987), pp. 18–33.

Reddaway, Peter. "Gorbachev the Bold." *New York Review of Books* 34:9 (May 28, 1987), pp. 21–25.

Slider, Darrell. "More Power to the Soviets? Reform and Local Government in the Soviet Union." *British Journal of Political Science* 16:4 (October 1986), pp. 495–512.

White, Stephen. "The New Program and Rules of the CPSU." *The Journal of Communist Studies* 2:2 (June 1986), pp. 182–191.

Yenaev, G. I. "Soviet Restructuring: The Position and Role of the Trade Unions." *International Labor Review* 126:6 (November-December 1987), pp. 703–713.

Index

Abalkin, Leonid, 216
Abuladze, Tengiz, 145(n15)
Accountability, 49–50, 60, 78, 135
Adamovich, Ales', 135, 210
Adzhubei, Aleksei, 128, 206
Afanas'ev, Viktor, 201, 207
Afanas'ev, Yuriy, 22, 113
Afghanistan, 54, 164, 184
Akhmatova, Anna, 135
Alexander II, 35(n30), 83–84(n29)
Aliyev, Geydar, 65, 87(n50), 92–93
"All-human considerations," 12
"All-people's state" concept, 5, 11
All-union Party conferences, 213–214
Amalrik, Andrey, 19–21
American Council of Learned
    Societies, 171
Andreyev, Sergei, 200
Andreyeva, Nina, 133, 203, 204, 207,
    208, 216
Andropov, Yuri, 6, 23, 65, 66, 93,
    136, 138–139, 214
"Anti-Party group" crisis, 47, 52,
    81(n13), 114
Anti-Semitism, 176–177, 186, 187,
    203. See also Pamyat'
Arab-Israeli War, 176, 177
Armenian National United Party, 161
Armenians, xiv, 149, 158, 171(n2),
    198, 199, 241
Arms control, 63, 64, 65, 66
Arms race, 62
A. S. Pushkin State Museum of Art,
    186
Australia, 181
Authoritarianism, 3, 4, 18–19, 21, 28,
    31. See also Stalinism

Authority building, 48–51
Azerbaijanis, xiv, 171(n2), 198, 199,
    241

Baltic states, xiv, 18, 20, 34(n13),
    159, 164, 170, 177, 183, 199
Basmachi movement, 164
Belorussians, 150, 163, 164, 171,
    171(n2)
Beriya, Lavrenty, 52, 65, 81(n13)
Bialer, Seweryn, 33(n4)
Bikkenin, Nail, 133
Bolshevik Party, 222
Bondarev, Yuri, 216
Bovin, Aleksandr, 25–26, 38(n75),
    39(n84)
Breslauer, George, 49, 82(n19)
Brezhnev, Leonid, xiv, 4, 5, 7, 11, 13,
    20, 23, 25, 28, 38(n75), 39(n80),
    48, 54, 55, 88–89(n70), 107,
    145(n16), 152–153, 156, 204, 220
    authority of, 50–51, 82(n21)
    coercion under, 12, 64–65, 66, 67,
    73
    defense policies, 65, 66–67
    foreign policy under, 54, 77,
    84(nn 30, 31)
    ideological impact of, 6, 42
    Party role under, 13, 14
    political economy under, 68–69, 71,
    72–76, 78, 85(n36)
    political order under, 44, 60, 66,
    69, 81(n15), 124, 225, 234, 239
    power consolidation by, 53, 69
    social sciences under, 205
    state authority under, 62, 63

Brezhnev era, 124, 127–128, 132, 138, 160, 168, 239
Bukharin, Nikolay, 145(n15), 164, 188
Bulgakov, Mikhail, 135
Bulganin, Nikolay, 53
Bureaucracy, xii, 143, 146(n33), 196, 197, 199–200, 202, 224–229
Bureaucratic centralism, 14
Bureaucratism, 137
Burlatsky, Fedor, 5, 21–22, 39(n84), 187, 235
Butenko, Anatoliy, 136–137

Canada, 181
Carnoy, Martin, 85(n44)
Centralism, 14–15, 222–224
Centralization, 42, 240
Chagall, Marc, 186
Checks and balances, xii, 29
Cherkess, 156
Chernenko, Konstantin, 23, 51, 214
Chernobyl incident, 134
Chernyshevsky, Nikolay, 35(n30)
Churchill, Winston, 205
Civil unrest, 20, 89(n76), 157–158, 198–199
Class struggle, 11–13
Clientelism, 58. See also Nomenklatura
Coercion, 46, 47–48, 49, 51, 81(nn 11, 13)
  under Brezhnev, 12, 64–65, 66, 67, 73
  under Stalin, 145(n15), 209–210
Collectivization, 30–31
Committee for the Release of Political Prisoners in Armenia, 161
Committee for the Release of Political Prisoners in Georgia, 161
Communism
  "construction" of, 5–6
  West European, 9
  See also Marxism-Leninism
Communist Party, xii
  authority of, 59, 150

membership, 52
military and, 67
in 1920s, 61
revitalization of, 51–54, 82–83(n22), 222
role of, 13–15, 42
transformation of, 222–224
See also Bureaucracy
Conference on Security and Cooperation in Europe (CSCE), 181, 185
Conservatism, 25, 26. See also Gorbachev, opposition to
Constitutionalization, 46–47, 59, 60, 80–81(n9)
Consumer demand, 126–127
Councils of Ministers, 230
Crimea, 20, 158
CSCE. See Conference on Security and Cooperation in Europe
Cultural change, 124–130
Cultural establishment, 128
Czechoslovakia, 9, 11, 18, 20, 28–29, 32, 84(n30), 177

Darkness at Noon (Koestler), 210
Decentralization, xiv, 166–169, 239–240
Defense spending, 65, 66–67
Dejevsky, Mary, 20
Democratic centralism, 14–15, 222–224
Democratization, 7, 8, 15, 19, 20, 21–22, 23–24, 27, 30, 32, 36(n37), 117, 118, 122–123, 130–131, 144, 161, 165, 168, 186, 187, 194, 195, 201, 203, 217, 220–222, 224, 235, 238
Deng Xiaoping, 201
De-Stalinization, 41–90, 131, 168, 188
  under Gorbachev, 204, 205–206, 207
  under Khrushchev, 39(n84), 47–48, 51, 60, 65, 81(n13), 92, 118, 122, 168, 204, 206
Détente, 128–129, 179, 180, 182, 241. See also Superpower relations

Devolution, 166–167
"Dictatorship of the proletariat," 5, 12, 150
Dissidents, 57, 73–74, 145(n16)
Doctors' Plot, 81(n13), 188
Doctor Zhivago (Pasternak), 210
Dogmatism, 132–133
Domestic order, 19–22, 23–24, 30, 63–64, 89(n76), 157–158
"Drop-out" phenomenon, 180
Dubček, Alexander, 28

Easton, David, 86(n44)
Economic reform movement, 68, 70–71, 168
Economy
  growth, 24, 69–72, 75–76, 78
  political effects of, 124–125
  reform, 7, 13, 29, 142–143, 218, 228–229, 238–239. *See also* Economic reform movement
  regional aspects, 153
Education, 27, 126, 155
Emigration, 37(n54), 175, 177–188, 189(n10), 189–190(n15), 190(n16)
Entrepreneurship, 144, 202
Estonians, 18, 34(n13), 171(n2)
Ethnic minorities, 17–18, 74, 79, 139, 144, 150–152, 153–155, 157–158, 160, 162–165, 169–171, 171(n2), 175–191, 198–199
Evans, Peter, 85(n44)
Executive Committee of the Soviet of People's Deputies. *See* Ispolkoms

Family reunification, 184
Federal Republic of Germany, 182, 190(n16)
First Party Secretaries, 233–236
Foreign policy, 28
  under Brezhnev, 54, 77, 84(nn 30, 31)
  post-Stalinist, 42, 77
  See also Superpower relations
Freedom
  of expression, xii, xiii, 6

  personal, xv, 18, 19, 22, 31
  of the press, 14, 134–135, 211
  See also Glasnost'; Political competition
Frolov, Ivan, 133

Gelman, Aleksandr, 212
Georgia, 168, 177
Georgians, 171(n2), 179
Glasnost', 7–8, 23, 26, 27, 30, 31, 35(n30), 91, 107, 108, 111–112, 115, 117, 118, 128, 134–135, 139, 140–144, 159–163, 168, 187, 194, 195, 197, 199, 201, 203, 216, 217, 237, 238
Glasnost' (Moscow journal), 161
Gomulka, Wladyslaw, 177
Gorbachev, Mikhail, xi–xv, 1, 5, 20, 25, 29, 39–40(n88), 43, 44, 51, 58, 71, 74, 76, 78, 79, 92, 95, 96, 97, 99, 145(n15), 153, 218, 238, 239, 240–241
  appointment of, 193
  authority of, 113–118
  ideological impact of, 4, 6–7, 10, 12–13
  Jews and, 175, 185–188
  nationality issue under, 161–166, 168–169, 171, 198–199
  opposition to, 199–204, 207–208, 219. *See also* Bureaucracy; Nationality issue; Yeltsin affair
  Party role under, 13–14
  political order under, 228–229, 230–232, 234
  power consolidation by, 91, 93, 114, 122, 194, 195, 198, 208–212, 214, 216–217, 234–235, 236, 239–240
  reform concepts of, 7–11, 15–17, 22–27, 29, 31, 32, 39(n86), 60, 117–118, 121–124, 130–141, 142–144, 161, 165, 194, 195–196, 199, 212, 220–237. *See also* Perestroika
  revisionism of, 205–207
  state security under, 67

support for, xii–xiii, 115, 122, 206, 240
Western skepticism about, 41
See also Yeltsin affair
Gorbachev, Raisa, 156
Gorbachev's Russia and American Foreign Policy (Bialer and Mandelbaum), xi
Gramsci, Antonio, 8
Gray, Jack, 34(n17)
Great Purge, 222
Grechko, Andrey, 66, 67
Greece, 125
Griffiths, Franklyn, 85(n39)
Grishin, Victor, 106, 109
Gromyko, Andrei, 114, 116, 217
Growth strategies, 69–72, 75–76, 78
Gustafson, Thane, 68

Hamilton, Malcolm B., 1–2, 33(n88)
Herzen, Alexander, 19
"High Stalinism," 34(n14)
Hirschman, Albert, 144(n5)
Historiography, 57, 203–207
Hodnett, Grey, 46, 56, 80(n9)
Holocaust, 176, 188. *See also* Jews
Hough, Jerry, 233
Hungary, 13, 32

"I Cannot Compromise Principles" (Andreyeva), 203–204, 206, 207, 208–211, 216
Ideology
  defined, 1–2
  democratization and, 8
  See also Marxism-Leninism; Political culture
Initiative Group for the Release of Ukrainian Prisoners of Conscience, 161
Institutions
  political, 43, 44, 46–47, 51, 58–60, 76, 77, 78–79, 80–81(n9), 84(n34)
  social-contract, 75
Intelligentsia, xii, xiii, 19, 27, 74, 115, 126, 128, 186, 206, 207

under Brezhnev, 12
under Gorbachev, 142, 144
participation of, 123
policy specialists, 55–58
International Society for Human Rights, 161
Ispolkoms (Executive Committee of the Soviet of People's Deputies), 230, 232–233, 235
Israel, 176, 178, 180, 181, 189(n12)

Jews, 37(n54), 155, 158, 171(n2), 175–191, 209–210
  emigration of, xiv, 175, 177, 178–188
  religio-cultural freedom for, xv
  See also "Refuseniks"
Journals, 9
Jowitt, Kenneth, 237

Kaganovich, Lazar, 47–48, 81(n12)
Kamenev, Lev B., 188
Karachai, 156
Karpov, V. V., 216
Karyakin, Yu., 204, 207–208
Katyn massacre, 164
Kazakhs, 171(n2)
Kazakhstan, xiv, 158, 199
Keenan, Edward, 26
Keenan, George F., 77–78
KGB, 64–65, 66, 67, 161, 162
Khrushchev, Nikita, xiv, 4–5, 13, 15, 45, 55, 59, 64, 72, 84(n33), 85(n39), 126, 128, 132, 138, 139, 145(n15), 152, 164, 214, 220, 222
  civil unrest under, 89(n76)
  defense policies, 65
  de-Stalinization under, 39(n84), 47–48, 51, 60, 65, 81(n13), 92, 118, 122, 168, 195, 204, 206
  ideological impact of, 5–6, 25–26, 136
  political economy under, 70–71, 73, 89(n75)
  political order under, 44, 66, 69, 225, 227, 234

power consolidation by, 51, 52–53, 122
reform attempts, 21, 42
removal of, 41, 53, 114
state authority under, 62–63
Kirgiz, 171(n2)
Kirilenko, Andrey, 51
Koestler, Arthur, 210
Kolakowski, Leszek, 3
Kolbin, Gennadi, 158, 165
Komsomol, 129, 158, 162
Korotych, Vitaly, 216
Kosygin, Aleksey, 29, 50, 51, 53, 60, 68, 71, 168. *See also* Economic reform movement
Kudryavtsev, V. N., 144(n7)
Kunayev, Dinmukhamed, 153, 155, 158, 165, 168
Kuusinen, Otto, 5
"Kuznetsov, A. V.," 35(n33)

Labor force, 126, 127
Labor policy, 85(n42), 87(n49)
Language, 154, 159–160, 162–163
Lapidus, Gail, 7
Latvia, 157, 158, 161
Latvians, 18, 34(n13), 171(n2)
Legal system, 236–237
Legitimacy, 77–78, 236–237
Lenin, V. I., 3, 8, 13, 16, 17, 21, 118, 131, 137, 145(n15), 146(n24), 205, 213, 222, 233
ideological impact of, 3–4, 14, 28, 223. *See also* Marxism-Leninism
political legacy of, 229–233
"Liberalization from above," 32
Liberman, Yevsey, 88(n69)
Liberman reforms, 70–71, 88(n69)
Ligachev, Yegor, 22, 94, 95, 96, 98, 108, 109, 115–116, 201–202, 204, 207, 208, 211, 212, 214, 216
Lindblom, Charles, 69
Literature, 135
Literaturnaya Rossiya, 201
Lithuanians, 18, 34(n13), 171(n2)
Luther, Martin, 237

Madison, James, 237
Malenkov, Georgiy, 52, 70, 72, 88(n68)
Mandelstam, Nadezhda, 19
Marx, Karl, 3–4, 8, 11, 13, 14, 17, 28
Marxism in the USSR (Scanlon), 31
Marxism-Leninism, xiii, 2–5, 8, 19, 27–28
flexibility of, 16–17, 29–30, 31
officialization of, 3
perestroika and, 200–201, 205
transformation of, 5, 10–11
See also Political culture
Materialism, 126–127
Mazurov, Kirill, 51
Medvedev, Roy, 123, 204
Meir, Golda, 176
Memory. *See* Pamyat'
Michels, Robert, 224
Mikoyan, Anastas, 84(n33)
Military
under Brezhnev, 77
force strength, 65–66
under Gorbachev, 195
political authority of, 66–67
social costs of, 86–87(n48)
Mlynář, Zdenek, 28, 39–40(n88)
Modernization, 161, 165, 166, 168.
See also Economy, reform; Perestroika
Moldavians, 171(n2), 177
Molodaya gvardiya, 201
Molotov, Vyacheslav, 81(n12)
Molotov-Ribbentrop Pact, 158
Morgun, Fedor, 83(n23)
Muslims, 153–154, 155, 183
Mzhavanadze, Vasilii, 153

Nationalism, 22, 128, 149–173, 198–199
Nationality issue, 138–139, 198–199, 241
decentralization and, 167–169
glasnost' and, 161–166
Jews and, 175–191
Western response to, 169–171

Nativization, 168
Neglasnost', 26
New Course, 70, 72, 88(n68)
New Economic Policy period, 8, 168
Newspapers, 9
New Zealand, 181
Nicholas II, 19
Night Frost in Prague (Mlynář), 28
1984 (Orwell), 210
Nineteenth Party Conference, 212–
    220, 237–238, 241
Nomenklatura, 68–69, 71, 77, 167,
    225, 226, 227–228, 229
Nove, Alec, 35(n30)
Novocherkassk riot, 89(n76)
Nuclear war, 12
Nuikin, Andrei, 204

Order. *See Poryadok*
Orwell, George, 210
Ownership, 15–16, 143

Pamyat', 10, 22, 108, 158, 161, 187,
    203
Pasternak, Boris, 135, 210
Patriotism, 28
"Peaceful coexistence," 42. *See also*
    Superpower relations
Peasant class, 63, 64
People's Republic of China, 13, 181,
    184
Perestroika, xii–xiii, 7, 22, 39(n83),
    122, 131, 141, 169–170, 171, 183,
    186, 187, 213, 218, 224, 238, 241
    effects of, xiv, 21, 142–144
    nationality issue and, 149, 160–161,
    163, 165
    opposition to, 199–204, 207–209
    phases of, 193–215
    popular support for, 219
    See also Modernization; Yeltsin
    affair
Perestroika (Gorbachev), 9, 195
Peter I, 121
Pioneer organizations, 162
Planning, 24

Pluralism, 8–11, 13–14, 19, 23, 29,
    35(n33), 36(n37), 130–141. *See
    also* Political competition
Podgornyy, Nikolay, 51
Polan, A. J., 3–4
Poland, 9, 10, 18, 32, 54, 67, 136,
    177, 178
Policymaking, 55–58
Politburo, 6, 51, 52, 59, 66
Political competition, 3, 4, 8–11, 19,
    23, 24, 27, 49, 69. *See also*
    Freedom, of expression
Political culture, xiii–xiv, 1–40, 143–
    144
Political debate, 137–138
Political economy, 76–77, 166, 168
    under Brezhnev, 68–69, 71, 72–76
    under Khrushchev, 70–71, 73,
    89(n75)
    reform of, 68, 70–71, 78, 79–80,
    125. *See also* Gorbachev, Mikhail,
    reform concepts of
    tsarist, 83–84(n29)
Political participation, 122–123. *See
    also* Democratization
Political system, xii, 76, 229–233
    authority building in, 48–51
    clientelism in, 58
    reform and, 43, 143, 220–237
    structure of, 44–48
Popov, Gavriil, 83(n29), 235
Population growth, 182–184,
    190(n19)
Portugal, 125
Poryadok, 19–22, 23–24, 30, 63–64,
    89(n76), 157–158
Power, defined, 82(n18)
Prague Spring, 6, 10, 28, 29, 54
Presidium of the Council of
    Ministers, 52
Protocols of the Elders of Zion, 187
Pushkin, Aleksandr, 21

Rashidov, Sharaf, 153, 155, 157, 168
Razumovsky, Georgii Petrovich, 116,
    211–212

Reagan, Ronald, 185
Recentralization, 169
Reddaway, Peter, 41
"Refuseniks," 22, 185, 186, 187
Regimes, 86(n44)
Repression. *See* Coercion; Freedom
"Revolution from above," 70, 130, 219
Rigby, T. H., 44–45
Robespierre, 193
Rueschemeyer, Dietrich, 85(n44)
Russians, xiv, 17–18, 27, 28, 31–32, 74, 128, 139, 144, 150–151, 163, 198
Russian Tradition, The (Szamuely), 18
Russification, 154–155, 163
Rust, Matthias, 195
Ryabov, Yakov, 54
Rybakov, Anatoli, 145(n15)
Ryzhkov, Nikolai, 96

Sakharov, Andrei, 123, 142
SALT. *See* Strategic Arms Limitation Talks
Samizdat journals, 161
Scanlon, James, 31
Science, 55
"Second economy," 123, 129, 130
Secretariat, 51, 52
Security, 43, 44, 61, 63, 67, 79, 161–162
Self-management, 15, 27
Shakhnazarov, Georgiy, 12
Shcherbitsky, Vladimir, 153, 155, 165
Shelest, Petr, 153
Shenfield, Stephen, 12
Shmelev, Nikolai, 166
Slavic republics, 183
Smirnov, Georgiy, 15, 16
Snieckus, Antanas, 153
"Social contract" concept, 72–73, 74–76, 78
Socialism, 3, 4
    "developed," 6, 7, 139
    under Gorbachev, 39(n86)
    ownership under, 16

replacement of, 5–6
transformation of, 28, 123–124, 130–131, 136–137
    See also Political culture
Social mobility, 71–72
Social problems, 130, 140
Social sciences, 140–141
Sokolov, Efrem, 164
Solomentsev, Mikhail, 114, 202
Solzhenitsyn, Aleksandr, 204
Sovetskaya Rossiya, 201, 211
Soviet Association of Political Sciences, 29
Sovietization, 154
Soviet-Polish Repatriation Agreement, 178
Soviets. *See* System of soviets
Soviet Ukrainian Academy of Sciences, 171
Soviet unity, xiv, 138–140, 149–173
Sovnarkhoz reform, 168
Spain, 125
Stalin, Iosif, xiii, xiv, 3, 13, 18, 19, 21, 27, 30, 34(n14), 45, 47, 52, 57, 59, 61, 62, 64, 65, 68, 73, 83(n24), 87(n49), 114, 121, 131, 135, 137, 146(n24), 150, 153, 156, 157, 159, 164, 188, 198–199, 209, 213, 214, 220
    coercion under, 71, 145(n15), 209–210
    growth strategies, 69–70, 71
    ideological impact of, 3, 4–5, 11, 17, 223
    Jewish policies, 176, 182, 188
    political legacy of, 41–43, 44, 51, 55, 69, 70, 71–72, 76, 77, 125, 131
    political order under, 225
    power consolidation by, 196
    purges under, 11, 21, 31, 46, 47–48, 81(nn 11, 12), 222
    state authority under, 61–62, 63
    See also De-Stalinization; Stalinism
Stalinism, 34(n14), 61–62, 64, 69, 75, 78, 209

State
  coercion by, 12, 46, 47–48, 49, 51,
    64–67, 71, 73, 81(nn 11, 13),
    145(n15), 167, 209–210
  defined, 85–86(n44)
  social performance of, 68–76
  -society relationship, xiii–xiv, 43,
    44, 72–74, 79, 121–147
State and Revolution, The (Lenin), 3–
    4, 34(n17)
Statebuilding, 61–64
"State of the whole people" concept,
    5, 11
Stolypin reform, 202
Strategic Arms Limitation Talks
    (SALT), 65, 179, 181, 184
Strelyanyy, A. I., 36(n43), 39(n83)
Subcultures, 17, 18
  ethnic, 17–18, 74, 79, 139–144,
    150–152, 153–155, 157–158, 160,
    162–165, 169–171, 171(n2), 175–
    191, 198–199
  generational, 25–27, 38–39(n80),
    48, 76, 90(n84), 126, 127–128,
    129, 145(n12)
  religious, 153–154, 155, 183
  See also Nationality issue
Succession, 52–54, 59, 71–72,
    82(n19)
Suslov, Mikhail, 145(n16)
Superpower relations, xi, 42, 54, 66,
    84(n30), 179, 180, 181–182, 184,
    185, 189(n14). *See also* People's
    Republic of China; United States
System of soviets, 229–233. *See also*
    Political system
Szamuely, Tibor, 18

Tadzhiks, 171(n2)
Tatars, 20, 158, 171(n2), 198
Technocracy, 128
Tikhonov, Nikolay, 51
Tito, 218
Tolkach, 228–229
"To Study Democracy" (Burlatsky),
    21

Totalitarianism, 3. *See also*
    Authoritarianism
Trotsky, Leon, 137, 164, 207
Tsvetaeva, Marina, 135
Tucker, Robert C., 22
Turchin, Valery, 123
Turkmen, 171(n2)
"Turnaround That Did Not Take
    Place, The," 211
Tvardovsky, Aleksandr, 145(n16)

Ukraine, 150
Ukrainian Association of Independent
    Creative Intelligentsia, 161
Ukrainian Culturological Club, 161
Ukrainian Helsinki Group, 161–162
Ukrainian Herald, 161
Ukrainian peace movement, 161
Ukrainians, 17–18, 37(n54), 161, 162,
    164, 168, 171, 171(n2), 177
Underground economy. *See* "Second
    economy"
United States, 79, 170, 178, 180–181,
    186, 205
  containment policies, 77–78
  Export-Import Bank, 189(n14)
  Jackson-Vanik amendment, 181,
    189–190(n15)
  Stevenson amendment, 181,
    189(n14)
  See also Arms race; Superpower
    relations
Urbanization, 125–128
Uskorenie, 7, 240
Ustinov, Dimitry, 67
Usubaliyev, Turdakun, 153, 168
Uzbeks, 171(n2)

Vorotnikov, Vitaly, 202

"We Need the Full Truth"
    (Ligachev), 22
Western influence, 129
Western relations, 11–12. *See also*
    Superpower relations

What Is to Be Done? (Lenin), 3, 34(n17)
Wiatr, Jerzy, 35(n33)
Working class, 202–203
Writers' congresses, 162. *See also* Intelligentsia

Yakovlev, Alexander, 117, 131, 132, 133, 164–165, 211–212
Yawning Heights, The (Zinoviev), 8
Yazov, Dmitry, 195
Yeltsin, Boris, 91–119, 197, 198, 216

Yeltsin affair, 91–119, 197–198
Yugoslavia, 9, 167

Zahrebelny, Pavlo, 162
Zalygin, Sergey, 26, 103
Zaslavskaya, Tat'yana, 88(n64), 134, 137, 141, 146(nn 32, 33)
Zaykov, Lev, 102
Zhdanov, Andrei, 203
Zhukov, Georgy, 66
Zinoviev, Alexander, 8
Zinoviev, Grigory Y., 188
Zionism, 176, 177–178, 180